BACK TO BASICS

BACK TO BASICS

Rediscovering the Richness of the Reformed Faith

EDITED BY

David G. Hagopian

CONTRIBUTORS

Douglas J. Wilson
Douglas M. Jones III
Roger Wagner
David G. Hagopian

P&R
P U B L I S H I N G
P.O. BOX 817 • PHILLIPSBURG • NEW JERSEY 08865-0817

Unless otherwise indicated, Scripture quotations are from the following translations:

In Part One, The Holy Bible, New King James Version. Copyright © 1979, 1980, 1982, Thomas Nelson, Inc.

In Parts Two and Four, the New American Standard Bible. Copyright by the Lockman Foundation 1960, 1962, 1963, 1968, 1971, 1973, 1975, 1977.

In Part Three, the Holy Bible, New International Version. Copyright © 1973, 1978, 1984 International Bible Society. Used by permission of Zondervan Bible Publishers.

Italics in Scripture quotations indicate emphasis added.

Printed in the United States of America

Library of Congress Cataloging-in-Publication Data

Back to basics : rediscovering the richness of the Reformed faith / edited by David G. Hagopian ; Douglas Wilson . . . [et al.].
    p.   cm.
    Includes bibliographical references and index.
    ISBN 0-87552-216-5
    1. Reformed Church—Doctrines. I. Hagopian, David G., 1963— . II. Wilson, Douglas J., 1953— .
BX9422.2.B33 1996
230'.42—dc20   95-34534

In memory of
my precious
Ariane Allyce Hagopian

From His sovereign and gracious hand you came,
and to His sovereign and gracious hand you returned.

CONTENTS

FOREWORD

I once sat in on a private debate between two prominent theologians, Cornelius Van Til of Westminster Theological Seminary and H. M. Kuitert of the Free University of Amsterdam. I was waiting to take an oral exam from Dr. Kuitert and was privileged to be a human fly-on-the-wall during this private exchange. As the discussion progressed, Kuitert repeatedly spoke of aspects of his thought that were in conflict with each other, "dialectical" concepts, which smacked of mutually exclusive categories.

Van Til pursued Kuitert with relentless logic. Kuitert continued to retreat into dialectics. Finally, in obvious exasperation, Dr. Van Til exclaimed, "Professor Kuitert, please tell me your theology without the dialectic so I can understand it!"

Outright contradictions have no place in biblical theology. Paradoxes— seeming contradictions that can be resolved under closer scrutiny—are another matter.

Let me give an example: On the one hand, Reformed theology has little, if anything, in its doctrine of God that differs from broader Christianity. On the other hand, the most distinctive dimension of Reformed theology is its doctrine of God.

How can both statements be true? The answer is that the Reformed doctrine of God is not distinct considered *by itself*. What distinguishes the Reformed doctrine of God is its relentless application to all other doctrines. For example, Reformed theology is not satisfied to say that God is sovereign. It insists that this sovereignty extends to God's plan of salvation. His providence indeed covers the whole scope of theology. In a word, the doctrine of the nature and character of God is *basic* to all of theology.

In this most commendable work, *Back to Basics*, the authors consistently demonstrate that the supreme "basic" or foundation of all true theology is the nature and character of God Himself. This book, both readable and instructive, is a marvelous exposition of the essence of Reformed thought. If Charles Spurgeon was correct in his assessment that Calvinism is merely a nickname for biblical Christianity, then *Back to Basics* shows that Reformed theology is the purest expression of basic Christianity. It is a clarion call to return to the foundation of faith that was laid in Christ by God our Father.

—R. C. Sproul

EDITOR'S PREFACE

My heart sank with unimaginable heaviness. Paralysis gripped my entire body. There on the ultrasound screen flashed the image of my precious little daughter—motionless.

Just moments before we had feared the worst. As I sat at the foot of my wife, the doctor tried to find my daughter's heartbeat. Silence. Calmly, but somewhat more deliberately, he pressed again, trying to register even a faint pulse. More silence. He then spread additional lubricant atop my wife's protruding abdomen and pressed even harder. Still more silence.

Then I saw it. The doctor turned away from my wife, and with one fluid motion, he swung toward me, his face now bearing an unmistakable wince. And I knew.

But I did not have the courage to ask. Instead, I tried to convince myself that everything was going to be all right. I told myself that my daughter was only in trouble and that all we had to do was move quickly.

I could not understand why the doctor and the nurse who now joined us were so sedate. Why were they moving so slowly? Didn't they know that this was an emergency? Was I the only one sensing the urgency of the moment?

And then the image flashed on the screen. Dead silence.

"How could this be!" I screamed inside.

Just one week before, my wife had gone into labor. My healthy daughter was about to be born. But she was slightly ahead of schedule. Fearful of the small chance that her lungs would not be fully developed and that she might experience other relatively minor complications associated with being born four weeks early, the doctor sent my wife to the hospital to have her contractions stopped. Two hours later, we left, and everything was under control—or so we thought.

A week later, however, the contractions kept coming with increasing frequency. We went back to the hospital only to learn that our little one had died just hours before. As we would discover in the painful days to follow, a rare bacterial infection had suddenly invaded her otherwise safe maternal environment. So rare was this infection that she was, at the time, the only baby ever known to have died from it.

But why? Why had we avoided a small chance of relatively minor complications only to encounter an unknown fatal infection? Why had we traded in a statistical improbability for a statistical impossibility? Why did my daughter have to die, never having seen the light of day?

With those questions tugging at my heart, we were driven like never before to our knees. From that vantage point, we learned that the sovereign and gracious God of Holy Scripture does make sense of what would otherwise have been a meaningless tragedy. Though this book was completed months before my family's recent loss, the truths contained in the pages to follow suddenly came to life anew for us, taking on a deeper, richer meaning. What, after all, could be more meaningful than finding our every solace in the sovereign and gracious God of Holy Scripture, the God who calls His people and their seed to Himself in *conversion*, draws them into an intimate *covenantal* relationship with Himself and His people, the *church*, and is glorified in their *Christian lives*?

These four truths—conversion, the covenant, the church, and the Christian life—not only offer great comfort to grieving families like mine; they also offer a deep and abiding comfort to all of God's people. Because these truths lie at the heart of the faith championed so passionately by the Reformers and those who count themselves as their heirs, they teach us what it means to have a vibrant faith that is truly reformed, yet always reforming, even amidst life's greatest trials.

The following pages seek to unfold these truths in a powerful yet practical way. While I must confess that I do not know all of the answers to the questions now tugging at my heart, there is one thing I do know: my family's loss, though painful, has been our daughter's gain, for though she is lost to us, she has been found to Christ as she now graces the sunnier plains above.

May our heavenly Father spare you the pain my family has recently experienced. But may He be pleased, nonetheless, to use the truths of this book in your life as He did in ours to bring about growth as never before!
[D. G. H.]

ACKNOWLEDGMENTS

The Preacher in the book of Ecclesiastes once proclaimed that "the writing of many books is endless, and excessive devotion to books is wearying to the body" (Eccl. 12:12 NASB). My heartfelt thanks and appreciation go out to those whose "devotion to books" helped lessen the weariness I otherwise would have experienced as this book made its way into print. Of course, I thank my coauthors, Douglas Wilson, Douglas Jones, and Roger Wagner, for their excellent contributions, as well as Thom Notaro and Barbara Lerch of P&R Publishing for their valuable guidance.

I also extend my thanks to the many people who reviewed the manuscript, in whole or in part, offering their encouragement and constructive comments along the way, including Jay Adams, E. Calvin Beisner, James Montgomery Boice, Jerry Bridges, Sinclair Ferguson, John Frame, D. James Kennedy, Ronald Nash, Marvin Olasky, Barry Traver, and G. I. Williamson. I am also grateful to R. C. Sproul for taking time out of his busy writing, teaching, and lecturing schedule to read the manuscript and write the foreword.

The families of Redeeming Grace Presbyterian Church in Orange County, California, and the students at the New St. Andrews College in Moscow, Idaho, offered much needed feedback as they were taught the contents of this volume.

Finally, I would be remiss if I failed to express my utmost love for, and appreciation to, my lovely wife, Jamie, and my three beautiful children, Brandon, Kirstin, and Anallyce, who perhaps too often let Daddy disappear into his study to pound away at his keyboard. [D. G. H.]

EDITOR'S INTRODUCTION

C. S. Lewis once quipped that he preferred to take his Christianity the same way he took his whiskey—straight. Though Lewis's analogy will startle some, his point should not be missed. True biblical Christianity is strong stuff. And because it is, the church has often succumbed to the temptation to water it down with all sorts of alluring admixtures. A dash of pragmatism here, a dash of mysticism there, and voilà—down it goes!

What goes down, however, is not the true biblical faith at all. It is, as Lewis aptly noted, a diluted, weakened faith. Even worse, many church goers are completely oblivious to that fact. While pretending to imbibe the strong stuff of true biblical faith, in reality they start with man-made formulas or water the strong stuff down to insipid solutions. Either way, what they ultimately consume bears little, if any, resemblance to the strong stuff of biblical truth.

It is no wonder that most Christians have forgotten not only how potent biblical faith really is, but even what it is about. They have forgotten that it is a faith that

- begins and ends with a sovereign and gracious God who plans all things—including the conversion of His people—in accordance with His will;
- anchors itself upon this sovereign and gracious God's past and future covenantal promise of union and communion with His people and their seed;

1

- grows in the company of God's covenant people as they, in union and communion with Him, are called out of the world together as His church; and
- calls God's people to glorify Him as they live their Christian lives in union with Him, knowing the glorious work He has done, is now doing, and will one day complete in them.

These are just some of the hallmarks of the glorious faith taught so clearly in the Bible and championed so boldly by those who rejected the admixtures that diluted the strong stuff of true biblical faith during the late Middle Ages. It is no surprise that this faith proclaimed by the Protestant Reformers in general, and the Swiss Reformers in particular, came to be known as the Reformed faith. Its sole aim was to reform the church as well as all of life—to call Christians back to the basics of true biblical faith in everything they believed and did.

As it was in the days of the Reformers, so it is in our own day of diluted, weakened faith. We, too, need to reject the alluring admixtures all about us, and to return to a Christianity made of strong stuff. We, too, need to get back to basics by learning what the Reformed faith—true biblical faith—is all about.

That is the reason for this book. Without pretending to be exhaustive, it provides an overview of the basic truths of the Reformed faith—a faith that is so much richer and deeper, so much more majestic and beautiful, than many people even imagine. Far from fitting into some "five point" shoe box, the Reformed faith, as we shall see, is a glorious faith that revolves around a sovereign and gracious God who calls us to conversion and into covenant with Him and His people, thus enabling us to worship Him with His people, the church, and to glorify and enjoy Him as we live the Christian life. This book, then, is a call back to basics—the basics about conversion, the covenant, the church, and the Christian life.

As you learn more about the basics of the Reformed faith in the pages that follow, you would do well to emulate the Reformers, who held steadfastly to all of Scripture and only Scripture as the foundation for everything they believed and did. That foundational commitment to Scripture, of course, was nothing new. After all, Luke commends to us a body of believers in the small town of Berea who shared the same commitment. How so? They compared even what the apostle Paul taught with the supreme standard of Scripture, to see whether the things he taught were true.

As you read this book, you should also search the Scriptures to see whether the things taught here are true. To help you in your search, this book comes equipped with a few brief study questions at the conclusion of each chapter, which should come in handy for further personal reflection or group study. And since this book is only a primer on some of the basic truths of the Reformed faith, an extended bibliography for further reading is also provided.

Whether you approach the Reformed faith with skepticism, unfamiliarity, or acceptance, we hope that you will find that this book sheds some light on what it means to be *reformed according to Scripture*, *yet always reforming according to Scripture*. May we live to see the day when the church will once again adopt that motto as her own. That can happen only if we all heed the call to get back to basics. [D. G. H.]

PART ONE

BACK TO CONVERSION

Douglas J. Wilson

INTRODUCTION

When you get back to basics, you have to start and stop somewhere, and for the Reformers and their heirs, that somewhere has always been the sovereign and gracious God who has revealed Himself in Scripture. Perhaps nothing brings our true starting and stopping point into sharper focus than the question of who gets the credit for our conversion. Does it go to God alone, or does man in some way share the spotlight with God?

The Reformed faith starts and stops—and indeed moves—with the triune God of the universe, who, as we shall see in this part of the book, has sovereignly planned all things according to the counsel of His own holy will and has graciously drawn us to Himself in conversion. God the Father appointed us to eternal life, God the Son bought us at the price of His own blood, and God the Spirit opened our hearts, enabling us to turn to Him in faith and repentance. He is the Alpha and the Omega, the First and the Last, not just in a general sense, but even when it comes to the nitty-gritty of our conversion. From beginning to end, our conversion is the result of His sovereign and gracious work for us and in us as His people.

In an age when many are tempted to edge their way on stage to share the spotlight with God, it is time to get back to basics—back to conversion. [D. G. H.]

ONE

IN THE BEGINNING

In the beginning was *God*. Before Adam made his first decision, there was God. Before Abraham believed the promise, there was God. Before Jesus wrestled with the will of the Father in the Garden of Gethsemane, there was God. And before any sinner ever heard forgiveness proclaimed, there was God—the One who, before the foundation of the universe, ordained that the Lamb would be slain to provide such forgiveness.

All biblical theology must begin and end where the Scriptures do—with God. Sadly, some Christians today tone down or completely ignore what the Bible really says about God. In the process, they end up destroying true theology altogether. By dethroning God and granting crown rights to man, some have fallen into one of the greatest sins plaguing the modern church: constructing a man-centered "theology" that makes a travesty of biblical teaching.

To be truly biblical, theology must be God-centered. That is, it must be centered on the one true God as He has revealed Himself in Scripture—not as we would like Him (or Her?) to be. If we neglect to focus on the one true God, we end up making a god in our own image—fashioned with our minds, if not with our hands. And that, the Bible says, is the sin of idolatry.

Like many well-intentioned Christians, I was for many years a stranger to what the Bible teaches about the sovereignty of God and His saving grace. In hindsight, I now realize that my ignorance stemmed primarily from my own prejudice, but my prejudice was amply reinforced by what I was taught. Because of my past prejudices, I will try to be especially careful to define and explain these crucial biblical doctrines. But caution born of humility is well worth it; after all, we are going to be on holy ground, and it is not too much to ask that the sandals come off. When the apostle Paul, with great wonder, asks, "Who has known the mind of the LORD? Or who has become His counselor?" (Rom. 11:34), he is not expecting an upstart in the back row to raise his hand.

CLEARING THE GROUND

There are two basic reasons why many Christians have trouble with the Bible's teaching on the sovereignty of God.

First, many Christians never really understand what the sovereignty of God is all about. This is partly due to the fact that many in the pulpit simply do not teach the whole system of truth found in the Bible. At the same time, those who do understand this doctrine rarely teach it, and when they do teach it, they do so in a whisper. Meanwhile, opponents of the doctrine often misunderstand it and misrepresent it with loud voices. As a result, many Christians reject not what the Bible teaches but a caricature of what the Bible teaches. For such people, the problem can be solved by carefully studying the Bible. This book is a gentle nudge in that direction.

Second, many do understand the biblical position, but reject it anyway. The solution to this sort of problem is not additional teaching, explanation, or proof texts—it is repentance. Those who knowingly reject any biblical truth need to stop running from God's Word. It is a sin for Christians willfully to reject what the Bible teaches. Of course, there are many godly Christians who do not embrace what the Bible teaches about God's sovereignty because they fail to understand it properly. But it is sinful to be unwilling to consider what the Bible teaches.

SOME CRUCIAL ASSUMPTIONS

The discussion of the sovereignty of God that follows, therefore, is based upon two crucial assumptions.

The first assumption is this: all who profess the name of Christ must accept whatever the Bible clearly teaches on any subject, including this one. In other words, we should adopt the Reformers' motto—*sola et tota Scriptura*—as our own. Our standard for determining what is true must be *only Scripture and all of Scripture.* We do not determine what is true. Nor do we determine what is important. What Scripture says, we must say, and where Scripture is silent, we must be silent. All Christians have an obligation to be open to what the Bible teaches on this subject, whatever that teaching may turn out to be. Nothing is to be dismissed, sight unseen, before we study the Word.

The second assumption goes hand in hand with the first: if Scripture is our only standard for all that we believe and do, finite human reason is not, and cannot be, the final arbiter of revealed truth. Human reason is a gift from God and must therefore be used within the boundaries established by Him. Those boundaries are set by the teachings of Scripture. The primary role of reason is to determine what Scripture actually says; the student of the Bible uses his mind to interpret and apply biblical truth. The role of reason is not to determine, on the basis of some extrabiblical philosophy, what Scripture can or cannot say. Our thoughts, like every other created thing, are to be subjected to the lordship and dominion of Christ (2 Cor. 10:4–5).

Recognizing the legitimate role of reason is crucial. One of the most common problems in the history of this discussion is that those who disagree with each other attempt to take their respective cases to different courts of appeal. One side appeals to Scripture, while the other appeals to "common sense" or reason. One side points to a passage that teaches the sovereign control of God over the choices of men, whereas the other responds by saying that such a view destroys human responsibility. One side says that God saves those whom He wills to save, while the other retorts that such a view would make it impossible for God to hold us responsible for our behavior. And so it goes.

What separates these two sides is not merely a difference of opinion. They not only disagree but appeal to different authorities for support. In fact, they disagree precisely because they appeal to different judges.

In the following pages, we will learn that God controls human choices perfectly but does so without violating the natural liberty of those making choices. From cover to cover, the Bible teaches that divine sovereignty and human responsibility are compatible with one another; nowhere does the Bible even suggest that the affirmation of divine sovereignty leads to the denial of human liberty. Yet, those who oppose the doctrine of divine sovereignty constantly appeal to the court of human reason and, from that vantage point, declare that sovereignty destroys liberty.

Because God, as our infinite Judge, has infallibly revealed Himself in Scripture, our final court of appeal—indeed, our only court of appeal—is

Scripture. Thus, we will address this subject with biblical statements, using biblical terminology and working within biblical categories. Toward that end, each section will review some relevant biblical passages and proceed to discuss and apply those passages. While there will be many evangelical readers who have not yet embraced the full Reformed faith, they nevertheless can quite cheerfully accept these conditions. As we are enabled by the Spirit of God, let us reason together within the boundaries established by Scripture.

S<small>TUDY</small> Q<small>UESTIONS</small>

1. Where must true theology begin—and why? Is this where your theology begins?
2. Why do Christians have difficulties with what the Bible has to say about divine sovereignty? What are the best ways to resolve such difficulties? Do you have difficulty with the doctrine of divine sovereignty? How should you resolve it?
3. What ultimately separates those who accept the biblical doctrine of divine sovereignty from those who deny it? Where do you fall on this dividing line? Where should you fall?

T W O

WHO'S IN CHARGE
AROUND HERE?

G od is not Zeus. He is not an oversized creature. He inhabits eternity;
from everlasting to everlasting, He is God (Ps. 90:2). He is over all,
in all, and through all. Nothing happens apart from His full knowledge
and presence (Heb. 4:13). Nevertheless, God does not live in the same
environment as we do, which is simply to say that He is not contained by
or shut up within the universe.[1] To the contrary, God created and controls
the universe in accordance with His plan and purpose.

While Christians readily believe and embrace the plan and purpose
of God as an obvious truth of the faith, many still succumb to the temptation to deny some of the ramifications of this truth. After all, if God is
sovereign over the created order, then He controls all natural events, including events that appear to be totally random. What, for instance, appears to be more random than a roll of the dice? Yet Solomon tells us,
"The lot is cast into the lap, but its every decision is from the LORD" (Prov.
16:33). And what is more chaotic to us than a battle? But when Micaiah
the prophet testified that Ahab would fall in an upcoming battle, he knew
that the Lord had certainly spoken through him (1 Kings 22:28). And
what happened in the battle? "Now a certain man drew a bow at random,
and struck the king of Israel between the joints of his armor" (v. 34).

Throwing dice and shooting an arrow in battle may indeed look to us
like random events. But our perspective is not the final word on the subject,

11

even though we may speak of "random" events all the time. Think for a moment about the word *sunset*. Why do we not refer to a sunset as an "earthturn"? The answer is simple: even though we know that the sun is not really setting, it nevertheless appears to be. So the way we talk sometimes mirrors the way things appear to us, as opposed to the way they really are. In the same way, we may speak of chance or random events, provided we remember what the Bible really teaches on these subjects. From the biblical vantage point, there is no such thing as ultimate chance, since, ultimately, God controls all aspects of creation, including arrows and dice.

Texts could be multiplied to show the Lord's control over all aspects of creation. To name just a few, He controls the weather (Job 36:32), the fall of sparrows (Matt. 10:29), the movement of the winds (Nah. 1:3), the rate of hair loss (Matt. 10:30), the rise and fall of nations (Dan. 4:17), the decisions of kings (Prov. 21:1), the natural disasters that afflict us (Amos 3:6), and even the traffic on the freeway (Prov. 16:9).

BOTH . . . AND

But what about the free choices of men? Does God control our choices? And if He does, how can they be free? As we shall see in the next chapter, far from destroying free choices, divine sovereignty actually makes them possible. What destroys free choices, therefore, is not divine sovereignty, but rather notions of autonomous free will. But before we see how free choice is possible only against the backdrop of divine sovereignty, we must first see what the Bible says about divine sovereignty and human responsibility. What does the Bible teach on these subjects? Does it really teach both that God controls human choices and that such choices are nonetheless genuinely free?

Allow Solomon to answer this all-important question: "The preparations of the heart belong to man, but the answer of the tongue is *from the* LORD" (Prov. 16:1).

Now, many Christians have no trouble admitting that a man can make plans, but that God ultimately controls his life. They pray and live as though God is superintending all their actions, which He is. For many, however, a problem is posed by the existence of sin. Does God's control include control over the sinful choices of men?

When I was first struggling with this issue, Acts 4:27–28 was my undoing: "For truly against Your holy Servant Jesus, whom You anointed, both Herod and Pontius Pilate, with the Gentiles and the people of Israel, were gathered together to do whatever *Your hand* and *Your purpose* determined *before* to be done."

The most heinous crime ever committed was the crucifixion of Christ. And no matter how hard some try to get around this important truth, the Bible declares that God decreed that Christ would be executed. But even though God decreed Christ's execution, He held those who executed Him (those who fulfilled God's decree) guilty of sin. Acts 2:23 teaches the same truth: "This Man [Christ], delivered up by the predetermined plan and foreknowledge of God, *you* nailed to a cross *by the hands of godless men and put Him to death*" (NASB). In the same breath, Acts 2:23 declares both that Christ was delivered up in accordance with God's sovereign plan and that those who put Him to death were responsible for their godlessness.

After wrestling with these passages, I did not initially come to the conviction that God controls *all* things. But when I finally admitted that God controlled even the crucifixion of Christ, I lost my major argument against God's sovereignty. Make no mistake about it: Herod, Pontius Pilate, and the people of Israel were not puppets; they were real men with real responsibilities before God. Christ told Pilate that he was guilty of sin (John 19:11). Nevertheless, Pilate's sin was predestined and was under God's perfect control.

Now as soon as I admitted that God could control human actions (including sinful actions) without turning human actors into robots, and without incurring the guilt of that sin Himself, I saw that there was no reason to deny that He exercises such control elsewhere. Once I understood that God's sovereignty did not destroy the responsibility of those who nailed Christ to the tree, so as to make God unjust, then I could not understand what all the fuss was about.

To be true to the plain meaning of Scripture, I had to admit that divine sovereignty and human responsibility live together comfortably in Scripture. Scripture presents no tension between sovereignty and responsibility. It is not *either* divine sovereignty *or* human responsibility. It is *both* divine sovereignty *and* human responsibility.

What is more, the coexistence of divine sovereignty and human responsibility is not a truth that is taught in just one passage (although one would be enough). Scripture constantly refers to human action that was under God's perfect control. Think for a moment about Joseph. After being reunited with his brothers who sold him into slavery, Joseph forgives them and declares: "And as for you, you meant evil against me, but God meant it for good in order to bring about this present result, to preserve many people alive" (Gen. 50:20 NASB).

Put somewhat differently, although Joseph's brothers sinned against him grievously, God's will was nonetheless fulfilled. God did not have perfect plan A until Joseph's brothers sinned and caused Him to switch to permissive plan B. All along, God had a single plan that encompassed the sin of Joseph's brothers without relieving them of the responsibility for their sin. God was sovereign; they were responsible.

Just a few pages later in Scripture, we read of Pharaoh's hardening his heart (Ex. 8:15, 32; 9:34). But just as Scripture informs us that Pharaoh hardened his own heart, so also it informs us that God hardened Pharaoh's heart (Ex. 7:13–14, 22; 8:19; 9:7, 12, 35; 10:1, 20, 27; 11:10; 14:8).

Eli's sons also come to mind. Although Eli rebuked them for their immorality, they "did not heed the voice of their father, because the LORD desired to kill them" (1 Sam. 2:25). Now, were Eli's sons responsible for continuing in their sinful rebellion against the authority of God? Of course they were. But why did they ignore their father's warning? The Bible says that they did so because the Lord desired to kill them.

Then there is the example of Job. Who did all the damage to Job? While it was clearly the work of Satan (Job 1:12; 2:6–7), Job saw the Lord's hand in it: "The LORD gave, and the LORD has taken away; blessed be the name of the LORD" (Job 1:21).

For those who assume that God cannot use the actions of His creatures to accomplish His perfect and holy purposes, such passages—and there are many—present a dilemma: did God take Job through his trials, or did Satan? But if we simply submit to the clear statements of Scripture, the dilemma vanishes. While Satan performed the actions in this drama, God controlled him perfectly all along. Therefore, it is completely accurate to attribute the outcome to both, although they obviously had different purposes.

In the same way, while we live out our lives according to our purposes and plans, God uses them to accomplish His foreordained purpose. This is exactly what Paul teaches us when he encourages the Philippians to "work out your salvation with fear and trembling; for it is God who is at work in you, both to will and to work for His good pleasure" (Phil. 2:12–13 NASB).

According to Paul, the fact that God sovereignly works in us to accomplish His good pleasure should motivate us to grow in sanctification. We work because He works. Thus, far from precluding human responsibility, divine sovereignty actually makes human responsibility possible.

Scripture itself is a testimony that divine sovereignty does not destroy human responsibility. The sovereignty of God pervades every page of the Bible—in fact, every word. And yet, who wrote the book of Romans? Whose words are they? Whose personality stands out on every page? The answer, of course, is Paul (Rom. 1:1). But every consistent Christian believes that Paul's words are *also* the very words of God. Unless we admit that God can use the free actions of His creatures to accomplish what He intends, we must abandon our belief that the Bible was infallibly inspired by God.

Put more bluntly, Christians who deny that God controls the free decisions of men have a real problem with inspiration. To be consistent, either they must assert that God destroyed the liberty of the biblical writers and that God alone speaks in the Bible through some sort of mechanical dictation, or they must abandon the verbal inspiration of the Scriptures as an impossibility. If they opt for the former, then they must explain how the personality of the various writers is so evident ("Bring the cloak that I left with Carpus at Troas"). But if they opt for the latter, then we must bid them farewell on their journey out of Christianity.[2]

THE WILLS OF GOD?

From what has been said so far, it should be plain that the will of God cannot be thwarted. If God fully intends that something will happen, it will happen. God's counsel will be done, and His eternal purposes will be accomplished.

But this is not the only sense we can give to the phrase "the will of God." There is a sense in which the will of God can be transgressed. Every time we sin, for instance, we violate the will of God. Accordingly, Paul tells the Thessalonians, "This is the will of God, your sanctification: that you should abstain from sexual immorality" (1 Thess. 4:3).

God does not will that Christians commit sexual immorality. He has prohibited it. Yet we know that Christians are capable of disobeying God in this matter—hence the warning to the Thessalonians. When Christians disobey God, the will of God, in a certain sense, is contradicted. For the sake of maintaining clear distinctions, let us call this will "the preceptive will of God." God has commanded us to do many things and has prohibited us from doing other things; He has given us His precepts. But because we are sinners, we transgress these precepts and thereby transgress God's preceptive will. Sinners do so every day. So the preceptive will of God can be disobeyed.

But there is another sense in which Scripture refers to "the will of

God." This is what we call "the decretive will of God," which refers to the fact that God has decreed what will happen. When God says, "Let there be light," the darkness is scattered. Through Isaiah the prophet, God proclaims that His decretive will cannot be thwarted: "I make known the end from the beginning, from ancient times, what is still to come. I say: My purpose will stand, and *I will do all that I please*" (Isa. 46:10 NIV).

A great deal of confusion results when one speaks of "the will of God" without indicating whether one is referring to His preceptive or decretive will. The distinction, however, is not difficult to make, and it is in fact required by Scripture. Everyone who has ever contemplated the sin in his own heart knows that there is much to be conformed to the preceptive will of God. But it is equally clear in Scripture that God's purposes cannot be thwarted. That truth was evident to Job—"Then Job replied to the LORD, 'I know that you can do all things; no plan of yours can be thwarted' " (Job 42:1–2 NIV). In Proverbs 19:21 we read, "Many are the plans in a man's heart, but it is the LORD's purpose that prevails" (NIV). No genuine Christian seriously doubts for a moment that God can do anything He wants. If God does not do something, it is only because He does not want to do it, not because He is incapable of doing it.

To acknowledge that God's plan cannot be thwarted is not to contradict the fact that people disobey God's moral law and revealed will. Disobedience, however, cannot overthrow the counsel of God. But when we begin to contemplate how God perfectly controls disobedience, numerous questions come to mind, perhaps the foremost of which is whether human choices are genuinely free. To that question we turn next.

STUDY QUESTIONS

1. Does the Bible endorse the view that certain things, such as the rolling of dice or the piercing of an arrow, happen at random? On this basis, explain from the Bible how the apparently random events in your life are not really random after all. How does this fact comfort you?
2. Cite biblical texts teaching that God is sovereign and that man is responsible. Based on these texts, can you ever blame your sin on God? Why not?
3. Given that Scripture refers to the will of God in two ways, can we accurately say that God has two wills? Can God's will ever be thwarted? Cite biblical texts in support of your answer.

Notes

1. "Some assume the following: we are little fish, and God is a big, big, big fish, so He has a lot to offer us. He can protect us, we can talk to Him. He is very smart, but we are really floating around in the same sea of possibility" (Steve Schlissel, "The Unchanging Character of God's Word," *Antithesis* 2, no. 1 [January/February 1991]: 11).
2. For further study of divine sovereignty, see Gen. 18:14; 50:20; Ex. 11:7; 12:36; 14:17; Num. 23:19; 2 Sam. 16:10–11; Ezra 6:22; 7:6; Neh. 9:6; Job 14:15; 36:32; 42:2; Pss. 33:10–11; 37:23; 104:21; 115:3; 135:6; 139:16; Prov. 21:1; Isa. 14:24–27; 45:7; 46:9–11; 55:11; 64:8; Jer. 32:17; Ezek. 36:27; Dan. 2:21, 28; 4:17, 35; Amos 3:6; 4:7; Hab. 1:6; Matt. 5:45; 6:26; 10:29; 25:34; Mark 14:30; Luke 22:22; John 6:64; Acts 1:24–26; 3:18; 17:28; Rom. 8:28; 11:36; 1 Cor. 4:7; Eph. 1:11; 4:6; Phil. 2:13; Col. 1:17; Heb. 1:3; James 4:15; 1 Peter 1:20.

THREE

WHERE THERE'S A WILL

Free will—who could be against it? But there is a better question: Free will—what is it?

Many of the staunchest advocates of free will encounter immediate difficulties when they are asked to explain what they mean.[1] By closely examining the definitions they offer, it soon becomes apparent that free will, as commonly understood, is not a biblical concept.[2]

OUT OF THE HEART

Contrary to popular belief, the Bible sheds much light on this important subject. In fact, Jesus plainly explains how the will operates—and His explanation is not what many suppose. In Matthew 12:33–37, He says to us,

> Either make the tree good and its fruit good, or else make the tree bad and its fruit bad; for a tree is known by its fruit. Brood of vipers! How can you, being evil, speak good things? For out of the abundance of the heart the mouth speaks. A good man out of the good treasure of his heart brings forth good things, and an evil man out of the evil treasure brings forth evil things. But I say to you that for every idle word men may speak, they will give account of it in the day of judgment. For by your words you will be justified, and by your words you will be condemned.

In this passage, Christ teaches that choices come from the heart. The will does not command the heart; the heart commands the will. Along these lines, consider the three key points that Christ makes.

First, words and actions are the fruit of our human nature; that is, they reveal our nature. A good nature will result in good words, and an evil nature will result in evil words. Good trees produce good fruit, and evil trees produce evil fruit. Our words and actions, therefore, are determined not by an autonomous will, but rather by our nature—whether good or bad.

Second, because our nature determines our words and actions, someone with an evil nature is incapable of speaking good words. But this inability, this bondage, is caused by his own heart. He is bound by what he wants; his heart acts as a limiting principle. And because wants emanate from the heart, he is not externally compelled to do what he does. Put simply, he wants what he wants because of his heart. Hence, while evil men are free to do what they *want*, they are not free to do what they *should*.

Third, just because our choices proceed from our hearts, our responsibility before God is not limited in the slightest. Our words are determined by our hearts, and we will be judged on the basis of our words precisely because they reflect our hearts.

In addition to explaining the relationship between the heart and the will by referring to fruit-bearing trees, Jesus also makes the same point by referring to treasure chests. In the passage above, He tells us that good deeds come from a good treasure chest, while evil deeds come from a bad one. Whoever reaches into a chest can only pull out of it what was already inside it. To amplify this point a bit, one chest may contain gold, while another chest may contain gravel. One who reaches into the chest containing gold will pull out gold, whereas one who reaches into the chest containing gravel will pull out gravel. Different chests, therefore, contain different things.

Likewise, different people have different hearts, and because different hearts contain different things, people make different choices. Seen in this light, the will is simply the arm that God has given us to reach into the chest in order to bring out the contents of the heart. Just as the arm has no power to determine the contents of the chest, so the will has no power to determine the contents of the heart. The will has power only to reveal the contents of the heart, and this it does very well.

As a result, no one is capable of making a choice contrary to his heart's strongest desire. This is an inexorable law; there are no exceptions.

The source of this law is found in God, whose choices proceed from His immutable and holy nature. Jesus taught us that no man can say, "Yes, I chose to do *this*, but my strongest desire was to do *that*." By definition, what we choose to do is what we want to do. We may certainly have other desires, and they may be very strong (Rom. 7:18–23), but what we finally do is what we ultimately wanted to do most. We are therefore responsible for the choices we have made.

If a particular choice did not stem from our strongest desire, we would not have made it to begin with. Suppose, for example, that I offer a man a bowl of cockroaches to eat, and he declines the invitation because he doesn't want to eat them. Suppose further that because he doesn't want to eat them, I proclaim, "Ah, your will is enslaved!"

"You're crazy!" he retorts. "How can you say that my will is enslaved?"

"Because you didn't use your will to eat the cockroaches," I say.

"My will," he contends, "is working perfectly well, thank you. I simply willed not to eat the cockroaches."

Quite true. His will chose just what he wanted, and he did not want to eat cockroaches.[3] But suppose that he tries to refute the notion that what we want to do is what we end up doing by saying, "I don't *want* to eat a cockroach, but I'm going to do so anyway. So there!" Has he now made his point? Not at all. He has simply acted on the basis of his strongest desire, which is now to win the debate.

In light of what we have considered, we see that it is inaccurate to talk about free will, as though there were an autonomous thing inside of us, capable of acting in any direction, regardless of the motives of our hearts. If such a thing existed—a creature who made choices apart from the desires of the heart—we would not applaud it as a paragon of free will but rather would pity it as a collection of random, arbitrary, and insane choices. Far from being a free and responsible agent, admired by all, such a creature would be a freak—a side show at the circus causing passers-by to recoil in abject horror. Choices made apart from the desires of the heart would be an exhibition, not of freedom, but of insanity: "Why did you throw the vase against the wall?" "Because I wanted to go for a walk."[4] The lights are on, but nobody is home!

It is far more biblical to speak of free men than of free will. A free man is someone who is free from external compulsion and is consequently at liberty to do what his heart desires. We shall refer to this kind of liberty as "natural liberty," which all men possess. It is true of liberty, and it is a gift from God. Under the superintendence of God, all men, Christian and non-Christian, have natural liberty to turn left or right, to choose chocolate or vanilla, or to move to this city or that—depending entirely upon what they want to do.[5]

Notice that this natural liberty is not the same thing as freedom from sin, which we shall refer to as "moral liberty." In Romans 6:20–22, Paul makes the distinction between natural liberty, which all men have, and moral liberty, which only believers have. He says, "For when you were slaves of sin, you were free in regard to righteousness. . . . But now having been set free from sin, and having become slaves of God, you have your fruit to holiness, and the end, everlasting life."

Slavery to sin is true slavery (i.e., the opposite of moral liberty). But even sin does not negate natural liberty. The slave to sin is free from righteousness, but is still not free from his own desires. Sin's slave loves sin, and consequently obeys his impulses. As a creature, the slave to sin is naturally free to do what he wants, which is to continue in sin. But he is not morally free to desire righteousness, because his sinful heart does not love what is right. Like all men, he is not free to choose what is repulsive to him, and true godliness is repulsive to him. In the realm of morality, he is free in a limited sense—free from the control of righteousness. When God by grace liberates him from the bondage of his own sin-loving heart, he becomes a slave to God. And as God's slave, out of a new heart, he freely follows Christ. The Christian is morally free from slavery to sin, and free to walk in righteousness.

TURNING THE TABLES

Now that we have cleared up many of the misunderstandings surrounding the definition of free will, we are in a position to clear up a misunderstanding that often arises when someone affirms the biblical doctrine of divine sovereignty, namely, that it destroys freedom. If God sovereignly foreordains all that comes to pass, some mistakenly conclude that human beings have no true freedom at all. This conclusion is quite false.

Over three hundred years ago, some of the greatest theologians ever assembled (the Westminster divines) declared that the sovereignty of God's eternal decree does not do violence "to the will of the creatures; nor is the liberty or contingency of second causes taken away, but rather established" (Westminster Confession of Faith, 3.1).

Note that the Westminster divines were saying that divine sovereignty is not merely consistent with human liberty, but indeed the very foundation for it. Hence, those who deny the doctrine of divine sovereignty are attacking the only true ground of human liberty.

The debate, then, is not between Christians who affirm the liberty and responsibility of creatures, and those who deny such liberty. Rather, it is between those who ground the liberty of creatures in the strength and power of God, and those who ground it in the strength and power of man.

To be sure, some people dismiss this affirmation of creaturely liberty as something "tacked on" to the biblical position—as a sort of sop to common sense.[6] Still others boldly proclaim that to assert both divine sovereignty and true human freedom is "illogical." There is a very simple answer to this bold proclamation: if asserting both divine sovereignty and human responsibility is illogical, then name the fallacy. There is a vast difference between logical contradictions and those high mysteries that, necessarily, are contained in the infinite wisdom of God. After all, something may be beyond human reason without necessarily being contrary to it.[7]

Dismissing divine sovereignty is a natural mistake to make, and people have been making it at least since the time of Paul (Rom. 9:19). When we consider the relationship of the infinite Creator to the finite creature, we do have a problem understanding how true natural liberty can coexist with a sovereign God superintending all events in the universe. But the reconciliation of these two biblical truths is ultimately to be found in the mind of God. It is not a problem that is keeping Him up nights, and we must recognize that our finite, creaturely minds are not capable of penetrating the glories of the infinite Creator.[8] The sovereign prerogatives of the Creator are not inconsistent with the natural liberty and true responsibility of creatures. How could they be? The Bible teaches them both, sometimes in the same verse (e.g., Matt. 18:7).[9]

Since the Bible teaches both truths, those who claim that divine sovereignty destroys true human liberty have a heavy load to tow. In the end, they destroy human liberty by rejecting its only proper foundation, which is divine sovereignty.[10]

We have already seen that the choices we make proceed from our hearts. Given this biblical fact, it is impossible for a choice to be truly autonomous. If there were an autonomous choice—a choice for which no reason at all could be given—we could no longer call it a choice in any meaningful sense. We would have to say that it was a random event. Speaking about an "autonomous choice" is as contradictory as speaking about a "round square."

Because all the influence flows from the heart to the will, and not vice versa, the question comes down to this: Since the will does not determine the direction of the heart, what does? The Bible teaches that God superintends the choices made by men. He may do so immediately through divine intervention, or mediately through the use of secondary agents.

If, for the sake of argument, we were to remove God's personal sovereignty from the realm of human choices, what would be left? Only a blind, inexorable, deterministic fatalism. Picture cupped hands around a guttering candle in a strong wind. This flame represent the human will. The wind is the world around us. The cupped hands are the Lord's. Within Christianity, advocates of "free will" want the Lord to remove His hands so that the candle may burn more brightly. The history of modern philosophy should teach us better than that. Those who begin such optimistic crusades in the name of free will always end up in the fever swamps of blind behaviorism and determinism.

The will simply cannot command the heart. But let us, for the sake of argument, remove the Lord's control of the heart because some well-intentioned Christians say it is inconsistent with free will. What is then left to influence the heart? Only the material universe—and the name of that philosophy is determinism. The candle is out.

The only biblical conclusion is that man, as a creature, is free to do as he pleases, but that he has this freedom only because God grants, sustains, and perfectly controls it.

DEAD ON ARRIVAL

We have established that men and women, as creatures, have true natural liberty. God has made the world in such a way that they are free to do as they please. But it does not follow from this that they are free to do as they ought.

Because we have true creaturely freedom, we are free to act on the basis of our desires and are free to do as we please. But because we are by nature sinners, what we desire to do is sinful. Our natural bondage to sin must therefore be seen as an expression of our creaturely freedom, not as a violation of it. As creatures, we are free to turn left or right. But as sinners, we will turn left into sin or right into sin. As creatures, we are free to choose pride or false humility, drunkenness or gluttony, self-righteousness or flagrant immorality. As creatures, we have freedom to do what we desire. But we always desire to sin because of our evil hearts.

Christ spoke about the relationship between an evil heart and evil deeds when He proclaimed: "For from within, *out of the heart of men*, proceed evil thoughts, adulteries, fornications, murders, thefts, covetousness, wickedness, deceit, licentiousness, an evil eye, blasphemy, pride, foolishness. All these evil things come *from within* and defile a man" (Mark 7:21–23).

Sinners have no desire to glorify God. In a moral sense, there is no freedom until the Spirit of God creates it. Consequently, salvation is not and cannot be the result of a cooperative effort between God and the sinner; it results from the unilateral act of God alone. Until God changes the sinner's heart, the sinner does not want true salvation. The Bible teaches that the unregenerate have no freedom at all in this moral sense. Ironically enough, it is precisely at this point—the choices that affect salvation—that many Christians are most eager to assert that the unregenerate actually have such moral freedom.

As we discuss what the Bible says about the condition of the unregenerate, we must keep in mind the distinction between natural and moral liberty, between man as a creature and man as a sinner. While man the creature has natural liberty from God, man the sinner does not have moral liberty.

> And you *He made alive*, who were *dead* in trespasses and sins, in which you once walked according to the course of this world, according to the prince of the power of the air, the spirit who now works in the *sons of disobedience*, among whom also we all once conducted ourselves in the lusts of our flesh, fulfilling the desires of the flesh and of the mind, and were *by nature children of wrath*, just as the others. (Eph. 2:1–3)

In this passage, Paul tells the Ephesian believers that before God made them alive, they were dead. They were not sick, not infected, not ailing, but dead. The messenger who first preached the gospel to them was not a doctor intent on persuading his patients to take their medicine, but rather was like the prophet Ezekiel, confronted with a congregation of bones.

The deadness of the unregenerate is not a temporary condition brought about by unfortunate circumstances; the unregenerate are all children of wrath by nature. And, as such, they have an inbred hostility toward the things of God—an inbred hostility about which they themselves can do nothing. Since they have natural liberty (i.e., the freedom to do that which emanates from their evil nature), they do not want to do anything about their present state: "The carnal mind is *enmity against* God; for it is not subject to the law of God, *nor indeed can be*. So then, those who are in the flesh *cannot please God*" (Rom. 8:7–8).

The natural man's inability to please God does not come about through external coercion. It is not as though God were holding a gun to his head, preventing him from repenting. He is not a hapless victim begging God to let him repent. It is not that way at all. As the passage above states, inability comes from enmity. The natural man cannot please God because he is at war with God.

In the earlier chapters of Romans, when Paul discusses the condition of the unregenerate, both Jew and Gentile, he leaves absolutely no room for doubt on this issue: "There is *none* righteous, no, *not one*; there is *none* who understands; there is *none* who seeks after God. They have *all* gone out of the way; they have together become unprofitable; there is *none* who does good, no, *not one*" (Rom. 3:10–12).

Remember, God gave us the Bible to reveal His mind to us. Since He chose specific words as the instrument of His revelation, we must treat those words as reliable indications of what God wants us to believe. And if the words in Romans 3 mean anything, not one unregenerate person has ever sought after God—not one.

The inability of the natural man to love God is a common theme in Paul's writings. It is not limited to the book of Romans. For example, we read in 1 Corinthians 2:14, "But the natural man *does not receive* the things of the Spirit of God, for they are *foolishness to him*; nor *can* he know them, because they are spiritually discerned."

The natural man can be saved only by the gospel. And this gospel, his only hope, is gibberish to him. Because the gospel is foolishness to him, Paul says that he cannot know it. Knowledge of the gospel requires spiritual discernment, and those without the Spirit do not have it. Nor will they have it until God graciously gives them a new heart.

Jesus also teaches that the natural man is unable to know God until God first draws him: *"No one can come to Me* unless the Father who sent Me draws him; and I will raise him up at the last day"* (John 6:44).

The point is clear enough. Unless the Father draws the unbeliever, the unbeliever cannot come to Christ. Later in the same chapter, when some withdraw from Him, Christ reiterates the same truth: "Therefore I have said to you that *no one can come to Me* unless it has been granted to him by My Father" (John 6:65). In other words, some withdrew from Christ because they wanted to, and the only way they could have had a different desire would have been if the Father had given it to them. In this case, He had not.

The Bible emphatically asserts that the unregenerate have no desire for God and, therefore, are unable to come to Him. Their inability is not an external constraint placed upon them; rather, it is an indication of the sinfulness of their hearts. They cannot because they will not. They will not because their wills are free to choose their hearts' desire. They are in moral bondage because they have natural liberty to do as they please.

In view of these truths, how can anyone be saved? If all are in this condition—and the Bible says that they are—how is it that some come to repentance and faith? How is salvation possible?

We have seen that because sinners love sin, they cannot choose God. But it does not follow from this that God cannot choose sinners. God loves sinners more than sinners love sin. His pure love is greater than our defiled love, and it goes forth conquering and to conquer. The Bible teaches us that our salvation is grounded in a loving God who chose rebellious and ungrateful sinners as His own before the foundation of the world.[11]

STUDY QUESTIONS

1. What are the two different kinds of liberty that God's creatures can possess, and what distinguishes one from the other? Do unbelievers possess these two different kinds of liberty? What about believers?
2. How does the advocate of free will blow out the candle of free will? Have you blown out the candle of free will in your attempt to keep the flame burning?
3. In what three ways does Ephesians 2:1–3 describe unbelievers? How do John 3:19; 1 Corinthians 2:14; Ephesians 4:17–19; 5:8; and Titus 1:15 describe the state of the unbeliever? Does an unbeliever, according to Romans 8:7–8, really want to please God? Is he even able to please God? Why not? Who brings those who are dead to life (see Col. 2:13)? When was the last time you expressed your gratitude to the One who made you alive together with Christ and forgave all your transgressions? How about doing so right now?

Notes

1. The embarrassment of Erasmus in his debate with Luther may be the archetypal example. Consider Luther's response: "For though what you think and write about 'free-will' is wrong, I owe you no small debt of thanks for making me far surer of my own view; as I have been since I saw the case for 'free-will' argued with all the resources that your brilliant gifts afford you—and to such little purpose that it is now in a worse state than before. That in itself is clear proof that 'free-will' is an utter fallacy. It is like the woman in the Gospel; the

more the doctors treat the case, the worse it gets" (Martin Luther, *The Bondage of the Will* [Old Tappan, N.J.: Revell, 1957], 65).

2. From Pelagius to Pighius, and from Pighius to Pinnock, free will has certainly been championed. But it has never been adequately explained, because it is an incoherent concept: "I shall consider whether any such thing be possible or conceivable, as that Freedom of Will which Arminians insist on" (Jonathan Edwards, *On the Freedom of the Will*, in *The Works of Jonathan Edwards*, 2 vols. [Edinburgh: Banner of Truth, 1974], 2:13).

3. "No one attempts to allure a hungry horse with bacon, or a hungry man with hay" (R. L. Dabney, *Systematic Theology* [Edinburgh: Banner of Truth, 1985], 129).

4. "If the will were able to make decisions contrary to reason, and to the likes and desires of the heart, it would be a monster. You would find yourself in a restaurant ordering all the foods you detest. You would find yourself selecting the company you loathe. But the will is not a monster. It cannot choose without consulting your intelligence, reflecting your feelings, and taking account of your desires. You are free to be yourself. The will cannot transform you into someone else" (Walter Chantry, *Man's Will—Free Yet Bound* [Canton, Ga.: Free Grace Publications, 1988], 5).

5. While the foreordination of God is the cause of such desires, it does not violate them. But more on this in a moment.

6. It is important to note the word "dismiss" and remember that it is not a synonym for *argue*. It is easy to assume that divine sovereignty is inconsistent with true human responsibility, but to argue that position is really impossible.

7. To say that anything beyond human reason is necessarily contrary to reason is to swallow the non-Christian view of mystery, which holds either that mysteries must exist for both God and man (thus dethroning God) or that no mysteries exist for God or man (thus exalting man). The Christian view of mystery, by contrast, holds that there are mysteries for man (as a finite creature), but not for God (as the infinite Creator). While the Christian view of mystery simply recognizes that there is a distinction between the infinite Creator and His finite creatures, the non-Christian view, in one way or another, denies this distinction.

8. I was once speaking with a woman in the Jehovah's Witnesses who said that she refused to believe in the Trinity because the concept was incomprehensible to her. I asked her if she believed that God was infinite. When she said that she did, I asked her to explain that infinitude in a way that would enable me to comprehend it. Of course, she could not. An infinite God is just as incomprehensible as a triune God. The human mind cannot be the court in which truth about God is established.

9. "God's sovereignty and man's responsibility are taught us side by side in the same Bible; sometimes, indeed, in the same text" (J. I. Packer, *Evangelism and the Sovereignty of God* [Downers Grove, Ill.: InterVarsity Press, 1961], 22).

10. "Instead of our doctrine of foreordination being the same with the heathen doctrine of fate, it is its absolute opposite and only alternative. We are shut up to a choice between the two—either a fatalism which results from mechanical coaction, or a fatalism which results from a mindless and purposeless chance, or an all-controlling providence of a heavenly Father who, in the exercise of his own personal freedom, has made room for ours. All thinkers who understand themselves know that they run along one or other of these lines. The wiseacres who plead the authority of philosophy and science as inconsistent with the scriptural doctrine of predestination may be safely left to themselves. They will not be found to be dangerous enemies even behind our backs" (A. A. Hodge, *Evangelical Theology* [Edinburgh: Banner of Truth, 1976], 135–36).

11. For further study of man's sin-induced inability to love or believe God, see Gen. 2:17; Job 14:4; 15:14–15; Ps. 51:5; Eccl. 9:3; Isa. 64:6; Jer. 13:23; 17:9; Matt. 7:16–18; 12:33; John 3:3, 5–7, 19; 5:21; 6:53; 8:34, 44; 14:16; Acts 13:41; Rom. 5:12; 6:20; 1 Cor. 1:18; 2 Cor. 5:17; Eph. 2:12; 4:17–19; 5:8; Col. 2:13; 2 Tim. 2:25–26; Titus 1:15; 3:3; 1 John 3:10.

FOUR

FROM THE SAME LUMP

D oes not a potter, asks Paul, have a right to make from the same lump of clay one vessel for honor and another for dishonor (Rom. 9:20–21)? Of course he does! It should come as no surprise that the same is true of the divine potter, who, before the foundation of the universe, chose from the same lump of humanity some to be vessels for honor and others to be vessels for dishonor. Or, to put it another way, He chose some and passed by others—or, elected some and hardened others—all in order to glorify His name.

THE "CHOOSING" PEOPLE?

When we discuss those whom God has chosen—the elect—we must first come to grips with the fact that the Bible itself again and again refers to Christians not just as saints but also as the chosen or the elect. It is only proper to conclude that these words actually mean something. Sadly, many deny the meaning of these words, or, worse yet, stand them on their head.

Once, for example, I was at a conference where a fine Christian gentleman gave a talk on Matthew 22. On the whole, it was a good and edifying talk—except for his treatment of verse 14: "For many are called, but few are chosen." Instead of explaining this verse, he explained it away. Later, when asked what I thought of the talk, I said that it was fine, except for the way the speaker turned the word "chosen" into "choose." The passage does not say, "For many are called, but few choose." Rather, it says that "few are chosen."

Elect does not mean "elector." *Chosen* does not mean "chooser." The Bible's teaching on this subject is so plain that denying it involves standing the words of Scripture on their head. When a man is chosen, he is not the one performing the action; that is, he is not the one who is choosing. Similarly, when a man is elected, he is not the one who is electing. So once we have agreed that God is the one who chooses (elects), and that people are chosen (elected), we may then proceed to discuss when and why God makes that choice.

A good starting point is found in Peter's first letter, where he describes the members of the church in this way: "But you are a *chosen* generation, a royal priesthood, a holy nation, *His own special people*, that you may proclaim the praises of Him who *called* you out of darkness into His marvelous light" (1 Peter 2:9). We are taught here that Christians are chosen and called to be God's special people. Christians are Christians because they have been chosen by God. But when was this choice made? When were the elect set apart from the rest of humanity? The Bible teaches that it happened before we were born—indeed, before time began.

> Therefore do not be ashamed of the testimony of our Lord, nor of me His prisoner, but share with me in the sufferings for the gospel according to the power of God, who has saved us and called us with a holy calling, *not according to our works, but according to His own purpose and grace which was given to us in Christ Jesus before time began.* (2 Tim. 1:8–9)

What does Paul say here? At conversion, we were called to Christ according to something. That something was not our own works, but rather God's purpose and grace. And God gave His purpose and grace to us before the beginning of time. His electing grace was not given when we believed; we believed because it had been given—before Creation. Consequently, God's electing grace does not depend upon anything we have ever done or anything we will ever do; it was given to us before we even had hands to receive it.

Because our election was settled before history, it is not possible for anything that occurs in history to unsettle it. This provides God's people with an unshakable confidence, which is precisely the way Paul applies this doctrine. God has secured the salvation of His elect in a way that cannot be undone: "Who shall bring a charge against *God's elect?* It is God who justifies" (Rom. 8:33).

If God has truly chosen someone, then no creature can undo that choice—including the fortunate individual upon whom the blessing has been bestowed. Notice also that if this doctrine is to serve as a ground for confidence, it must not be hidden away in a book in the pastor's study. Pastors must proclaim it, and Christians must learn to take comfort in it during times of trial.

The truth of election is not just a comfort in affliction, but also the foundation for godly living: "Therefore, *as the elect of God,* holy and beloved, put on tender mercies, kindness, humbleness of mind, meekness, longsuffering" (Col. 3:12).

The Colossians were not simply to be tender, kind, humble, meek, and so forth—they were to do so as the elect of God. In other words, simply inculcating such characteristics is not enough. They must be put on for the reason that God has elected us to be His holy, beloved people.

The concept of God's election is found elsewhere in the pages of Scripture. In Acts 13:48, for instance, we learn that God's election precedes belief: "Now when the Gentiles heard this, they were glad and glorified the word of the Lord. *And as many as had been appointed to eternal life believed.*" In this passage, we see that the gospel was proclaimed. And, just like countless other times, some believed and some did not. Luke clearly tells us why it turns out this way—those who are appointed to eternal life believe, while the others continue in sinful unbelief.

In the first chapter of Ephesians, Paul points out that God's election is not something that sinners can manipulate in order to remain in sin. The choice, the election, has as its intended goal the holiness of the saints: "*He chose us* in Him before the foundation of the world, that we should be holy and without blame before Him in love, *having predestined us* to adoption as sons by Jesus Christ to Himself, according to the good pleasure of His will" (Eph. 1:4–5).

Before the world was created, God chose certain individuals to live holy and blameless lives, and He predestined those individuals to persevere in that holiness until the day when they would receive the adoption as sons, the final redemption of the body (Rom. 8:23). According to Scripture, there is no question about whether the elect will remain elect. They receive the gift of salvation through God's choice, and the God "who changes not" does not waver in His choices.

Just a few verses later, Paul anchors the point further: In Christ "we have obtained an inheritance, *being predestined* according to the purpose of

Him who works *all things* according to the counsel of His will" (Eph. 1:11).

It is impossible to evade the force of this language by saying that predestination applies only to the apostles, or to first-generation Christians (Eph. 1:12). God works *all things* according to the counsel of His will. Not only was the conversion of Saul established before the world came into being—so was the conversion of every believer.

Of course, the classic passage discussing the doctrine of election is the ninth chapter of Romans. Consider verses 10 through 16 of that chapter:

> And not only this, but when Rebecca also had conceived by one man, even by our father Isaac (for the children not yet being born, *nor having done any good or evil, that the purpose of God according to election might stand, not of works but of Him who calls*), it was said to her, "The older shall serve the younger." As it is written, *"Jacob I have loved, but Esau I have hated."*
>
> What shall we say then? Is there unrighteousness with God? Certainly not! For He says to Moses, *"I will have mercy on whomever I will have mercy, and I will have compassion on whomever I will have compassion."* So then it is *not* of him who *wills*, nor of him who *runs*, but of God who shows mercy.

Paul takes care to emphasize several things that are pertinent to our discussion. One is that God selected Jacob over Esau prior to their birth, *so that* His purpose in election would stand. If we say that God based His election upon His foreknowledge of the choices made by Jacob and Esau, then why does Paul emphasize that God elected one of them prior to their birth, before they did good or evil? He makes this point in order to assert that God's choice had nothing to do with the relative merits of Jacob and Esau. Before they were born, before they had done any good or evil, God chose Jacob and rejected Esau so that His purpose might stand. He did not choose Jacob because of his good works.

This passage is not, as some suggest, about the nations of Israel (descended from Jacob) and Edom (descended from Esau). That suggestion confuses the precise problem Paul is addressing with the solution he offers. In this chapter, Paul is solving a problem. He is answering the objection that ethnic Israel was elect in a certain sense, yet remained in unbelief. How could this be? In the first five verses of Romans 9, Paul laments the unbelief of his fellow Jews, who were possessors of the adoption, the glory, the covenants, the law, the promises, the service of God, and from whom the Christ came. So this is the problem: How could ethnic Israel, the chosen nation, reject their own Messiah?

In verse 6, Paul tells us that we are not to infer from ethnic Israel's unbelief that God's Word had no effect. He then argues that not all who are elect with regard to national privilege are elect with regard to personal salvation. "For they are not all Israel who are of Israel, nor are they all children because they are the seed of Abraham" (vv. 6b–7a).

In other words, Paul argues that God's Word will never be nullified. From verse 6 on, he shows how the failure of the national election of the Jews was only apparent, and that God's real election of individuals was sovereign and efficacious.[1] If Paul is discussing national election throughout the chapter, then the Word of God *can* be of "no effect," which Paul expressly denies. National election is the problem, not the solution.

So what conclusion may we properly draw from Romans 9? God reserves the right to show mercy and compassion as He sees fit, and He does so without unrighteousness on His part. Because this is how He saves sinners, we may also conclude, with Paul, that salvation is not the result of sinners' *willing*, nor of sinners' *running*. It is the result of the pure mercy of God, with human choices and merit nowhere in sight (v. 16).[2]

FORGETTING THOSE "PASSED"?

Turn the coin over and look at the other side: if God chooses those who are saved, and not everyone is saved, then God also chooses *not* to give salvation to some—those who ultimately remain lost. One side of the coin is called election, while the other is called hardening—the process by which God passes by those who are not elect. Coming to grips with what the Bible says about hardening is crucial if we are ever to understand election.

The passages that discuss hardening are important because they show that election (choosing some and not others) is not indiscriminate. If, as some argue, God does not harden the nonelect, then we must reject the notion that God chooses the elect, since hardening is simply the flip side of election.[3] Consider further the words of Romans 9:17–24, where Paul, by the inspiration of the Holy Spirit, explains that God both has mercy on some and hardens others.

> For the Scripture says to Pharaoh, "Even for this same purpose I have raised you up, that I might show My power in you, and that My name might be declared in all the earth."

Therefore *He has mercy on whom He wills*, and *whom He wills He hardens*. You will say to me then, "Why does He still find fault? For who has resisted His will?"

But indeed, O man, who are you to reply against God? Will the thing formed say to him who formed it, "Why have you made me like this?" Does not the potter have power over the clay, from the same lump to make one vessel for honor and another for dishonor? What if God, wanting to show His wrath and to make His power known, endured with much longsuffering the *vessels of wrath prepared for destruction*, and that He might make known the riches of His glory on the vessels of mercy, *which He had prepared beforehand for glory, even us whom He called*, not of the Jews only, but also of the Gentiles?

In this passage, God's sovereign mercy is clear. Equally clear is His sovereign hardening of sinners. God shows mercy to whom He wills, and He hardens whom He wills. When we react to this notion, and kick against the goads (and virtually all of us have done so), we want to cry out, "Why?" We want to demand an answer. An answer is not directly given in the passage, but after he rebukes the spirit of the reaction, Paul does give us a hint about what the answer should be.

The elect, he tells us, are vessels of mercy. They were prepared as such beforehand. Those vessels not prepared for glory are described as vessels of wrath, prepared for destruction. Paul says here that God, in order to demonstrate His wrath and power, endured with great patience these vessels of wrath. In other words, God was patient with those vessels He had bound over for destruction. They were eventually destroyed as part of His purpose, but He put up with them longer than they deserved.

Pharaoh serves as a good example of this truth. God told Moses before his mission to Egypt began that Pharaoh would be uncooperative (Ex. 3:19). The response of Pharaoh and the outcome of the conflict were not at all up in the air. Even so, God endured Pharaoh's stubbornness with great patience. With each plague, Pharaoh had a new opportunity to obey the voice of the Lord, but he would not. He disobeyed because he was a sinner, enslaved to his own sinful desires. God hardened him in those sins even while showing great patience with him.

God did all this, Paul tells us, in order to make His power and wrath known. There is no indication that God wants this doctrine hidden away somewhere. There is no reason for Christians to be embarrassed by, or to shy away from, these matters. They are plainly taught in the Bible, and those who believe the Bible should affirm them just as plainly.

Two chapters later, Paul sets forth the contrast between the elect and the nonelect again.

> Even so then, at this present time there is a remnant according to *the election of grace*. And if by grace, then it is no longer of works; otherwise grace is no longer grace. But if it is of works, it is no longer grace; otherwise work is no longer work. What then? Israel has not obtained what it seeks; but *the elect have obtained it,* and *the rest were hardened.* Just as it is written: "*God has given them* a spirit of stupor, eyes that they should not see and ears that they should not hear, to this very day." (Rom. 11:5–8)

Note that Paul is not contrasting grace and works. He is contrasting the election of grace and works. There is a fundamental antithesis between human works and the election of grace, as long as such grace is biblically understood. And what conclusion does he draw from this contrast between the election of grace and works? He concludes that the elect have obtained salvation, and that the rest were hardened. How were they hardened? Who hardened them? God gave them a spirit of stupor.

This contrast is not found just in Romans. To the church in Thessalonica, Paul writes, "For God did not appoint *us* to wrath, *but to obtain salvation* through our Lord Jesus Christ" (1 Thess. 5:9). Believers are appointed to their salvation. Unlike unbelievers, they are not appointed to wrath.

Each human being is headed for one of two destinations—wrath or salvation. All individuals are foreordained to one or the other, and this foreordination is accomplished without injustice to anyone. Unbelievers who retort that God's foreordination is unjust take these wonderful doctrines of grace as an occasion to rail at God, thereby demonstrating that they are among those destined for wrath. And if that is the case, we should not take their railings seriously. They are under the just condemnation of God. There is no need to walk through the corridors of hell in search of profound insights on the nature of justice. They experience it there, but they still do not know what it is.

Nor does this teaching of God's hardening of sinners come only through the apostle Paul. Referring to unbelieving Jews, Peter says in 1 Peter 2:8, "They stumble, being disobedient to the word, *to which they also were appointed.*" In this text, Peter gives us two reasons why the nonelect stumble. The first reason mentioned is disobedience to the Word. These men are clearly responsible for their own condemnation. But there is another reason behind their disobedience—they were appointed to this stumbling. In the next verse, Peter contrasts such men to the elect, the "chosen generation."

These *are* hard words. But those who receive them from God find that they result in soft and tender hearts. And those who, on their own authority, soften or ignore these words of God will find the end result to be hard hearts. We are Christians. We must, therefore, believe what God tells us to believe.[4]

OBJECTIONS OVERRULED

Some, however, refuse to embrace this marvelous truth of the faith, claiming that it makes God either unjust or the author of sin.

Is God Unjust?

Some believers object to the biblical doctrine of divine sovereignty by shifting the blame: they ask how an all-sovereign God can find fault with His creatures. The simplest response to this objection is to point out that Paul answers it in the ninth chapter of Romans. There Paul states the prerogatives of divine sovereignty in the strongest possible terms when he writes that God "has mercy on whom He wills, and whom He wills He hardens" (v. 18).

Paul understood human nature well. He knew exactly what would follow on the heels of such an assertion—no doubt he had heard it many times before. So he goes on to put words in the mouth of an imaginary opponent: "You will say to me then, 'Why does He still find fault? For who has resisted His will?' " (v. 19).

Notice the nature of the objection thrown at Paul. If God shows mercy on whom He wills and hardens whom He wills, then how can God justly blame us for doing what He has willed beforehand? Notice Paul's response. Quite bluntly, Paul turns the tables on the objector: "On the contrary, who are you, O man, who answers back to God? The thing molded will not say to the molder, 'Why did you make me like this,' will it? Or does not the potter have a right over the clay, to make from the same lump one vessel for honorable use, and another for common use?" (vv. 20–21).

By a series of rhetorical questions, Paul puts this objection in its place.

The creature has no right to talk back to the Creator. The one who is molded has no right to interrogate the molder. The molder, however, has every right to make vessels for one use or another. Instead of shying away from divine sovereignty, Paul uses this very objection as an occasion to affirm it. The fact of the matter, according to Paul, is that God elects some and hardens others so that He might demonstrate the riches of His glory upon His vessels of mercy. Far from causing us to raise an angry fist at God, this marvelous truth should drop us to our knees in humble gratitude for the mercy God has bestowed upon us.

I was a pastor for about eleven years before I came to understand the thoroughness of God's grace in salvation. Up to that time, my teaching on the subject was a typical hodgepodge of confusion and evasion. As I look back at that time, I now find it interesting, if not somewhat curious, that no one ever objected to my teaching as did the objector in Romans 9. No one ever said, "Douglas, if what you're saying is true, then doesn't that make us puppets? And if we are puppets, then how can God blame us for what we do?"

But since I have come to these truths—meaning that I am now willing to make the same sort of blunt assertions that Paul makes—I have heard this objection countless times. It is almost as though the objectors (who are all Christians) are unaware that this objection is in Scripture, that Paul places it in the mouth of one who resists the truth, and that he kicks the legs out from under it.

I was once conversing with two men, both of whom attempted to deny the sovereignty of God. One of them understood that my theology generates the same objection that Pauline theology does. But the other man proceeded to present that objection to me: "Why does God still blame us?" When I was talking to the second man later, I found out that he thought I was somehow tricking my opponents into talking this way, because the objection was so obviously unbiblical. But there is no trick to it at all. All one has to do is assert that God shows mercy as He sees fit, and that He hardens whom He sees fit—and then the objections start to fly. It is not a big mystery why this happens. Men do not want to submit to what the Bible says, especially when what it has to say is so unflattering.

So, if we preach the gospel as Paul preached it, we will inevitably encounter this objection. If it is not forthcoming, then we are not preaching the gospel as Paul preached it. Finally, those who deny that God elects and hardens whom He wills must explain how their theology can possibly generate this objection.

Is God the Author of Sin?

While some respond to God's sovereignty in salvation by asking how God can still find fault, others actually come right out and claim that on that view men are tempted by God. There are two ways to respond to this objection.

The first is to point out that it is totally improper for Christians to "defend" God from the "slanders" attributed to Him by His own revelation. Mockers and fools may be rebuked, but Isaiah, John, Paul, and Christ are not among them.

We know that God is holy because He has revealed Himself as such in Scripture. We know that He is sovereign for the same reason. We have no authority to reject one portion of Scripture for the sake of another portion. If we do, we demonstrate that we do not understand either portion.

The Bible does teach that God is all-holy, and that He is not the author of sin: "Let no one say when he is tempted, 'I am being tempted by God'; for God cannot be tempted by evil, and He Himself does not tempt anyone" (James 1:13). And since Scripture cannot contradict itself, this teaching must be consistent with God's sovereignty. The objection supposedly based on the holiness of God comes not from Scripture but from humanistic philosophy. No verse says, "Do not say or think in your hearts that I control sin and evil."

The objection that appeals to the holiness of God takes passages asserting God's perfect holiness (which neither side in this debate denies) and builds upon them with unbiblical reasoning drawn from the notion of human autonomy. According to this reasoning, a holy God would not exercise sovereignty over His creatures, and therefore does not do so. The premise of a holy God is biblical enough, but the conclusion cannot be derived biblically from it—and indeed is expressly denied by Scripture.

The second problem is that this objection does not really remove the difficulty. All Christians believe that God has the power to destroy sin at any moment. Yet, He chooses not to do so. Why? If God can be held culpable by men (and He cannot be), then there is no reason to restrict our accusations to the sovereign God as understood by those of Reformed persuasion. Those of non-Reformed persuasion charge the God of Scripture with sins of commission—"Do you mean to say that God perfectly controlled the murder of the little girl I read about in the papers this morning?" But why stop there? The atheist charges the God of non-Reformed believers with a sin of omission—"Do you mean to say that God knew all about the murder of this girl, and refused to prevent it?"

If God can be charged with sin (as Paul would say, I am out of my mind to talk like this), then there is no reason to limit the list of accusations. The proud humanist looks at the God of the Reformed faith and sees a tyrant and murderer. And then he turns and looks at the God of non-Reformed theology and sees one who is guilty of culpable negligence and reckless disregard for human life.

For those fevered enough in their imaginations to suppose that God can be indicted in one of our courts, God must cease to be all-controlling and all-powerful, and perhaps even cease to exist. This, of course, is intolerable for all Christians—God does not have to answer to us. We know that God is perfect; He is without iniquity. We also know that He is sovereign; He perfectly controls those who hate Him, and will finally destroy them. We will not have these discussions in front of the judgment seat of Christ.

The reason this objection surfaces within Christianity is that some Christians are consistent enough to say out loud what all Christians, at some level, believe. The charge leveled at those who affirm the sovereignty of God is a charge that can be made against all Christians. But those Christians who affirm God's sovereignty are the only ones who have a biblical answer—"Who are you, O man, to reply against God?"

STUDY QUESTIONS

1. Answer the following questions on the basis of Ephesians 1:12; 2:10; John 15:16; Philippians 2:12–13; 2 Thessalonians 2:13–14:

   a. Is divine election an excuse to neglect walking with God, or is it rather the very foundation for walking with God?
   b. Were believers just appointed to believe, or were they also appointed to glorify God by their good works?
   c. Are you glorifying God by your good works?

2. In Romans 9, Paul argues vigorously in favor of divine election and hardening. Some have attempted to evade the force of Paul's argument by suggesting that God's election depends upon His foreknowledge—specifically, that God elected those whom He knew would come to believe in Him. How do Paul's comments about Jacob and Esau in verses 10–13 refute this reasoning? In particular, when did God choose Jacob

and reject Esau? Do your good works have anything to do with your salvation? Explain.

3. How can believers continue to assert objections to biblical truths when those objections are answered in the Bible? Are we omniscient? Is God? Can the ultimate mysteries of divine sovereignty be known to God but not to us? Who are we to reply against God?

Notes

1. "How does an appeal to the collective election of Israel or the election of Jacob and his seed to earthly, historical prominence solve the problem of unbelieving, eternally lost Jews? How can that solve the problem when that *is* the problem?" (C. Samuel Storms, *Chosen for Life* [Grand Rapids: Baker, 1987], 80).

2. For further study of election, see Ex. 33:19; Ps. 65:4; Matt. 11:27; 22:14; 24:22, 24, 31; Mark 13:20; Luke 18:7; John 6:37, 65; 13:18; 15:16; 17:9; Rom. 8:18–11:36; 1 Cor. 1:27–29; Eph. 2:10; 1 Thess. 1:4–5; 5:9; 2 Thess. 2:13–14; 1 Tim. 5:21; 2 Tim. 2:10; Titus 1:1; James 2:5; 1 Peter 1:1–2; 5:13; Rev. 13:8; 17:8, 14.

3. "Hard experience had made Calvin's judgment, that without preterition [passing by] election itself cannot stand, the deep conviction of the whole Reformed church" (B. B. Warfield, *The Works of Benjamin B. Warfield*, vol. 9: *Studies in Theology* [Grand Rapids: Baker, 1981], 227).

4. For further study of God's hardening of sinners, see Ex. 4:21; Deut. 2:30; Josh. 11:20; Ps. 105:24–25; Prov. 16:4; Isa. 6:9–10; Matt. 7:6; 11:25; 13:10–15; Mark 4:12; Luke 2:34; 8:10; John 9:39; 12:39–40; Acts 13:41; 28:27; Rom. 11:9–10; 2 Thess. 2:11; 2 Peter 2:12; Jude 4; Rev. 13:8; 17:17.

FIVE

BOUGHT WITH A PRICE

M any Christians are in general agreement with the Reformed faith until they come to what it teaches about the power of the Cross. While such Christians may be sympathetic to a consistent biblical theology, they have difficulty accepting that Christ did not die for everyone. They reject out of hand the Reformed idea of "limited atonement." After all, there is a sense, as we will see, in which the Atonement is unlimited.

Admittedly, the atonement of Christ has engendered quite a bit of controversy through the years. For this reason, we must begin to discuss it at the proper place. Otherwise, we will rapidly find ourselves in one of two opposing camps, each of which hides behind a wall of proof texts. Contrary to this party spirit, the teaching of the Bible is consistent when it comes to the Atonement. One side cannot rightly say that it has *these* verses, while the other side has *those* verses, as though God did not make Himself clear on this crucial doctrine. Scripture is not divided against itself. All of the Bible belongs to all Christians.

BACK TO NATURE

We must begin our discussion of the Atonement by focusing on its *nature*, not its *extent*. Once we understand its nature, we will find that we understand its extent. By learning *why* Christ died, we will also learn *for whom* He died.

The key question we must ask ourselves is, What exactly does the Cross of Jesus Christ *do* for sinners? Christians have adopted two basic answers to this question. The popular answer is that the Cross creates the *possibility* of saving everyone, while the biblical answer is that the Cross *actually saves* those who believe in Christ. The popular answer holds that those who are saved can attribute their salvation to the Cross plus their decision to apply for its benefits, while the biblical answer holds that those who are saved can attribute their salvation to the Cross alone.

In the fifth chapter of Romans, Paul draws several parallels between the First Adam and the Last Adam (Christ) in order to demonstrate that the Cross alone actually saves. One of the strongest points of comparison has to do with the efficacy of their respective actions. Adam, through his disobedience, plunged all his descendants into disobedience and death. Similarly, Christ, through His obedience, created righteousness for all His descendants. Adam, when he sinned, did not create the mere possibility of his descendants sinning. Similarly, Christ did not create the mere possibility of His descendants being saved. Whereas Adam brought destruction, Christ brought eternal life. To whom were these things brought? Remember, we are talking about the two Adams—the two heads of two races. Adam brought death to all his descendants, and Christ brought life to all His descendants.

> For if by the one man's offense death reigned through the one, *much more those who receive abundance of grace and of the gift of righteousness* will reign in life through the One, Jesus Christ. . . . For as by one man's disobedience many were made sinners, *so also by one Man's obedience many will be made righteous.* (Rom. 5:17, 19)

It is important to see that Christ's obedience creates righteousness in the same way that Adam's disobedience created unrighteousness. There is no uncertainty here. When Adam sinned, he secured a miserable future for his descendants. Therefore, when Christ was obedient, even to death on the cross, He secured eternal glory for His descendants.

This is what I meant when I spoke earlier of the nature of the Atonement. Does the Cross actually secure the salvation of anyone? The answer of many who misunderstand the gospel is no. The Cross of the popular gospel secures only the possibility of salvation. But Adam did not secure the possibility of sin; he actually brought in sin and death. Since Paul's crucial point of comparison between the two Adams is the efficacy of their respective actions, and since Christ's obedience was greater than Adam's disobedience, the Cross of the ancient and eternal gospel actually secures the salvation of countless sinners.[1] And what a wonderful security it is!

The Cross is a source of security because Christ died for a purpose, and not for mere potentiality: "Therefore Jesus also, *that He might sanctify the people with His own blood,* suffered outside the gate" (Heb. 13:12). Jesus suffered outside the gate in order to sanctify His people with His blood. Often the New Testament describes the death of Christ by using a purpose clause to teach us that Christ died to accomplish something in particular.

The Bible does not say that Christ died for the possibility of redemption; it says that He died to redeem—to purchase—His people as His own (Gal. 3:13; Col. 1:13–14; Titus 2:14; Heb. 9:12). He did not die for the possibility of justification; He died to justify, to put us right with God (Rom. 3:24–25; 5:8–9). He did not die for the possibility of making propitiation; He died to make propitiation, to turn away the wrath of an all-holy and all-just God (Rom. 3:25; 4:10). He did not die for the possibility of expiation; He died to expiate, to cleanse us from the guilt and pollution of our sin (Eph. 5:25–26; Titus 2:14; Heb. 9:14; 1 John 1:7). He did not die for the possibility of reconciliation; He died to reconcile, to restore our fellowship with God, which had been severed by sin (Rom. 5:10; 2 Cor. 5:18–19; Eph. 2:15–16; Col. 1:21–22).

To What Extent?

Now we can see how our view of the nature of the Atonement profoundly affects our view of its extent. If Christ's death actually secures salvation for His descendants, and if, as we already know, not all men are saved, then Christ did not die for all men. The Bible states this fact explicitly. In the gospel of John, Christ Himself tells us about what He came to do.

> I am the good shepherd; and *I know My sheep,* and am known by My own. As the Father knows Me, even so I know the Father; *and I lay down My life for the sheep.* And other sheep I have which are not of this fold; them also I must bring, and they will hear My voice; and there will be one flock and one shepherd. Therefore My Father loves Me, because I lay down My life that I may take it again. No one takes it from Me, but I lay it down of Myself. I have power to lay it down, and I have power to take it again. This command I have received from My Father. (John 10:14–18)

This passage reveals that Jesus knows the identity of His sheep and that He came to lay down His life for them. At this point, some may be tempted to say that all men are His sheep, but Jesus eliminates this possibility just a few verses later.

> Jesus answered them, "I told you, and you do not believe. The works that I do in My Father's name, they bear witness of Me. But you do not believe, *because you are not of My sheep*, as I said to you. *My sheep* hear My voice, and I know them, and they follow Me. *And I give them eternal life*, and they shall never perish; neither shall anyone snatch them out of My hand. My Father, who has given them to Me, is greater than all; and no one is able to snatch them out of My Father's hand. I and My Father are one." (John 10:25–30)

Christ's teaching is very clear indeed. He knows the identity of His sheep, and He gives His life for them. There are certain individuals who are not His sheep. Note that Jesus does not say that they are not His sheep because they do not believe, but rather, that they do not believe because they are not His sheep. The cause of their unbelief is to be found in the fact that they are not among the sheep for whom Christ gave up His life. Jesus goes on to say that He gives eternal life to His sheep. Now how does Christ secure eternal life for His sheep? He does so through the Cross.

It is important to meditate upon two statements uttered by Christ in the same discourse: "I lay down my life for the sheep" (v. 15), and "You are not of my sheep" (v. 26). If Christ laid down His life for His sheep and if He told certain hearers that they were not His sheep, then Christ did not lay His life down for them. And if He did not lay down His life for them, then He did not lay it down for every person. But He did actually secure, by His death, the salvation of countless people.

For this reason, Scripture applies the death of Christ to His people and does not apply it indiscriminately to all men: "And as it is appointed for men to die once, but after this the judgment, so Christ was offered once to bear the sins of *many*. To those who eagerly wait for Him He will appear a second time, apart from sin, for salvation" (Heb. 9:27–28).

In this passage, we learn that Christ bore the sins of *many*; He did not bear the sins of every last person who ever lived. Just a few verses before, the author of Hebrews makes the same point: "And for this reason He is the Mediator of the new covenant, *by means of death*, for the redemption of the transgressions under the first covenant, *that those who are called may receive* the promise of the eternal inheritance" (v. 15).

No one who desires to be faithful to Scripture can deny the truth explicitly proclaimed here. Christ died in order that "those who are called may receive" the promise of eternal life. Jesus did not throw the gospel out into the world, hoping that someone would respond to it. Rather, His death was designed to accomplish a certain objective, which is described in Hebrews 9:15, namely, that those who are called might receive it. And not all are called.

In the gospel of John, one who hated Christ even went so far as to testify as to the saving design of the Cross.

> And one of them, Caiaphas, being high priest that year, said to them, "You know nothing at all, nor do you consider that it is expedient for us that one man should die for the people, and not that the whole nation should perish." Now this he did not say on his own authority; but being high priest that year he prophesied that Jesus would die for the nation, *and not for that nation only, but also that He would gather together in one the children of God who were scattered abroad.* (John 11:49–52)

In other words, Jesus did not just die for the Jews, but for the children of God all over the world. In this sense, therefore, we may scripturally say that Christ died for the world (John 1:29); we may say that He died for the Jewish nation (John 11:51), and that He died for all tribes and nations (Rev. 5:9). We may not say, however, that He died for those within those nations who were not His sheep—whether Pharaoh, or Judas, or Nero, or anyone else who has died in unbelief.

But Jesus did efficaciously die for all kinds of men everywhere—Jews, Greeks, slaves, free, male, female, kings, and peasants (1 Tim. 2:1–6). But on the glorious day when the wheat is gathered into the barns, there will be no one in heaven maintaining that Christ died to bring in the chaff and weeds as well, and wondering out loud why it did not happen.[2]

WHAT IN THE WORLD?

But what about those passages which teach that Christ died for the sins of the world? Do not such passages teach that Christ died for every human being? After all, John tells us that "He Himself is the propitiation for our sins, and not for ours only but also for the whole world" (1 John 2:2).

What could be clearer? Jesus died for the sins of everyone, right? No, that is not what this passage says. To see why this is the case, let us reduce the relevant part of it to a simple proposition:

Jesus is a propitiation for the sins of the whole world.

Now we know who Jesus is, but what is propitiation? When Scripture says that Christ made "propitiation" for sin, it means that He turned away God's wrath brought about by sin. When Christ made propitiation, He fully satisfied the demands of divine justice. So now our proposition reads as follows:

Jesus turned away divine wrath for the sins of the whole world.

Notice that there is nothing iffy about these words. John does not say that Jesus is a propitiation if the world believes. He simply states that the wrath of God is turned away from the whole world. If we listen to this text speak with all its force, it becomes quickly evident that we have a problem. The passage does not teach that Christ brought about a possible or potential propitiation for everyone in the world, if they believe. It teaches that Christ actually made propitiation for the sins of the whole world.

Whereas *propitiation* in the New Testament always refers to an actual turning aside of divine wrath, the word *world* means many different things. The Greek word translated *world* is *kosmos,* and it is used in at least seven different ways in the New Testament. It can mean

(1) the universe as a whole (Acts 17:14),
(2) the planet earth (John 13:1; Eph. 1:4),
(3) the world-system (John 12:31; 1 John 2:15),
(4) the entire human race (Rom. 3:19),
(5) humanity, not including believers (John 15:18),
(6) Gentiles in contrast to Jews (Rom. 11:12), and
(7) humanity, considered in the light of God's eschatological, redemptive design (John 3:16–17; 6:33).[3]

Now it is very easy to assert that Jesus was a propitiation for every last person (definition number 4), but does this definition fit the context of 1 John 2:2? In particular, why should we not take the word *world* in the sixth or seventh sense listed above—especially since John is fond of contrasting Jews and Gentiles and of speaking about this great eschatological hope? It is therefore quite biblical to say that Jesus died for the world, and because the death of Christ is efficacious, the world, in this sense, will be saved.[4] God's wrath will not fall on the world; this passage says it will not.

Moreover, since this passage says that Christ is a propitiation (and not a potential propitiation) for the sins of the whole world, were we to interpret the word *world* to mean every human being, we would slide down the slippery slope to universalism—the notion that all are saved. In other words, if the death of Christ actually turned God's wrath away from all humanity without exception, then all are saved. But we know that Scripture does not teach that. Therefore, the word *world* in 1 John 2:2 cannot refer to every last human being.

THAT'S ALL FOLKS?

Many appeal not only to 1 John 2:2, but also to 1 Timothy 2:3–4: "For this is good and acceptable in the sight of God our Savior, *who desires all men to be saved* and to come to the knowledge of the truth."

At first glance, this passage appears to contradict everything we have said up to this point. If God desires everyone to be saved, yet everyone is not saved, then is it not true that sinful men can reject God's redemptive work? And if that is the case, how can we really say that God controls everything?

In this passage, the Greek word translated "all" is *pas*. This word can be used in at least three ways. First, it can be used in a universal sense to refer to every member of a particular class without exception. As we saw above, Adam's sin plunged all his descendants—without exception—into the misery of sin and death (Rom. 5:17–19).

Second, the word *all* can sometimes be used in a hyperbolic sense to refer to a large number of a particular class—as a synonym for *many*. When Christ, for example, told His followers that they would be hated by all (Matt. 10:22), He certainly did not mean that every human being would hate them, since their fellow Christians would not hate them in this way. Christ is using a hyperbole, an intentional overstatement, to emphasize that many unbelievers will hate believers on account of Him.

Third, the word *all* can also be used in an explanatory sense to refer to all kinds of, or all sorts of, a given thing. At one point, for instance, Matthew literally says that Christ healed "all" sicknesses and "all" disease in Galilee. Bible translators quite properly render this sense of *all* as "all kinds of ": "Jesus went about all Galilee, teaching in their synagogues, preaching the gospel of the kingdom, and healing *all kinds of sickness* and *all kinds of disease* among the people" (Matt. 4:23).

Of these three possible meanings, the universal sense cannot apply to 1 Timothy 2:3–4 since such a rendering would result in universalism. If God decretively willed that "all" men be saved, and if the word "all" here meant "everyone without exception," then everyone would eventually be saved. But, as we have seen above, not all will be saved. Therefore, the word "all" cannot be taken in this universal sense.

But what about the hyperbolic or explanatory senses? Either sense fits. Thus, this passage teaches either that God desires that many be saved, which is perfectly true, or that He desires all kinds of men to be saved.

While either sense fits the context of this passage, the explanatory sense fits particularly well. Paul begins this chapter by urging that prayer be offered up for "all men." Note how he puts it: "Therefore I exhort first of all that supplications, prayers, intercessions, and giving of thanks be made for *all men, for kings and all who are in authority,* that we may lead a quiet and peaceable life in all godliness and reverence" (vv. 1–2). Thus, the context of this passage lends support to the conclusion that the word *all* should be taken in the explanatory sense.

The explanatory sense also corresponds with a common theme in the New Testament, namely, that the gospel is not limited to a particular race or sex or social class. In Christ there is neither Jew, Greek, white, black, slave, free, male, female, king, nor peasant (Gal. 3:28). As Christians, therefore, we are instructed to pray for all sorts of men. In the next breath, Paul goes on to specify a particular class or category of men that should be included—kings and all those in authority. But why should we pray for all kinds of men? This question brings us to the passage at hand. We are to pray for all kinds of men because God wants all kinds of men to be saved.

Thus, "all kinds of men" is a perfectly legitimate translation of the word *pas* in 1 Timothy 2:4. It fits nicely with the immediate context, as well as with the larger context of the New Testament. We must never forget that one of the biggest controversies in the first-century church was whether one could become a Christian without first becoming a Jew. The church answered that question biblically—becoming a Jew is not a prerequisite to salvation. Christ did not come for the Jews alone; He came for all kinds of men. Christ did not come for the rich alone; He came for all kinds of men. Christ did not come for the poor alone; He came for all kinds of men. And this is the point made in 1 Timothy 2:4, as well as in similar passages that teach that Christ died for all.

STUDY QUESTIONS

1. What are the two basic views of what the Cross of Christ does for sinners, and how do they differ from one another?
2. For whom did Christ die, according to the following passages: Matt. 1:21; 20:28; 26:28; John 11:50–53; Acts 20:28; Rom. 5:8–10; 8:32–34; 2 Cor. 5:18–21; Gal. 1:3–4; 3:13; Eph. 1:3–12; 2:14–16; 5:25–27; Col. 1:2, 13–14, 21–22; Heb. 2:17; 3:1; 9:15, 28; Titus 2:14; 1 Peter 2:24; 3:18; Rev. 1:5?
3. How does knowing that Christ died specifically to save you help strengthen your faith? How does it comfort you?

Notes

1. "Now, who is it that limits the death of Christ? Why, you. You say that Christ did not die so as infallibly to secure the salvation of anybody. We beg your pardon, when you say we limit Christ's death; we say, 'No, my dear sir, it is you that do it.' We say Christ so died that he infallibly secured the salvation of a multitude that no man can number, who through Christ's death not only may be saved, but are saved, must be saved and cannot by any possibility run the hazard of being anything but saved. You are welcome to your atonement; you may keep it. We will never renounce ours for the sake of it" (Charles Spurgeon, as quoted by J. I. Packer in his introduction to John Owen, *The Death of Death in the Death of Christ* [reprint, Edinburgh: Banner of Truth, 1959], 14).
2. For further study of the nature of the Atonement, see Matt. 1:21; 20:28; 26:28; Luke 19:10; John 17; Acts 20:28; Rom. 3:24–25; 5:8–10; 8:32–34; 2 Cor. 5:18–19, 21; Gal. 1:3–4; 3:13; Eph. 1; 2:15–16; 5:25–26; Col. 1:13–14, 21–22; 1 Tim. 1:15; Titus 2:14; 3:5–6; 1 Peter 2:24; 3:18; Heb. 2:17; 3:1; 9:12, 14–15, 28; Rev. 5:9.
3. "To ascertain the precise meaning of the word *world* in any given passage is not nearly so easy as is popularly supposed" (A. W. Pink, *The Sovereignty of God* [Grand Rapids: Baker, 1930], 253).
4. This argument takes us into the field of eschatology, specifically as an example of postmillennial hope. Suffice it to say that a significant number of Reformed Christians have also held that God was in the process of saving the entire world. "The abundant and continuous testimony of Scripture is that the kingdom of God is to fill the earth, 'from sea to sea, and from the River unto the ends of the earth' " (Loraine Boettner, *The Reformed Doctrine of Predestination* [Philadelphia: Presbyterian and Reformed, 1963], 132).

SIX

SIGNED AND SEALED

So far we have established that men are dead in their sins, totally incapable of desiring or effecting their own resurrection. Yet God the Father, out of His great mercy, selected some of these wretched sinners to receive eternal life. This election or choice was made before the foundation of the world, before the beginning of time.

Because God the Father elected some to salvation, God the Son took on flesh, came to earth, and purchased their salvation. Christ said He came to do the will of the Father (John 6:39), and that is just what He accomplished. He died to save those whom the Father had given to Him.

THE APPLICATION OF REDEMPTION

We come now to consider the application of salvation to those for whom Christ died. That is, we come to the work of God the Holy Spirit in our regeneration.

In Titus 3:5, Paul gives us a glimpse of the Spirit's active role in regenerating those whom the Father has elected and for whom the Son bled and died: "Not by works of righteousness which we have done, but according to His mercy He saved us, *through the washing of regeneration and renewing of the Holy Spirit.*"

The salvation of the elect was certain long ago. Their number was established long ago and cannot be changed. Although the elect are known to God, they are not known to us until the Holy Spirit reveals their identity through a supernatural transformation of their lives. This transformation begins when the Spirit regenerates them, continues to sanctify them, and seals them for glorification. In his first letter, Peter alludes to the saving work of the Father, Son, and Spirit by referring to true believers as "elect according to the foreknowledge of God the Father, *in sanctification of the Spirit,* for obedience and sprinkling of the blood of Jesus Christ" (1 Peter 1:2).

Those who are chosen by the Father and purchased by the Son are sealed and set apart by the Spirit. The beauty of salvation is to be found not only in its logical consistency, but also in the harmony we see within the triune God in the outworking of salvation. Father, Son, and Spirit all work together toward the same end, the salvation of the same group of people. It is not as though the Father selects some for salvation, and the Son goes off on His own, seeking to purchase the salvation of everyone. Nor does the Spirit transform anyone who was not marked out beforehand by the Father for that transformation. The Father, Son, and Holy Spirit are *one,* and although each accomplishes a different aspect of our salvation, they are in complete harmony in accomplishing that work.

Regeneration by the Spirit is a truth that corresponds to a truth discussed earlier—that we were dead in our sins before we were regenerated. This means that the Spirit works in us to raise us from the dead. Being spiritually dead, we obviously do not cooperate with Him in this work. He resurrects us by His own power and will. When Jesus raised Lazarus from the dead, it was not a work that He and Lazarus accomplished together— even though the power of the work was evident in Lazarus, it was not something done by Lazarus.

In the same way, when the Spirit raises us up to walk in newness of life, His power is evident within us, but our resurrection does not originate with us. The Bible calls this resurrection from the dead a new birth: "Jesus answered, 'Most assuredly, I say to you, unless one is born of water *and the Spirit,* he cannot enter the kingdom of God. That which is born of the flesh is flesh, and *that which is born of the Spirit is spirit*'" (John 3:5–6).

The order of events is apparent in all the images that the Bible gives us of this new birth. The dead do not work on their own resurrection. The unborn do not work at their own birth. I do not recall doing anything to bring about my physical birth in 1953. I was not even consulted. Nor was I consulted about my new birth. The work of the Spirit is to bring life. At the risk of sounding simplistic, before He brings it, it is not there. The Spirit gives life (2 Cor. 3:6).

HORSES AND CARTS

After He gives us this new life, we are the ones who live it out. We are the ones who experience it. Because the Spirit has given life, evidence of that life is apparent immediately. But what are the first evidences that the Spirit has done His efficacious work? The first indications of the Spirit's quickening are repentance and belief. The new birth does not result from repentance and belief, as many mistakenly imagine. It is the other way around. Repentance and faith are gifts from God that He bestows through the Spirit. We must keep the horse and the cart in the right places.

Some may object that if we must repent, and we must have faith, then these things cannot be the gift of God. If God gives them, how are they ours? The answer is that they are ours because God gives them to us. If He did not give them to us, we would never have them. Once again we must allow Scripture itself to settle this issue: "Him God has exalted to His right hand to be Prince and Savior, *to give repentance to Israel and forgiveness of sins*" (Acts 5:31). Again, "When they heard these things they became silent; and they glorified God, saying, 'Then God has also *granted* to the Gentiles *repentance* to life' " (Acts 11:18).

In fact, Paul instructs believers to correct those given to false teaching in the hope that God would grant them the gift of repentance: ". . . in humility correcting those who are in opposition, *if God perhaps will grant them repentance*, so that they may know the truth, and that they may come to their senses and escape the snare of the devil, having been taken captive by him to do his will" (2 Tim. 2:25–26).

We may say the same thing about saving faith. It, too, is described as a gift from God. It does not come from us, lest any of us should boast. When Paul preached the gospel at Philippi, Lydia was granted salvation. Note carefully the order of events: "Now a certain woman named Lydia heard us. She was a seller of purple from the city of Thyatira, who worshiped God. *The Lord opened her heart to heed* the things spoken by Paul" (Acts 16:14).

Lydia believed because the Lord was good to her and opened her heart. The Lord's work in Lydia's heart preceded her response to Paul's preaching, not the other way around. When Paul later wrote to the church that had been established in Philippi, he spoke to them about this gift of faith: "For to you it has been *granted* on behalf of Christ, *not only to believe in Him*, but also to suffer for His sake" (Phil. 1:29). God gave faith to the Philippians, as well as the privilege of suffering. Both were gifts from Him.

The same point about faith is made with regard to the Christians in Achaia. When Apollos ministered in that region, he helped those whom

God had saved through grace: "And when he desired to cross to Achaia, the brethren wrote, exhorting the disciples to receive him; and when he arrived, he greatly helped those who had *believed through grace*" (Acts 18:27).

Luke does not say that those in Achaia believed "in" grace, but rather that they believed "through"—by means of—grace. In other words, God gave them grace, and that grace produced their faith. Given Scripture's explicit teaching that faith is a gift from God, we have no reason for refusing to take this as the obvious meaning of Ephesians 2:8–9: "For by grace you have been saved through *faith*, and *that* not of yourselves; *it is the gift of God*, not of works, lest anyone should boast."

Paul is extremely zealous to maintain the purity of salvation by grace. He knows that human merit can be smuggled into the process by the most unlikely means. Here it seems that he is guarding against the one who would take credit for his own faith, thinking, "At least I had the good sense to believe."[1] Paul will have none of that. No one can have faith unless it is first given by God. That way, no one can ever take credit for his own salvation.

A LONG-DISTANCE CALL

In addition to teaching us that repentance and faith are gifts of God, Scripture also communicates the same point by telling us that God has called us into His light. Over and over in Scripture, Christians are identified as "the called." When the time for salvation for each one of the elect arrives, each is called into the salvation prepared ages before: ". . . among whom you also are *the called* of Jesus Christ; to all who are in Rome, beloved of God, *called to be saints*" (Rom 1:6–7).

While election occurred before Creation and thus long before the Atonement was accomplished, the call occurs every time someone is converted. It is a crucial part of God's work in us and for us. "Moreover whom He predestined, these He also *called*; whom He *called*, these He also justified; and whom He justified, these He also glorified" (Rom. 8:30).

The instrument that the Holy Spirit uses in calling men out for Himself is the gospel of Christ crucified: "But we preach Christ crucified, to the Jews a stumbling block and to the Greeks foolishness, but to those who are *called*, both Jews and Greeks, Christ the power of God and the wisdom of God" (1 Cor. 1:23–24).

This gospel does not make sense to everyone who hears it. The Jews of Paul's day stumbled over it, while the Greeks thought it was gibberish.

But to the called, it was the power and wisdom of God. Notice that not everyone is called. This call is efficacious; it is an effectual call. All who hear it, and there are many, are saved everlastingly.[2]

CHOICE PRESERVES

Many Christians wonder if they can lose their salvation. Given what we have discussed thus far, we can see that this is not the real question. The real question is, Can God lose a Christian? Salvation is not a possession of ours, like car keys, which we may misplace. Those who have been elected from eternity, purchased by the Cross, and raised from the dead are consequently God's *eternal* possession. We are not our own—we were bought with a price (1 Cor. 6:20; 7:23). God chose us, and because He chose us, He will preserve us.

If we were to lose our salvation, God would do the losing, not us. However, in many places He assures us that He does not lose those who are His.

Although "eternal security" is a doctrine full of comfort, it cannot be built on a foundation of sand. There is no biblical ground for "eternal security" apart from confidence in the fact that God elected us, Christ purchased us, and the Spirit raised us from the dead. Apart from the saving work of the triune God, believing in "eternal security" will usher in carnal comfort—the notion that allows professed Christians to live like the Devil while expecting an eternal home with the Lord. Unless the believer's security is undergirded by the whole counsel of God, it will become corrupt—a cushion for sin.

The Bible very clearly grounds the believer's security in God. We do not save ourselves, and we do not keep ourselves saved. Listen to the way Paul makes this point:

> Who is he who condemns? It is Christ who died, and furthermore is also risen, who is even at the right hand of God, who also *makes intercession for us. Who shall separate us from the love of Christ?* Shall tribulation, or distress, or persecution, or famine, or nakedness, or peril, or sword? As it is written: "For Your sake we are killed all day long; we are accounted as sheep for the slaughter." Yet in all these things we are more than conquerors through Him who loved us. For I am persuaded that neither death nor life, nor angels nor principalities nor powers, nor things present nor things to come, nor

height nor depth, nor any other created thing, *shall be able to sepa-rate us* from the love of God which is *in Christ Jesus* our Lord. (Rom. 8:34–39)

In this passage, we learn that nothing created can separate us from the love of God in Christ. Now it is common for those who dispute this truth to say that all of the things Paul mentions are external threats to our salvation. We can separate ourselves, so the argument goes, from the love of God in Christ if we choose to leave. But why would a true believer choose to do something so foolish? Would it not be in response to the temptations created by all those things Paul lists here (life, death, angelic forces, future events, any created thing, etc.)?

In addition, our decisions are included in the list—we are "created"— and so we cannot separate ourselves from the love of God in Christ. Our future decisions are certainly among the things to come, and so they cannot separate us from the love of God in Christ. Can we really take comfort in an unbelieving modification of Christ's words—"Be of good cheer, I have overcome the world, if you make sure the world does not overcome you, which, of course, it might"?

Christ promises to keep His own. We are His sheep, and He, as the Good Shepherd, promises to keep us safe: "My sheep hear My voice, and I know them, and they follow Me. And I give them eternal life, and *they shall never perish;* neither shall *anyone* snatch them out of My hand. My Father, who has given them to Me, is greater than *all;* and *no one* is able to snatch them out of My Father's hand" (John 10:27–29).

Our security lies not in our faithfulness, but in the faithfulness of God and His Word. Left to our own devices, we *would* fall away. But we are not in our own hands; we are in Christ's hands, and in the Father's. We cannot be removed from that eternal haven.

Those who are foreknown in the Father's electing love, are predes-tined to a final conformity to the image of Christ. This means that the question is settled: "Whom He foreknew,[3] He also *predestined to be con-formed* to the image of His Son, that he might be the firstborn among many brethren. Moreover whom He predestined, these He also called; whom He called, these He also justified; and whom he justified, these He also glorified" (Rom. 8:29–30).

God's promise of that coming glory is sufficient, but He was gracious enough to seal His Word in our hearts by means of His Spirit: "In Him you also trusted, after you heard the word of truth, the gospel of your salvation; in whom also, having believed, you were *sealed* with the Holy Spirit of promise, who is *the guarantee of our inheritance* until the redemption of the purchased possession, to the praise of His glory" (Eph. 1:13–14).

God does not promise to keep us if we, of ourselves, fulfill certain conditions. Rather, it is His sovereign grace that keeps us on course and guarantees that we will arrive safely at our destination. This is because our destination is a predestination. God settled the matter before we were born. So our faithfulness is not the ground of our confidence; rather, our confidence is the ground of our faithfulness. And if a professing believer is not faithful, then that is simply a good reason for questioning whether he has genuine confidence. If someone says he loves God, but hates his brother, he is a liar; the truth is not in him (1 John 4:20; 2:4). If someone claims to have eternal security, but lives like the Devil, then let him make all the claims he wants! Such claims do not save—the Lord Jesus Christ saves, and He transforms those whom He saves.

While some seek to abuse this truth, it cannot be abused. For the whole truth is this: the Father has predestined His people to be made holy, and He has foreordained that they shall be safely kept in that holiness until they are glorified. How such a wonderful doctrine can be interpreted as a license for sin—by both antinomians and legalists—shows how easily we can go astray if we refuse to submit to God as He has revealed Himself in His Word.

Suppose someone were to say that Smith was predestined to be saved from drowning, and that he was foreordained to spend the rest of his life in the Sahara. Suppose still further that an opponent were to reply that if this were so, there would be nothing keeping Smith from sinking to the bottom of the Pacific. The opponent's reply would indicate that he had missed the point entirely.[4]

STUDY QUESTIONS

1. What role does God the Father play in saving sinners? God the Son? God the Spirit? Explain how the members of the Trinity work in harmony in saving sinners. How does knowing that the persons of the Trinity work together to save you give you hope and comfort?

2. Does the new birth result from repentance and faith? Is the sinner responsible for mustering up this repentance and faith of his own accord? Who grants repentance and faith to those who are saved (see Acts 5:31; 11:18; 13:48; Phil. 1:29; 2 Tim. 2:25–26)? How can we rightly say that repentance and faith belong to us?

3. Who saves sinners? Based on this fact, why is it wrong to ask if believers can lose their salvation? Have you ever asked yourself if you can lose your salvation? What is the real question you should ask yourself from now on? What comfort does this truth give you?

Notes

1. Some argue that the Greek term translated "that" or "this" in Eph. 2:8 refers to "grace," not to "faith." Clark Pinnock, for example, writes, "Often Eph. 2:8 is given as a proof text that faith is a gift. The gender of the Greek form of the pronoun 'this' has as its antecedent 'grace' rather than 'faith' because the antecedents must agree in gender" (Clark Pinnock, ed., *Grace Unlimited* [Minneapolis: Bethany Fellowship, 1975], 200). Contrary to Pinnock, however, Gordon Clark correctly points out that authors who argue like Pinnock are "unaware that feminine abstract nouns frequently take the neuter in these constructions" (Gordon Clark, *Predestination* [Phillipsburg, N.J.: Presbyterian and Reformed, 1987], 153).
2. For further study of resurrecting grace, see the following passages: Deut. 30:6; Ezek. 36:26–27; Matt. 11:25–27; 13:10–11, 16; Luke 8:10; 10:21; John 1:12–13; 3:3–8; 5:21; 6; 17:2; Acts 13:48; Rom. 1:6–7; 9:23–24; 1 Cor. 1; 6:11; 2 Cor. 3:17–18; 5:17–18; Gal. 1:15–16; 6:15; Eph. 2:1–10; 4:4; Col. 2:13; Phil. 2:12–13; 2 Tim. 1:9; Heb. 9:15; James 1:18; 1 Peter 1:3, 15, 23; 2:9; 5:10; 2 Peter 1:3; 1 John 5:4, 20; Jude 1; Rev. 17:14.
3. The phrase "whom He foreknew" here "means 'whom he set regard upon' or 'whom he knew from eternity with distinguishing affection and delight' and is virtually equivalent to 'whom he foreloved' " (David N. Steele and Curtis C. Thomas, *The Five Points of Calvinism* [Phillipsburg, N.J.: Presbyterian and Reformed, 1963], 87).
4. For further study of God's preservation of His saints, see the following passages: Ps. 34:7; Isa. 43:1–3; 54:10; Jer. 32:40; Ezek. 11:19–20; Matt. 18:12–14; 24:24; Luke 10:20; John 3:16, 36; 4:14; 5:24; 6:47, 51; 17:11–12, 15; Rom. 5:8–10; 8:1; 14:4; 1 Cor. 1:7–9; 2 Cor. 4:8–9, 14; 9:8; Eph. 1:5, 13–14; 4:30; Phil. 1:6; Col. 3:3–4; 1 Thess. 5:23–24; 2 Thess. 3:3; 2 Tim. 2:19; 4:18; Heb. 9:12, 15; 10:14; 1 Peter 1:5; 1 John 2:19, 25; 5:11, 13; Jude 1, 24–25.

SEVEN

TO SUM IT ALL UP

We began by showing that ultimate truth is something one cannot determine by means of autonomous human reason. The ability to reason is a gift to us from the God revealed in Scripture, and consequently, we cannot use that gift to deny any other revealed truth. To do so is to commit theological suicide. Christians must begin and end their search for spiritual truth within the Bible's covers.

The God revealed in the Bible cannot be contained in our finite minds. He is not the sort of Being we would have invented. He is the Transcendent One, and He sits on the circle of the heavens—the nations and all their universities and seminaries are but dust in His sight. Because He is the Almighty, He is capable of creating and controlling free creatures. This He has done. We look around us and everywhere see men acting out the desires of their hearts. We know that these desires are not capable of unsettling the eternal counsels of God. Through these desires, God accomplishes His wonderful plan. If we refuse to believe that we are in His hands, we do not thereby dethrone Him. All such unbelief inevitably destroys whatever we set in His place. Like Dagon, the idol of free will topples, and God is glorified even when it comes to such disobedience.

Although men as creatures are free to do as they want, as sinners they are not free to do as they ought. All descendants of Adam are by nature objects and vessels of wrath. All of us were dead in transgressions and sins. But God decreed, before the foundation of the world, that some of these vessels of wrath would be spared. He chose to show mercy on them, while He passed by others.

When the time was fulfilled, God sent His Son to be a sin offering for His people. Jesus Christ, our Savior, poured out His life for the church, and secured for her an everlasting salvation. Because of Him, she will forever be without spot or blemish or any such thing. When it is time for each one of the elect to be added to the church, the Holy Spirit of God replaces his or her heart of stone with a heart of flesh. Out of a new heart the believer cries out to God in repentance and faith. This same Spirit indwells the heart of each new believer as a seal and guarantee that the newborn saint will never perish.

Because this grace is too wonderful for the finite mind to grasp, many object to it. The central objection is that grace undermines justice. But our only solid idea of justice comes from the Bible in the first place, and we can scarcely defend the biblical concept of justice by denying other biblical truths. In the final analysis, this problem is solved when we recognize two fundamental truths: there is a God, and we are not God. Consequently, we dare not rail against Him.

The Bible speaks uniformly throughout, and if we submit to the Word of God, we can be confident that God will teach us. But as we learn these precious truths, we must not use them to separate from other genuine Christians in a factious manner. We are not becoming Calvinists; we are becoming consistent in our affirmation of the Bible. And if that is so, then we will be distinguished not only by our doctrinal rigor, but also by our love of peace, our love of the brothers, and our humility of mind. And this brings us to the place where we put what we believe into practice as members of God's covenant community.

At the heart of sin is the refusal to honor God as God and give Him thanks. This sin is not limited to the ranks of those outside the church. At the conclusion of the twentieth century, this sin has flooded our homes, churches, seminaries, publishing houses, and music studios. We are no longer known in the world as a God-fearing people.

If God is pleased to turn our hearts back to Him in repentance, the results will show in more than just our theological attachments. As we find ourselves humbled under the mighty hand of God, that humility will be seen elsewhere. If a man is a "Calvinist without reserve," and is arrogant at home and in the church, he is no true Calvinist at all.[1] A true glimpse of the sovereignty of the Most High will always result in visible humility and love in the community of saints.

The apostle Paul firmly condemned the sin of factionalism. He had no use at all for it in any form. "For when one says, 'I am of Paul,' and another, 'I am of Apollos,' are you not carnal?" (1 Cor. 3:4). This carnality is not removed if we take away the names of Paul and Apollos and substitute the names of Luther, Calvin, or Wesley. Nor is it removed if we seek to take the high moral ground by feigning to take on the name of Christ (1 Cor. 1:12). With our hearts we must repent from the carnality of having a party spirit; only then will a humble spirit permeate the words of our books and discussions—even when we must differ with our brothers in Christ. And let us never forget that truth is determined by what the Bible says, not by loyalty to any individual, living or dead.

A true understanding of the doctrines of grace will not only replace factionalism with visible love and humility, but also usher in powerful gospel preaching. In an age when the church thinks more of marketing herself than preaching her crucified Lord, such a result is greatly to be desired. We may lament the fact that our age has no Whitefield, Spurgeon, or Edwards, but it would be far more profitable for us to lament the fact that we have very little soil in which such preachers grow.

As a recovered gospel is preached in power, Christians will deepen their understanding of grace—God be praised, we do not begin with grace and finish with human effort. It is all grace, from beginning to end. And because God is good, the day will come when the prayer of the apostle Paul will be answered, and all the saints will come to see the glory in grace— grasping the ungraspable, knowing the unknowable, and marveling at how unworthy wretches can be dressed in a righteousness not their own. May the triune God—the Father who loved us before time, the Christ who purchased us on the cross, and the Spirit who brought us out of the grave— hasten that day. Amen.

STUDY QUESTIONS

1. What lies at the heart of sin? How has it affected our homes, churches, seminaries, publishing houses, and music studios?
2. How does a true glimpse of the sovereignty of the Most High result in visible humility and love? Have you gained such a glimpse lately?
3. What are you doing to recover the true gospel in your own life? Your family? Your church? Your workplace? Your culture?

Notes

1. "And I am afraid there are Calvinists, who, while they account it a proof of their humility that they are willing in words to debase the creature, and to give all the glory of salvation to the Lord, yet know not what manner of spirit

they are of. . . . Self-righteousness can feed upon doctrines, as well as upon works; and a man can have the heart of a Pharisee, while his head is stored with orthodox notions of the unworthiness of the creature and the riches of free grace" (John Newton, *The Works of John Newton* [Edinburgh: Banner of Truth, 1985], 1:272).

PART TWO

BACK TO THE COVENANT

Douglas M. Jones III

INTRODUCTION

B ecause the Reformed faith starts and stops and moves with God as He has revealed Himself in Scripture, it is not surprising that it emphasizes His sovereignty in converting us from darkness to His marvelous light. God's grace, to be sure, is sovereign. But that is only part of the story. His grace is also covenantal, which is simply to say that God has sovereignly and graciously established a redemptive relationship of union and communion with His people and their offspring.

In this part of the book, we will take a look at this covenantal relationship between God and His people. We will focus on its anticipation of, and fulfillment in, the person and work of Christ, both in the past and in its glorious future. From the past to the future, the sovereign and gracious God of the universe covenantally promises to redeem us and to bring us and our offspring into a covenantal relationship with Him. He promises not only that He will be our God and the God of our offspring after us, but also that we will be His people both now and forever.

In an era when few have ever heard of the covenant, we need, more than ever, to get back to basics—back to the covenant. [D. G. H.]

EIGHT

THE BEAUTY OF IT ALL

W hat is it that strikes you as extremely beautiful? What type of beauty moves you to the very depths of your being? The sounds of a live symphony? The riches of a Rembrandt? The rhythm and power of a Shakespearean soliloquy? A sunrise across a silver ocean? A snow-covered prairie? The secure embrace of a spouse? The heartfelt prayer of a child?

Magnify greatly whatever you find exceptionally beautiful in order to begin approaching the beauty of *God's covenantal work*. God's covenantal work involves stunning patterns and silencing choruses, breathtaking landscapes and warm rhythms, tragedy and triumph, and fearful awe. Nothing can really compare to the beauty of God's gracious covenantal work, which He has laid before us magnificently from Genesis to Revelation.[1] In the pages that follow, we will get a better glimpse of the moving mosaic of God's covenantal work.

But what is covenantal work? For that matter, what is a covenant? For the moment, think of it as a marriage bond between God and His people. This covenant work, as we shall see, is simply the *core* of biblical faith and history; *it is the gospel*. As God's good news, it continues to set aflame every aspect of faithful Christian living and culture.

As the faithful Ursinus penned, "What is your steadfast comfort in life and death?—That in His infinite and immutable lovingkindness, God has received me into His covenant of grace."[2] This rich comfort has been the hope and faith of God's people since the Fall. This comfort—that despite the ferocity and despair of sin that surrounds us, the "God of all comfort" (2 Cor. 1:3) has mercifully condescended to "save His people from their sins" (Matt. 1:21) by means of a covenant—is the very gospel of Christ, the work of the Father, and the promise of the Spirit.

A CRUCIAL CONCERN

But why is God's covenant work so crucial to Christian thought, piety, and culture? First, if the Lord has mercifully condescended to reveal Himself to us by means of a covenant, then we cannot know Him correctly if we ignore His chosen means of expression. Christ declares that "this is eternal life, that they may know Thee, the only true God, and Jesus Christ whom Thou hast sent" (John 17:3). If we ignore God's manner of relating to us, we do so at our own peril: "My people are destroyed for lack of knowledge" (Hos. 4:6).

Second, as New Covenant believers, God has commissioned His people to proclaim, teach, and defend His gospel; yet, the New Testament writers identify Christ's gospel with God's covenant promises (Gal. 3:8; Heb. 4:2; Rom 1:1–2). So, if we fail to recognize the gospel as God's covenantal work, we cannot faithfully proclaim, teach, or defend the gospel.

Third, if we fail to appreciate the covenant, then we cannot properly understand Scripture. If everything in Scripture is so intricately tied to God's covenantal work, then we cannot properly comprehend the history, poetry, law, prophecy, and doctrines of Scripture apart from their covenantal foundations. Harold O. J. Brown notes that covenantal faith, the Reformed faith, "is the most Jewish branch of Christianity, and as such was the first to develop an interest in the Jews and their institutions."[3] The New Covenant does not describe itself as some new, unconnected period in history, completely separated from the Old Covenant, as modern dispensationalism, popular evangelicalism, and Lutheranism suggest. Rather, as we will see, the New Covenant message is a continuous and progressive outgrowth of Old Covenant promises. The Lord reveals one continuous work in Scripture, not two or seven. To miss the covenant is to miss Scripture.

Fourth, by properly embracing God's covenant, we will grow in assurance, steadfastness, boldness, thankfulness, and fear of God. Our faithfulness can do little but grow as we recognize and embrace Him as our covenant Lord. And by recognizing the uniqueness and the deep interconnections of the covenant from Genesis to Revelation, we can better appreciate the apologetic importance of God's covenant work. Who but the Lord could have done such a magnificent work?

In everything, then, the covenant is important. Without it, we cannot properly know God, proclaim the gospel, understand Scripture, or live the Christian life.

THE SKELETON OF SCRIPTURE

What is God's covenantal work all about? Covenant theology focuses, in part, on history—the history of God's work in salvation, which has come to be known as redemptive history. But that does not tell us enough. What particular view of redemptive history does God's covenantal work involve? What is the "skeleton" of redemptive history?

Covenant theology maintains that God has organized redemptive history in terms of covenants and a promise, or, as the apostle Paul declares, "the covenants of promise" (Eph. 2:12). This covenant work, this "marriage bond" from Genesis to Revelation, He unifies by the promise that He is redeeming a people for Himself, a promise most gloriously expressed throughout Scripture by the formula, "I will be your God, and you will be My people."

To see how this covenantal view of God's Word contrasts with other views, consider some of the ways in which God could have structured the history of redemption. He could have structured it, for example, in terms of "the great heroes of the faith." On this view, redemptive history would simply be a disconnected story of noteworthy saints, like a sports hall of fame. Or He could have structured the history of redemption in terms of repeating cycles, never progressing or ending. Or He could have done so in terms of an ongoing class struggle for political liberation. Or, as much of modern evangelicalism maintains, He could have structured redemptive history in terms of broken and inwardly changing time periods, called dispensations. Clearly, then, all these options for redemptive history—heroes, cycles, class struggles, and dispensations—differ greatly from covenant theology, not only in their understanding of Scripture's skeleton, but also by their radically different consequences for the gospel and the Christian life.

PUTTING FLESH ON THE BONES

Having seen something of the skeleton of covenant theology, we now need to put some flesh on its bones by looking at some of its important features. What, in more detail, is a covenant? The word *covenant* is not used often in our culture. However, in various ancient cultures—especially in that of the Old Testament and its neighbors—covenants played a central role. They stood at the heart of the relationship that bound ruler to citizen, nation to nation, person to person, husband to wife, child to parent, and so on.

From just these examples, then, we can see that a covenant is, first of all, a relationship between persons. But not just any personal relationship will do; a covenant is a *binding personal relationship*. Scripture contains several examples of covenants that bind persons to certain conditions and obligations (Gen. 21:22–34; Josh. 9; 1 Sam. 18:3; 2 Sam. 3:6–21; 5:3; 1 Kings 5). Think, for instance, of Jacob and Laban. After God blessed Jacob at Laban's expense, and then Jacob fled, Laban caught up with him, demanding an explanation. After each man accused the other of injustices, they determined to resolve their dispute by making a covenant: "Let us make a covenant, you and I, and let it be a witness between you and me" (Gen. 31:44). While appealing to God as their witness and avenger, Jacob bound himself not to harm his wives (Laban's daughters) or add other wives, and Laban bound himself not to intervene in Jacob's life. As a sign or token of the covenant, they set up a specially designated heap of stones and demonstrated the peace between themselves by offering a sacrifice and breaking bread with one another (v. 54).

In a covenant between two people, then, each person makes certain binding promises, agreeing that God will serve as judge and avenger against the person who breaks the agreement. Such a covenant between people, however, must be distinguished from a covenant between God and man (i.e., a covenant between the Lord and His servants). A covenant between men assumes a general equality and mutual agreement between the persons involved, which is obviously not the case with covenants between God and man. Equal participants may each suggest conditions, set terms, and barter benefits, but no such bargaining is possible between the sovereign Lord and His finite creatures. While Jacob and Laban could negotiate with each other, Adam and Abraham were in no position to negotiate with God.[4]

We always find this hierarchy when we examine the covenants made between the Lord and His servants (i.e., Adam, Noah, Abraham, Moses, David, and Christ). The servants do not set any terms or conditions for the Lord; rather, God sovereignly and graciously imposes all stipulations, conditions, sanctions, promises, and rituals. These covenants are unilaterally (one-sidedly) rather than bilaterally (two-sidedly) set up.[5] God's covenants declare His lordship in salvation and over all creation. John Frame expresses this connection between lordship and covenant well when he writes,

Lordship is a covenantal concept. . . . God brings His covenant servants into existence (Isa. 41:4; 43:10–13; 44:6; 48:12f.) and exercises total control over them (Ex. 3:8, 14). As Lord, He sovereignly delivers them (Ex. 20:2) from bondage and directs the whole environment (cf. the plagues in Egypt) to accomplish His purposes for them. Authority is God's right to be obeyed. . . . Over and over, the covenant Lord stresses how His servants must obey His commands (Ex. 3:13–18; 20:2; Lev. 18:2–5, 30; 19:37; Deut. 6:4–9). To say that God's authority is absolute means that His commands may not be questioned (Job 40:11ff.; Rom. 4:18–20; 9:20; Heb. 11:4, 7–8, 17, passim), that divine authority transcends all other loyalties (Ex. 20:3; Deut. 6:4f.; Matt. 8:19–22; 10:34–38; Phil. 3:8), and that this authority extends to all areas of human life (Ex.; Lev.; Num.; Deut.; Rom. 14:32; 1 Cor. 10:31; 2 Cor. 10:5; Col. 3:17, 23).[6]

Thus, the Lord-servant covenants of Scripture are not mutual compacts between equals, but rather are sovereignly and unilaterally imposed bonds. Adam does not offer God any advice; Abraham does not negotiate any clauses; David does not propose any terms; the covenant is exclusively the sovereign Lord's gracious mandate.

Up to this point, we have observed that a Lord-servant covenant (1) is a mutually binding relationship between persons (Lord and servants), (2) involves conditions (commandments, promises, and sanctions), (3) is, in all aspects, sovereignly imposed by God. One final and prominent characteristic of Lord-servant covenants flows from the conditional promises mentioned above: God's promises always focus on union and communion, the mutual bonds of love and faithfulness between the Lord and His servants. This designation, "union and communion," is a precious and long-standing description in covenant theology, which summarizes the intimacy, peace, faithfulness, devotion, and reverential fear that we find in Scripture. In short, the glorious, central, and unifying promise of redemptive history, "I will be your God, and you will be My people," is the promise of union and communion.

Scripture expresses this promise of union and communion in terms of both the husband-wife relationship—"For your husband is your Maker, whose name is the LORD of hosts" (Isa. 54:5; see also Jer. 31:31–32; cf. 3:1, 6–10; Ezek. 16:5–8; Hos. 1:2; 3:1; Eph. 5:24–25, 32; Rev. 21:9)—and the parent-child relationship—"I will be a father to you, and you shall be sons and daughters to Me, says the Lord Almighty" (2 Cor. 6:18; cf. 2 Sam.

7:14; Ex. 4:22; Deut. 1:31; 8:5; Hos. 11:1; Rom. 8:15; 1 John 3:1).

The covenant, then, is not some hollow, external, legal relationship between the Lord and His servants. It is a bond of union and communion, like a precious, intimate, faithful, and loving marriage. The Lord as husband has laid down His life in service to His bride, and His servants as the bride are to respect and honor the husband. Likewise, the Lord as Father warmly loves, protects, and disciplines His people as children, who are to obey, reverence, and rejoice in the presence of their Father. Notice also in these images how the Lord excludes merit (earning God's favor); neither a bride nor children "earn" their keep; each of them serves out of love. Such are the Lord's gracious covenantal promises of union and communion: "The tabernacle of God is with men, and He will dwell with them, and they shall be His people, and God Himself will be with them and be their God" (Rev. 21:3 NKJV).

The elements of a covenant between God and man, then, are

- a mutually binding relationship between the Lord and His servants,
- sovereign administration,
- conditions (commandments, sanctions), and
- promises of union and communion.

More briefly, a Lord-servant covenant is a *God-ordained bond of union, peace, friendship, and service between the Lord and His people.* This is what we find when we examine God's covenants made with Adam, Abraham, Moses, David, and Christ.

In the chapters that follow, we will enter into more of the rich mosaic of God's covenantal work for His people, considering both its past and its future aspects. While Scripture reveals much about the beautiful development of God's covenant work from Adam to Christ, it also gives us a glimpse of its glorious culmination in the future. We will examine each of these parts of covenant life and redemptive history in turn, beginning with God's covenant work in the past.

STUDY QUESTIONS

1. Is your steadfast comfort in life and death that God, in "His infinite and immutable lovingkindness, . . . received [you] into His covenant of grace"? Why or why not?

2. What is redemptive history, and what are some of the organizing principles that characterize God's work in redemptive history? What are the implications of each organizing principle for Christian thought, piety, and culture? What organizing principle best describes your view of redemptive history, and how has it affected your life?
3. Would it be correct to characterize God's covenant with His people as a hollow, external, legal relationship? Why not? How does knowing that you are married to God or are His child affect your relationship with Him?

Notes

1. I dedicate this section to my sister Lucy Zoe Jones, who, over the years, has taught me so much about beauty.
2. Zacharias Ursinus, *Explicationum catecheticarum* (Heidelberg, 1612), cited in William Hendriksen, *The Covenant of Grace* (1932; reprint, Grand Rapids: Baker, 1978), 13.
3. Harold O. J. Brown, *Heresies: The Image of Christ in the Mirror of Heresy from the Apostles to the Present* (Grand Rapids: Baker, 1984), 114.
4. John Murray, *The Covenant of Grace* (London: Tyndale, 1953), 9.
5. Ibid., 12.
6. John Frame, *The Doctrine of the Knowledge of God* (Phillipsburg, N.J.: Presbyterian and Reformed, 1987), 12, 15–16.

NINE

BACK TO THE FUTURE

We often hear Scripture portrayed as an unconnected mishmash of hero stories, when in fact the Lord has gloriously developed one message, an interlaced and many-faceted outworking of His central promise, "I will be your God, and you will be My people." This most central promise first appears in the Lord's revelation to Abraham, but we find its roots and motive in God's covenantal dealings with Adam and Noah. This section's brief survey begins with Adam and Noah and then moves through the more explicit features of God's subsequent covenantal work, examining in each

- the connections to the previous covenant,
- the promise of a people,
- the promise of a land,
- the covenant summary promise, and
- the further unveiling of the main covenant.

By following this pattern, we can more readily comprehend the richness of God's covenant.

In the end, what we will find is the following picture: The Lord began His work of union and communion by covenanting with Adam as our representative at Creation. But Adam violated that initial covenant, and so the Lord graciously provided another covenant—a covenant for the fallen, a covenant of salvation or redemption. Beginning immediately after the Fall, the Lord progressively unveiled this gracious, redemptive covenant through His promises to the fallen Adam, His preservation of the world for redemption after Noah, His promises of a people and a land to Abraham, and His greater revelation of these promises to Moses, David, and the prophets. Each new stage beautifully developed from, and expanded upon, a prior covenant, like one intricate chain. Ultimately, this single, unified, and glorious redemptive covenant culminated in the work of Christ, the Last Adam, our representative who, in covenant with the Father before the world began, restored the union and communion that the First Adam discarded. In all, God's covenantal work was the revelation and realization of the loss of union and communion, followed by the regaining of them, with the Lord demonstrating His supreme glory and graciousness throughout.

WHAT IS IN A NAME?

The most prominent distinction that appears in God's covenant work is that between God's covenant before the Fall and His covenant thereafter. Before the Fall, the Lord graciously condescends to covenant with Adam (and humanity) in his condition of genuine righteousness. But after the Fall, the Lord establishes a covenant to redeem rebels alienated by their sin.

These two distinct covenants have gone by many names in the history of Christian thought, but we will call them the Covenant of Creation and the Covenant of Redemption. These labels highlight the different conditions of humanity with respect to each covenant.

Regardless of the names we apply to these two covenants, the more interesting point is that the distinction between them is prior to, and more foundational than, the distinction between the Old and New Covenants, which sometimes receives undue emphasis. The important distinction between the Old and New Covenants is really between anticipation (the Old Covenant) and fulfillment (the New Covenant) within the Covenant of Redemption. The intricate covenantal chain of redemption runs unbroken through both Old and New Covenants.

THE COVENANT OF CREATION WITH ADAM

Before we discuss the Covenant of Redemption and the contrasts between the Old and New Covenants within it, we first need to grasp the features and beauty of the Covenant of Creation.

Union and Communion

In the opening pages of Genesis, we read not only of God's glorious cre-
ative work, which He judged to be "very good," but also of His grace in
establishing union and communion with our first parents. God first demonstrated His grace by creating man in His own image, male and female.
He further demonstrated His grace by blessing our parents (1:28), providing sustenance for their lives (1:29), giving them gifts of plants and trees
(1:29), surrounding them with beauty (2:9), supplying fruitful labor (2:15),
granting them stewardship authority (1:28; 2:19), and, when Adam was
the only human being, blessing him with intimate communion and help
through one of his own kind—Eve, "flesh of my flesh." Added to these
blessings, if they continued in perfect righteousness, were the prospect of
holy children and a holy family life.

Into this paradise of union and communion between God and man,
the Lord introduced a particular commandment beyond those already
given (labor, stewardship, family fruitfulness, Sabbath rest), and, by so
doing, He revealed the covenantal nature of His relationship with Adam.

The Lord commanded Adam and Eve, "From any tree of the garden
you may eat freely; but from the tree of the knowledge of good and evil you
shall not eat, for in the day that you eat from it you shall surely die" (Gen.
2:16–17). In this commandment, we find the four essential parts of a covenant (even though the word *covenant* is not used).

1. *A mutually binding relationship between the Lord and His servant:* God
bound Adam by the specific command forbidding him to eat, and the Lord
bound Himself to preserve Adam for faithful obedience to the command
and "surely" to bring death for disobedience to it.

2. *Sovereign administration:* The Lord Himself determined the framework for His creature; Adam set no terms.

3. *Conditions (commandments, sanctions):* Conditions are always indicated by if-then statements. In this case, if Adam faithfully obeyed, then
he would keep on living and never face death. However, if Adam disobeyed God's command, then he would "surely die."

4. *Promises of union and communion:* As noted above, Adam had al-
ready been living in perfect union and communion with God. Now the
Lord promised to preserve this precious relationship on the condition of
Adam's loyalty and faithfulness.

Some people hesitate to call God's relationship with Adam a covenant, since the word itself does not appear in the text. But the word *marriage* does not appear in Genesis 2, either; nonetheless, we understand that

a marital union was established at the end of the chapter. We learn much about marriage in that context, even though the specific word is absent (Gen. 2:24; cf. Matt. 19:3ff.). Similarly, all the specific and unique parts of a covenant are present in Eden before the Fall, even though the word *covenant* does not come into use until later in Scripture. Furthermore, Scripture itself later refers to this relationship with Adam as a covenant when Hosea rebukes the Israelites by proclaiming that "like Adam they have transgressed the covenant" (Hos. 6:7).[1]

Alienation and Enmity

As we know so painfully, Adam rebelled against and rejected God's gracious covenant: "Our first parents being left to the freedom of their own will, through the temptation of Satan, transgressed the commandment of God in eating the forbidden fruit; and thereby fell from the estate of innocency wherein they were created."[2] As a result, Adam not only put himself at war with God, but also, as the representative of all mankind, alienated the human race from God and put the whole human race at enmity with God. As Scripture declares, "Through one man sin entered into the world, and death through sin, and so death spread to all men, because all sinned" (Rom. 5:12).

By violating the covenant, Adam brought upon himself the curse that God had promised. He forsook the covenant relationship of union and communion and instead embraced the covenant-breaking relationship of alienation and enmity. Adam despised God's grace by disobeying Him and then attempted to avoid personal responsibility for his transgression.

The curses that the Lord imposed, in fulfillment of His promise, were foundational for everything that happened in history from that point forward. The Lord poured out His curses on all three parties to the crime: Satan (as the serpent), Eve, and Adam, in that order. In particular, Adam and Eve were cursed to face toilsome labor at odds with each other and their world, and, even more significantly, they unleashed the reign of death on all humanity (Rom. 5:17).

Many popular accounts of the Fall leave the curse at this. Notice, however, that the Lord not only imposed the promised curse of pain and death, but also imposed a war—a deep-seated and long-lasting war—between the seed of the woman and the seed of the Serpent, between the friends of God and the enemies of God, between the City of God and the City of Man: "I will put enmity between you [the Serpent] and the woman, and between your seed and her Seed; He shall bruise your head, and you shall bruise His heel" (Gen. 3:15 NKJV).

Thus, the Lord Himself imposed a hostile alienation—an antithesis—in history, which shows itself throughout scriptural history and beyond. This hostility between the faithful and the rebellious rages everywhere and at all times. It is prominent throughout Scripture, as the seed of the woman—Abel, Seth, Noah, Shem, Abraham, Isaac, Jacob, Moses, faithful Israel, David, the remnant of Judah, and ultimately Christ and His seed to the end of history—battle relentlessly against the seed of the Serpent—Cain, the Nephilim, Ham, Nimrod, Ishmael, Esau, Egypt, Korah, the Canaanites, Saul, the Northern tribes, Assyria, Babylon, apostate Judaism, Rome and others.

Although this enmity sometimes manifests itself in physical violence, it most powerfully erupts in spiritual and philosophical warfare. Paul, himself a powerful combatant in this war, reminds us that "we do not wrestle against flesh and blood, but against principalities, against powers, against the rulers of the darkness of this age, against spiritual hosts of wickedness in the heavenly places" (Eph. 6:12 NKJV). Our weapons are not the weapons of "flesh and blood." They are not physical, "but mighty in God for pulling down strongholds, casting down arguments and every high thing that exalts itself against the knowledge of God, bringing every thought into captivity to the obedience of Christ" (2 Cor. 10:4–5 NKJV).

This war is so pervasive that there is no room for compromise. Peaceful coexistence is impossible. Neutrality is impossible: "For what fellowship has righteousness with lawlessness? And what communion has light with darkness? And what accord has Christ with Belial? Or what part has a believer with an unbeliever? And what agreement has the temple of God with idols?" (2 Cor. 6:14–16).

When our representative, Adam, rebelled, he cast all of creation and history into a state of alienation, division, hostility, and enmity—total war—against the Lord. Everything after Adam's rebellion falls under the curse and wrath of God. "The whole creation groans and labors with birth pangs" and "eagerly waits" for redemption (Rom. 8:19, 22 NKJV).

THE COVENANT OF REDEMPTION

Yet, the Lord did not forsake us in our rebellion. Within the very curse on the human race, the Lord demonstrated His mercy and grace by declaring to those who so high-handedly rebelled against Him, "He shall bruise your head, and you shall bruise His heel" (Gen. 3:15 NKJV). One would come from the woman and triumph over the enemies of God. We would not always be trapped in alienation and enmity. In this promise, we have the beginnings of the Covenant of Redemption—the promise of victory and salvation. As the Westminster Confession, 7.3, summarizes, "Man, by his fall, having made himself incapable of life by that covenant, the Lord was pleased to make a second."

Noah

Scripture does not portray Adam and Noah as two unrelated persons; nor does it portray their times as two disjointed periods of history. In Noah's time, God's revelation explicitly built upon the foundations of the covenantal work established with Adam. Accordingly, we should not think of Noah's covenant simply as one among many. Rather, it was an unfolding or development of God's one Covenant of Redemption. Or, using an earlier image, Noah's covenant was another more intricate link in the chain of one redemptive covenant.

Between the Fall and Noah's time, the enmity between the two seeds had manifested itself in Cain's murder of Abel, the intermarrying of the daughters of men and the "sons of God," and the pervasive wickedness that invited judgment by the Flood. Alienation and enmity dominated.

In the midst of this corruption, the Lord poured out His grace on Noah and his family, out of all the families on the earth. The Lord said He was "bringing the flood of water upon the earth, to destroy all flesh . . . ; everything that is on the earth shall perish" (Gen. 6:17). "But," declared the Lord, "I will establish My covenant with you; and you shall enter the ark—you and your sons and your wife, and your sons' wives with you" (v. 18).

In these dealings with Noah, the Lord renewed features of the Adamic covenant, highlighting the links between Adam and Noah. First, the Lord commanded Adam to "be fruitful and multiply" (Gen. 1:28), and He used the same language with Noah (9:1, 7). Second, the Lord granted Adam stewardship and dominion over the animals (1:28), and He granted Noah the same privileges (9:2–3). Third, we find that the summary description of animals for Adam (1:24–25) was virtually the same as that for Noah (6:20; 8:17). Fourth, for Adam the family served as the redemptive center of society (1:24; 3:17), and likewise for Noah the family was the object of redemption and the agency of stewardship (6:18; 9:9). Fifth, the Lord related to Adam by means of a covenant (2:16–17), as He did with Noah

(6:18). Sixth, Genesis 5 highlights the antithesis of seeds by showing that Noah descended from Seth, a faithful son of Adam (4:25–26). Throughout the Lord's redemptive dealings with Noah, we are regularly reminded of the covenantal foundation laid with Adam.

After the Flood and all its destruction, the Lord more explicitly inaugurated His covenant with Noah. Again, we see the characteristics of a divine covenant.

1. *A mutually binding relationship between the Lord and His servant:* The Lord bound Himself to preserve creation from cataclysm, and He bound Noah to be fruitful, subdue the earth, and impose a death penalty on those who slay others made in His image (Gen. 9:6).

2. *Sovereign administration:* "I Myself do establish My covenant with you" (9:9). The Lord sought no input from Noah, but sovereignly set the terms and made the promises of the covenant.

3. *Conditions (commandments, sanctions):* The Lord not only renewed the original creation ordinances of fruitfulness and stewardship, but also instituted a death penalty for murder and required faithfulness to this commandment (9:5).

4. *Promises of union and communion:* We find covenantal intimacy expressed in terms of a nurturing preservation of seedtime and harvest (8:22), protection from cataclysm (9:15), stewardship of creation (9:2–3), and the gracious sign of the rainbow (9:13, 17). The Lord further showed this covenantal union by repeatedly declaring that this covenant was "between Me and you" (Gen. 9:9, 11–13, 15–17). This provided a foretaste of the central promise, "I will be your God, and you will be My people."

Finally, Noah's covenant was foundational in the Covenant of Redemption in that it focused on preserving creation. The Lord not only bound Himself to preserve seedtime and harvest, summer and winter, and withhold future cataclysmic floods, but also set the death penalty as a restraint within society so that murder could no longer run rampant and go unpunished. As O. Palmer Robertson notes, this focus on preservation was foundational to the entire future work of redemption in that "God commits himself to preserve the present order of the world so that the work of redemption may be accomplished. Seedtime and harvest, cold and heat, summer and winter, day and night will never cease as long as the earth endures (Gen. 8:22). The world will be kept free of massive disturbances like Noah's flood. Regularity and order will preserve the human race and the environment."[3] In other words, the covenant made with Noah preserved the creation from further divine destruction and preserved humans from destroying one another so that the Lord could securely unfold His covenant work from then onward.

Abraham

We may often hear people treating the genealogies in Scripture lightly, as if they were some bothersome fillers. When we see a genealogy, however, the first thing we should think about is war. Yes, war. Genealogies, among other things, should remind us of the ongoing spiritual war between the seed of the woman and the seed of the Serpent (Gen. 3:15).

Just as Scripture takes care to demonstrate the lineage from Adam and Seth to Noah (Gen. 5:3–32), so it also takes care to show how the seed of the woman developed through Noah and his faithful son Shem to Abraham (Gen. 11:10–32). With Abraham, the Lord did not just begin anew in an unconnected manner. Instead, He continued to extend His covenantal mercy and grace selectively to the seed of the woman, from Adam and Seth, through Noah and Shem, to Abraham—one covenantal chain.

Genesis 12, 15, and 17 record God's three covenantal encounters with Abraham. In the first one (12:1–4), the Lord called Abraham and gloriously declared the gospel: "In you all the families of the earth shall be blessed" (v. 3). You may not think of this as containing the gospel. Much of contemporary Christianity tends to have an overly narrow understanding of the gospel, one broken off from its Abrahamic foundations. Nevertheless, the Holy Spirit, speaking through Paul, declares most significantly that "the Scripture, foreseeing that God would justify the Gentiles by faith, preached *the gospel* beforehand to Abraham, saying, 'All the nations shall be blessed in you' " (Gal. 3:8; cf. Heb. 4:2; Rom. 1:1–2).

Sadly, we often tend to minimize this glorious gospel promise. The Lord did not promise that in Abraham a significant minority would be blessed or that a good number of nations would be blessed, but that all families of the earth would be blessed! The Lord also promised Abraham a land (Gen. 12:1). These two things—a people and a land—are the specific promises around which all of God's subsequent covenant work revolved.

In the second covenantal encounter between the Lord and Abraham (Gen. 15), Abraham sought assurance of the promise, and the Lord provided that assurance—His own word: "Since He could swear by no one greater, He swore by Himself " (Heb. 6:13). The Lord presented His word in the form of a special covenantal ceremony—a self-maledictory oath— that was common to many cultures at that time. In this ceremony, two persons would "cut" a covenant by mutually agreeing to the conditions in their covenant and then dividing one or more animals in half and walking down the bloody path between the cut pieces. This gruesome and solemn ceremony showed that each party had promised to abide by and accomplish the conditions agreed upon or else have his own blood shed, like that of the divided animals. In other words, a person taking part in a self-maledictory or self-cursing oath was saying, "May this same end befall the covenant breaker."

The self-maledictory ceremony in Genesis 15 is rather odd when compared to the normal practice of the ritual. Normally, both parties to the covenant would walk through the animal halves together, but here only a representation (a lamp) of the Lord passed through. Perhaps, by passing through the pieces by Himself, the Lord was emphasizing the fulfillment of the promises on the pain of His own death, rather than Abraham's (although both were obligated to be faithful). In essence, the Lord brought the curse of death upon Himself to ensure that the promises were kept. In the end, we know that in order to accomplish what was promised, the Lord had to do just that. God in Christ would have to "become a curse for us" (Gal. 3:13) so that we could be brought into union and communion with Him. But we are getting ahead of our survey.

In this encounter between God and Abraham, we also learn more about the promise of a people and a land. We learn that God was selective in determining the seed of the woman. He rejected Abraham's servant (Eliezer) as an heir, and promised an heir from Abraham's own body (Gen. 15:1–4). The Lord also described the greatness of Abraham's descendants by saying that they would be uncountable—as many as the stars in the sky (v. 5). As for the promise of a land, the Lord foretold that Abraham's seed, though suffering under captivity (Egypt), would eventually triumph and inherit the land from the river of Egypt to the Euphrates (v. 18).

After these first two encounters between Abraham and the Lord, we find yet another one (Gen. 17). Again, we should not think of these encounters as instituting three separate covenants. Their content was the same, and it was common to renew a covenant in this manner. In each encounter, the Lord revealed more details of the Covenant of Redemption. In Genesis 17, four items stand out. First, the Lord rehearsed the promises of a land and a people, but this time added that through Abraham and Sarah "kings shall come forth" (vv. 6, 16).

Second, we find the first expression of the covenant slogan ("I will be your God, and you will be My people"), which the Lord would repeat regularly from that point on: "I will establish My covenant between Me and you and your descendants after you . . . to be God to you and to your descendants after you . . . and I will be their God" (vv. 7–8).

Third, the Lord elaborated on the conditions of the covenant by introducing the sign and seal of circumcision (vv. 11–14). Although only circumcision is mentioned here, the Lord gave other conditions as well, for we know that He later declared that "Abraham obeyed Me and kept My charge, My commandments, My statutes, and My laws" (Gen. 26:5). The Abrahamic covenant required Abraham's trust and obedience, as he evidenced from the start: "For I have chosen him [Abraham], in order that he may command his children and his household after him to keep the way of the LORD by doing righteousness and justice; in order that the LORD may bring upon Abraham what He has spoken about him" (Gen. 18:19).

The words "in order that" teach us that Abraham was obligated to obey the Lord faithfully "by doing righteousness and justice," thus meeting the gracious conditions of God's covenant.

Fourth, we see a narrowing process with respect to the seed of the woman. Initially, God narrowed the human race by judgment, pouring out His grace only on Noah's family. Then the Lord narrowed the recipients of His redemptive grace down to Abraham and his seed. After rejecting Eliezer as Abraham's heir (Gen. 15:4), the Lord narrowed down even Abraham's physical seed by excluding Ishmael and choosing instead to pour out His redemptive grace on the line of Isaac: "But My covenant I will establish with Isaac" (Gen. 17:21). So, we learn from the very beginning that not all of Abraham's physical descendants will automatically be beneficiaries of God's redemptive grace. Finally, although we see this narrowing process, we remember that the Lord promised Abraham a vast number of descendants!

In these three passages describing the covenants between the Lord and Abraham, we see clearly all the parts of a covenant as described previously, namely

1. *A mutually binding relationship between the Lord and His servant:* The Lord bound Himself to fulfill His promises "on pain of death," and He required Abraham to serve in faithful obedience.

2. *Sovereign administration:* The Lord alone called Abraham out of his homeland, and, most significantly, He alone passed through the animal halves in the covenant ceremony.

3. *Conditions (commandments, sanctions):* The Lord required Abraham to circumcise all his physical and adopted male descendants, and "Abraham obeyed Me and kept my charge, My commandments, My statutes and My laws" (Gen. 26:5).

4. *Promises of union and communion:* In the Abrahamic covenant, the

Lord first made explicit use of the union and communion formula: "I will establish My covenant between Me and you and your descendants after you . . . to be God to you and to your descendants after you . . . and I will be their God" (Gen. 17:7–8).

The period from Abraham to Moses (when the next major step in the development of the Covenant of Redemption occurred) was characterized by continuity. The Lord explicitly reaffirmed His covenant with Abraham's immediate descendants, extending union and communion to the seed of the woman (Isaac, Jacob, and Joseph), while inviting alienation and enmity from the seed of the Serpent (Ishmael, Esau, and Egypt).

After Abraham's death, the Lord repeated the covenantal promises of a land and a people to Isaac on the basis of His promise to Abraham (Gen. 26:3–4, 24). Isaac's seed then divided between Jacob and Esau, and once again we see that the Lord narrowed the faithful covenantal line: "For they are not all Israel who are descended from Israel; neither are they all children because they are Abraham's descendants" (Rom. 9:6–13). From the earliest times, the seed of the woman—the seed of Abraham—was characterized by faithful obedience, not biological heritage. Jacob, as part of the selected covenantal line, subsequently received the Abrahamic promises of a land and a people (Gen. 28:13–15; cf. 48:4; 50:24). Similarly, as the covenantal chain continued from Jacob to Joseph and his brothers (Gen. 50:24), so it extended to the sons of Joseph, Ephraim and Manasseh, via Jacob (Gen. 48:15–16).

Redemptive history from Adam to Joseph's sons consisted not of disjointed hero stories or unrelated dispensations, but of the unfolding of God's covenantal work. The intricate and beautiful chain of divine covenants united the seed of the woman into one people. The covenants progressively elaborated God's promises of triumph over Satan, preservation for redemption, a land for God's people, and a blessing to all the families of the earth. We see a beautiful continuity of God's covenant work from Adam to Abraham to Moses.

Israel

The seed of Abraham, Isaac, Jacob, and Joseph was fruitful in Egypt and multiplied to such an extent that the seed of the Serpent, Egypt, grew fearful of the seed of the woman. Pharaoh

> said to his people, "Behold, the people of the sons of Israel are more and mightier than we. Come, let us deal wisely with them,

lest they multiply and . . . join themselves to those who hate us, and fight against us, and depart from the land." So they appointed taskmasters over them to afflict them with hard labor. (Ex. 1:8–11)

From this passage alone, we see that the book of Exodus does not start with a new story, but picks up with the immigration of Jacob's sons (1:1–5) and the death of Joseph (v. 6). Hence, the history of Jacob and Joseph continued. In fact, just prior to his death, Joseph had assured his brothers, "God will surely take care of you, and bring you up from this land to the land which He promised on oath to Abraham, to Isaac and to Jacob" (Gen. 50:24). But even beyond this connection with all that had preceded, the Lord explicitly dealt with His people in Egypt on the basis of His promises to Abraham (Ex. 2:23–25).

After liberating the people of Israel from Egypt, the Lord inaugurated His covenant with them: "If you will indeed obey My voice and keep My covenant, then you shall be My own possession among all the peoples, for all the earth is Mine; and you shall be to Me a kingdom of priests and a holy nation" (Ex. 19:5–6). The people promised to be His covenant servants and accepted the conditions of the covenant—faithful obedience—as expressed through the Ten Commandments and their specific applications, ceremonies, and sacrifices (vv. 7–8). The Lord explicitly revealed the sanctions of the covenant as well; that is, He revealed the blessings for faithfulness and the curses for unfaithfulness. Furthermore, the Lord not only promised union and communion, but actually dwelt among His people in the Tabernacle. Hence, we have all the parts of a covenant relating to the prior covenant with Abraham, Isaac, and Jacob.

1. *Continuity with previous covenants:* The seed of the Serpent in the form of Egypt oppressed God's people, and so the people cried out to the Lord for help. But the Lord did not respond to them as some new group in the middle of the desert. Scripture explicitly teaches that "God heard their groaning; and God remembered His covenant with Abraham, Isaac, and Jacob" (Ex. 2:24). He responded to their cries because of His existing covenant with Abraham. Even more, consider Exodus 6:1–8 and notice how God affirmed His covenant with the patriarchs.

I am the LORD; and I appeared to Abraham, Isaac, and Jacob, as God Almighty, but by My name, LORD, I did not make Myself known to them. . . . And furthermore I have heard the groaning of the sons of Israel, because the Egyptians are holding them in bondage; and I have remembered My covenant. Say, therefore, to the sons of Israel, "I am the LORD, and I will bring you out from under the burdens of the Egyptians, and I will deliver you from their bondage. I will also redeem you with an outstretched arm and with great judgments."

Notice how the Lord used the Abrahamic covenant as a reason and motive for redeeming Israel from slavery, thereby connecting His redemptive work to the Abrahamic covenant.

2. *The promise of a people:* The Lord promised Abraham that his descendants would "be enslaved and oppressed" (Gen. 15:13), but that they would be released (v. 14). The Lord kept His promise to Abraham by acting to rescue Abraham's enslaved and oppressed descendants. Even more, when the Israelites later rebelled and worshiped the golden calf, Moses pleaded for their lives on the basis of the Abrahamic promise of a people: "Remember Abraham, Isaac, and Israel, Thy servants to whom Thou didst swear by Thyself, and didst say to them, 'I will multiply your descendants as the stars of the heavens' " (Ex. 32:13).

3. *The promise of land:* Similarly, the Lord acted on behalf of the Abrahamic promise of a land. He declared: "And I also established My covenant with them, to give them the land of Canaan, the land in which they sojourned. . . . And I will bring you to the land which I swore to give to Abraham, Isaac, and Jacob, and I will give it to you for a possession; I am the LORD'" (Ex. 6: 4, 8). Moses invoked the promise of a land when entreating the Lord not to destroy the Israelites: "Remember Abraham, Isaac, and Israel, Thy servants to whom Thou didst swear by Thyself, and didst say to them, '. . . [A]ll this land of which I have spoken I will give to your descendants, and they shall inherit it forever' " (Ex. 32:13).

4. *The summary promise of the covenant:* The Lord continued to express the covenant in terms of the promise of union and communion: "I will take you for My people, and I will be your God" (Ex. 6:7). Moses later reminded the people that they should keep God's commandments "in order that He may establish you today as His people and that He may be your God, just as He spoke to you and as He swore to your fathers, to Abraham, Isaac, and Jacob" (Deut. 29:13).

5. *Expanded understanding of the covenant:* In each new expression of the Covenant of Redemption, the Lord amplified or elaborated on its details. With Noah, He amplified the promise of preservation. With Abraham, He amplified the promises of a land and a people, and introduced the covenant sign of circumcision. Now, with Moses, we find a tremendous

expansion of God's revelation. To begin with, the Lord revealed a comprehensive expression of His will, the law of God, which detailed His principles for personal, familial, ecclesiastical, and national faithfulness. Moreover, by revealing His holiness in this manner, and having it committed to writing, the people would more clearly see their sin and better recognize their need for a Savior.

Along with the moral and ceremonial codes in His law, the Lord also revealed much more about His covenantal work through set feasts, such as Passover, all of which served to fill out the rich mosaic of the Covenant of Redemption.

In this expression of the covenant with Israel, part of the promise of a people involved an individual who would be "a Prophet," a brother whom the people would obey (Deut. 18:15–19 NKJV). He would obey and teach every commandment of God, and whoever would refuse to obey Him would be destroyed (Deut. 18:19; cf. Acts 3:22–23; 7:37).

As we read the history of redemption from Moses through Joshua and the judges up to King David, we see that it is the history of Israel's relation to the Abrahamic-Mosaic covenant as it battles the seed of the Serpent outside and within its community. The covenant and its conditions are the determining factor of history. God acts and sanctions in accordance with His covenant. Through Israel's faithfulness and unfaithfulness, we see the Lord pursuing His promises of building a people and securing a land; nevertheless, the people of Israel do not acquire the peace and security implicit in the promises.

David

From the Fall to Noah to Abraham to Moses, we have an interconnected sequence of covenants, each dependent upon what preceded and each progressively amplifying God's redemptive promises of a people and a land. King David, the man after God's own heart, marked the next major stage in the development of the Covenant of Redemption. Because everyone unavoidably places some significance on God's covenant with David, many have sought to separate or unhinge David's covenant from those which preceded it. But, once again, the Scriptures clearly argue against such an interpretation. As we will see, the Lord covenanted with David not in spite of, but in explicit dependence upon, the one existing covenant He had unfolded and developed through both Abraham and Israel.

The key text detailing God's covenant with David is found in 2 Samuel. After the era of the judges, the Lord raised up King Saul in judgment

(1 Sam. 8), finally replacing him with His servant, David. David fought fearlessly for the name of God, extending the land of Israel and battling the seed of the Serpent. After David secured Jerusalem (2 Sam. 5) and defeated the Philistines, the Lord covenanted with him, renewing and securing the Abrahamic-Mosaic promises of a land and a people. In 2 Sam. 7:8–17, the Lord declared to David through Nathan,

> I will make you a great name, like the names of the great men who are on the earth. I will also appoint a place for My people Israel and will plant them, that they may live in their own place and not be disturbed again, nor will the wicked afflict them any more as formerly. . . . When your days are complete . . . I will raise up your descendant after you, who will come forth from you, and I will establish his kingdom. He shall build a house for My name, and I will establish the throne of his kingdom forever. I will be a father to him and he will be a son to Me; when he commits iniquity, I will correct him with the rod of men . . . but My lovingkindness shall not depart from him, . . . and your house and your kingdom shall endure before Me forever; your throne shall be established forever.

David later described this declaration of God to him as "an everlasting covenant" (2 Sam. 23:5). And of this encounter the Lord said, "I have made a covenant with My chosen; I have sworn to David My servant" (Ps. 89:3; cf. Ps. 132:11–12). In other words, God specifically described this encounter as a covenant. It manifested all of the characteristics of a divine covenant: (a) mutual binding, (b) sovereign administration, (c) conditions (Ps. 132:10–12), and (d) promises of union and communion (1 Sam. 7:13, 24). So is this covenant discontinuous with previous covenant work or is it characterized by continuity?

1. *Continuity with previous covenants:* David recognized his and Israel's place when he exhorted the people to "Remember His covenant forever . . . the covenant which He made with Abraham, and His oath to Isaac. He also confirmed it to Jacob for a statute, to Israel as an everlasting covenant" (1 Chron. 16:15–17; cf. Ps. 105).

And, in the Davidic covenant itself, the Lord spoke of the current covenant as following from His salvation of Israel from Egypt (2 Sam. 7:6) and from the covenant (i.e., the covenant with Israel) governing the era of judges (2 Sam. 7:11). Furthermore, He covenanted with David on the basis of the promise of a land and a people (see below). Thus, David is one

further link in the chain of the Covenant of Redemption. The Lord covenanted with him on the basis of His promises to Israel and Abraham.

2. *The promise of a people:* The Lord promised to preserve and protect
His people from their enemies (2 Sam. 7:10), and David responded by
rehearsing God's redemptive work for His people: "And what one nation
on the earth is like Thy people Israel, whom God went to redeem for Himself as a people and to make a name?" (2 Sam. 7:23).

Since the Mosaic expression of the covenant, we have more readily
understood the dual nature of the promise of a people: general and particular. It always contained the more general promise of an innumerable people, but it also contained the promise of a particular individual. In Moses'
era, we were promised "a Prophet" (Deut. 18:15ff.) who would faithfully
obey and declare God's commands. Similarly, in 2 Samuel 7:12, we learn
of a promised descendant who would build a more permanent temple for
the Lord, as we see in Solomon. We also learn of a descendant for whom
God "will establish the throne of his kingdom forever" (2 Sam. 7:13). Even
further, David spoke of a kingly figure, his "Lord" (Ps. 110:1), who would
serve as "a priest forever according to the order of Melchizedek" (Ps. 110:4),
the priest who blessed Abraham. As we get more and more of a description
of this coming descendant, we learn that three offices will belong to one
person, the Branch of David—prophet, priest, and king.

3. *The promise of a land:* As for the promise of a land, the Lord promised to "appoint a place for My people Israel and . . . plant them, that they
may live in their own place and not be disturbed again" (2 Sam. 7:10).
And, in giving thanks, David himself rehearsed the Abrahamic-Mosaic
promise of land (2 Sam. 7:23).

4. *The summary promise of the covenant:* Again, showing the common
chain with Abraham and Moses, David cited the promise of union and
communion: "For Thou hast established for Thyself Thy people Israel as
Thine own people forever, and Thou, O LORD, hast become their God" (2
Sam. 7:24).

5. *Expanded understanding of the covenant:* Each covenant expanded
upon what had preceded it, and the Davidic covenant was no different.
Two amplifications stand out. The first was the new focus on rest and
peace from Israel's enemies. Since 2 Samuel 7 repeatedly invoked the notions of rest, peace, stability, and security, these features should be taken as
part of the goal of God's covenant work.

The second amplification concerned David's eternal throne—"Your
throne shall be established forever" (2 Sam. 7:16). While the Lord, long
before, had promised Abraham that kings would arise among his descen-

dants (Gen. 17), we do not learn of a more glorious throne until David's time. All the while, the Lord evidently had far more in mind than David's physical throne and kingdom, since both were soon lost after Solomon, and all Israel was sent into exile for violating God's covenant conditions (2 Chron. 36:11–21). What became of the Abrahamic-Mosaic-Davidic promises of a land and a people in union and communion with their God? To find out, we turn to the post-Davidic prophets.

The Prophets

With the loss of David, Solomon, and a united kingdom, all hope appeared to be lost for Israel. Because they had rejected God's gracious covenant and repeatedly turned to idolatry, the Lord kept His covenantal promises and poured out His wrath on the unfaithful. First, the northern kingdom was turned over to Assyria, and then the southern kingdom was turned over to Babylon, both captors being fierce expressions of the seed of the Serpent. As Daniel confessed, "Indeed all Israel has transgressed Thy law and turned aside, not obeying Thy voice; so the curse has been poured out on us, along with the oath which is written in the law of Moses the servant of God, for we have sinned against Him" (Dan. 9:11). By their gross idolatry, Israel had violated the conditions of the covenant, forfeiting their inheritance of a people and a land. As the Lord had previously declared: "Those blessed by Him will inherit the land; but those cursed by Him will be cut off" (Ps. 37:22; cf. Jer. 12:7–9, 15; Deut. 28:63). The Lord sold Israel into slavery and cut off its inheritance.

Nevertheless, in the midst of all the captivity, violence, and tears, the Lord continued to hold up the Abrahamic-Mosaic-Davidic promises for His faithful remnant. And to them He sent prophets, not only to declare the people's violation of the covenant, but also to show forth the fulfillment of the covenant.

1. *Continuity with previous covenants:* Through the prophets, the Lord continually justified both judgment and hope by appealing to His covenants with Abraham, Moses, and David. Through Isaiah, the Lord spoke to Israel as "the descendant of Abraham My friend" (Isa. 41:8; cf. 29:22; 63:16). The Lord, "who caused His arm to go at the right hand of Moses" (Isa. 63:12: cf. v. 11), promised to "make an everlasting covenant . . . according to the faithful mercies shown to David" (Isa. 55:3; cf. 9:7; 16:5; 22:22).

Likewise, Jeremiah declared that the Lord would restore the fortunes of "the descendants of Abraham, Isaac, and Jacob" (Jer. 33:26), turning them from the curses of the Mosaic covenant (Jer. 32:23–44; cf. 31:33; 44:10ff.) to "serve the LORD their God, and David their king, whom I will raise up for them" (Jer. 30:9; cf. 17:25; 21:12; 23:5; 33:15ff.).

Similarly, Ezekiel referred in one passage to the covenant work with Abraham, Moses, and David, prophesying that the Lord would bring His people to "live on the land that I gave to Jacob My servant" (Ezek. 37:25), that "they will walk in My ordinances, and keep My statutes" (v. 24), and that "My servant David will be king over them" (v. 24).

Through the minor prophets as well, the covenantal chain continued. Micah reminded the people how God had ransomed them from slavery, sending Moses (Mic. 6:4); he also spoke of God's "unchanging love to Abraham" (7:20). Hosea described Israel returning to seek "David their king" (Hos. 3:5), and Amos foretold that God would "raise up the fallen booth of David" (Amos 9:11; cf. Acts 15:16). In another astounding passage, the Lord promised to "pour out on the house of David and on the inhabitants of Jerusalem, the Spirit of grace and of supplication, so that they will look on Me whom they have pierced. . . . They will call on My name, and I will answer them; I will say, 'They are My people,' and they will say, 'The Lord is my God' " (Zech. 12:10–13:9).

2. The promise of a people: Apart from the direct connections between the prophets and Abraham, Moses, and David, what became of the promise of a people? On this point, the prophets amplified the covenant with David by detailing the two aspects of this promise—a general seed and a particular individual within that seed. We find the general covenant promise of a people detailed as never before, but we also find a particular individual descendant described in more detail—the prophet, priest, and king still to come.

As far as the general seed is concerned, the Lord repeatedly promised to revive and unite the faithful remnant living in exile (e.g., Ezek. 37; Dan. 9), but we find even more than that important promise developing. From the very beginning of the Abrahamic covenant, blessings (salvation) were promised for "a multitude of nations" (Gen. 17:5) and "all the families of the earth" (Gen. 12:3). The promises were never limited to one family line or one nation, and the prophets proclaimed this truth most gloriously. They declared that God would adopt the Gentiles as His people as well.

Hosea prophesied that "the number of the sons of Israel will be like the sand of the sea. . . . Where it is said to them, 'You are not My people,' it will be said to them, 'You are the sons of the living God' " (Hos. 1:10), and the apostle Peter revealed that this speaks of God's adoption of the

Gentiles (1 Peter 2:10). Isaiah promised that the restored Israel would be "a light of the nations" (Isa. 49:6), which the apostles Paul and Barnabas understood as a command to preach to the Gentiles (Acts 13:46–48). Amos spoke of God's people possessing "the remnant of Edom and all the nations who are called by My name" (Amos 9:12), and James saw this fulfilled in the work of the apostles (Acts 15:17). Significantly, the Lord promised through Joel, "I will pour out My Spirit on all mankind" (Joel 2:28), and Peter saw this fulfilled in the outpouring of the Spirit at Pentecost (Acts 2:14ff.).

But, as we learn later, for the Lord to adopt the Gentiles into the Abrahamic line, a Redeemer would have to arise—one particular and prominent descendant of Abraham. Although David was long dead, the prophet Ezekiel described this individual as "My servant David," who "will feed them" and "be their shepherd" (Ezek. 34:23). Jeremiah spoke of this "righteous Branch" of David, who "will reign as king" (Jer. 23:5). For, as the Lord promised long before, "David shall never lack a man to sit on the throne of the house of Israel" (Jer. 33:17). Moreover, Isaiah declared that the one who would sit on the throne of David would be the "Prince of Peace" and that His name would be "Mighty God" (Isa. 9:6), but that this servant, though kingly and conquering (52:13; 53:11–54:3), would be "pierced through for our transgressions," bearing "the sin of many" and interceding "for the transgressors" (53:5, 12).

As these last passages demonstrate, the coming descendant of David would be not only a prophet (Deut. 18:15ff.), priest (Ps. 110:4), and king (Jer. 23:5), but even more prominently a redeemer—specifically, a kinsman-redeemer. Although this truly profound title does not mean much in our own culture, separated as it is from biblical times, the position of the kinsman-redeemer throughout the history of Israel (and in some surrounding nations) was central to Old Testament life and culture. The word *redeemer* and its variants appear numerous times in Scripture, describing God's work for His people. Most of the time, the word translates the Hebrew word *go'el*, literally, a "kinsman-redeemer." The notion of a kinsman-redeemer was central to God's covenant work.

So what was a kinsman-redeemer? As the English suggests, he first had to be a close blood relative (a kinsman), such as a brother, uncle, or cousin (Lev. 25:48–49). Second, he had to be able to pay a ransom to rescue a poor and vulnerable relative. Specifically, the kinsman-redeemer had at least four duties: (1) to ransom a relative who had sold himself into slavery and oppression (Lev. 25:47–55), (2) to marry the wife of a widowed kinsman (Ruth 3; 4), (3) to avenge the name of oppressed and/or

murdered relatives (Deut. 19:12; Num. 35:16–21, 31), and (4) to regain a
poor relative's forfeited inheritance (Lev. 25:23, 34).

So when the prophets speak of the coming descendant as a redeemer
in the context of God's covenant work (Isa. 52:3; 54:5, 8; 61:1–2; 63:4ff.;
Jer. 31:11; Ps. 72:14), we should understand the covenant work of the
Branch of David to include ransoming His poor and irresponsible kin from
slavery, winning back their forfeited inheritance, marrying the widowed,
and avenging them against their enemies, the seed of the Serpent. As the
coming kinsman-redeemer declared through Isaiah, "The LORD has anointed
me to bring good news to the afflicted; He has sent me to bind up the
brokenhearted, to proclaim liberty to captives, and freedom to prisoners;
to proclaim the favorable year of the LORD, and the day of vengeance of
our God" (Isa. 61:1–2).

3. *The promise of a land:* In the prophets, the Lord amplified the
promise of a land, just as He amplified the promise of a people. Although Israel had violated the covenant and forfeited her inheritance of
a land and a people (Ps. 37:22; cf. Jer. 12:7–9, 15; Deut. 28:63), the
Lord, in His loving-kindness, promised to return the faithful remnant of
His people to the land promised to Abraham. When the Lord did restore
the faithful remnant, as recorded in the books of Ezra and Nehemiah,
the people recognized their restoration as a fulfillment of His covenant
with Abraham, Moses, and David. The actual confession of these faithful Israelites stands as one of the most remarkable summaries of covenant
history recorded in Scripture. Although not reproduced here, the ninth
chapter of Nehemiah deserves a full reading and thoughtful meditation.
The people confess that their restoration is in fulfillment of God's standing covenant: "Thou art the LORD God, who chose Abram . . . and gave
him the name Abraham. And Thou didst . . . make a covenant with him
. . . to give it to his descendants. And Thou hast fulfilled Thy promise,
for Thou art righteous" (Neh. 9:7–8). The confession of Nehemiah 9
goes on to trace God's covenant work from Abraham through Moses and
David in a most moving and glorious manner. Yet, even the glories of
Nehemiah's days did not last forever. The people become complacent
and idolatrous, and forgot the Lord's covenant mercy.

But even beyond the temporary restoration of the people to Israel,
the prophets understood the promise of a land to include much more than
just the original token lands. Through the prophets, the Lord revealed
that the promise of land to Abraham included the whole earth. For example, Daniel interpreted Nebuchadnezzar's divinely given dream to picture
a kingdom that would arise after that time and become a "great mountain"

and fill "the whole earth" (Dan. 2:35, 44), not just the lands originally specified for Abraham. Isaiah also speaks of this holy mountain, saying that "all the nations will stream to it" (Isa. 2:2).

4. *The summary promise of the covenant:* The covenant promise of union and communion was continually asserted throughout the prophets: "I am the LORD your God, . . . 'You are My people' " (Isa. 51:15–16; see also Jer. 31:1, 33; 32:38; Ezek. 34:24; 36:28; Hos. 2:23; Zech. 2:11; 8:8). This central promise of union and communion appeared in many other forms as well, sometimes partial or elliptical, but it followed the contours of the intricate covenant chain from Genesis to Malachi.

As we have seen in the prophets, the Covenant of Redemption built to an especially high level of anticipation. The faithful hearers of the prophets anticipated a glorious culmination of the promises of a land and a people, especially in the form of the coming Redeemer, the right-eous Branch of David, still to be raised. To that glorious culmination, we turn next.

STUDY QUESTIONS

1. Identify the two covenants instituted after Creation. How do these two covenants relate to the Old and New Covenants? How should this fact change the way you look at Scripture?
2. What special form of the promise of union and communion is expressed for the first time in Genesis 17:7–8? According to Genesis 15:4 and 17:21, did God's promise automatically extend to Abraham's physical offspring? Explain. How does Paul express this same point in Romans 9:6–8?
3. In what ways does the Covenant of Redemption anticipate an individ-ual seed of the woman who would function as our prophet, priest, and king? How is He expected to fulfill His offices as prophet, priest, and king as our kinsman-redeemer (see Lev. 25:23–34, 47–55; Ruth 3; 4; Deut. 19:12; Num. 35:16–21, 31)?

Notes

1. See O. Palmer Robertson, *The Christ of the Covenants* (Phillipsburg, N.J.: Pres-byterian and Reformed, 1980), 22-25, for a discussion of this passage. Further evidence that the Covenant of Creation was made with Adam is provided by the fact that Christ, as the Last Adam, successfully completed the First Adam's failed work. Since, as we will see, the Last Adam was in covenant with God,

we should expect that the First Adam was also in covenant with Him.
2. Westminster Larger Catechism, Q. 21.
3. O. Palmer Robertson, *Covenants: God's Way with His People* (Philadelphia: Great Commission Publications, 1987), 34.

TEN

NOTHING NEW UNDER THE SON?

In the Old Testament, the Lord graciously revealed His Covenant of
Redemption like a beautiful mosaic, rich in features and deep in color—
through merciful promises of a people and a land, gracious and pure commandments of His holy will, comforting pledges of union and communion,
assurances of a coming kinsman-redeemer who would hold the offices of
prophet, priest, and king, and so much more. This covenantal work began
with the promises given after the Fall and preserved with Noah, was established with Abraham and amplified through Moses, and was exalted with
David and glorified through the prophets.

After such glorious anticipation, what do we find in the pages of the
New Testament? We find that generations after the last of the prophets,
the angel Gabriel returned and quietly declared the glories of the covenant,
the holy promises of the ages, to a young, faithful woman: "You will con-
ceive in your womb, and bear a son, and you shall name Him Jesus. He will
be great, and will be called the Son of the Most High; and the Lord God will
give Him the throne of His father David; and He will reign over the house
of Jacob forever; and His kingdom will have no end" (Luke 1:31–33).

It is the same story. The same promises continue. The past covenant
work is not forsaken, but fulfilled. The New Testament cannot stand on
its own. It stands on the unified promises made to Adam, Noah, Abraham,
Moses, David, and the prophets. These promises have determined all of
redemptive history up to the first chapter of Matthew's gospel, and they
continue into the fulfillment stage of the Covenant of Redemption.

NOT TO ABOLISH BUT TO FULFILL:
CONTINUITY WITH PREVIOUS COVENANTS

While the angel Gabriel declared Christ to be the fulfillment of God's Covenant of Redemption, other connections appear as well. On the opening pages of Matthew and Luke we find genealogies manifesting the blood connections between Jesus and David and Abraham. In fact, Matthew opens with the words, "The book of the genealogy of Jesus Christ, the son of David, the son of Abraham" (Matt. 1:1). In these genealogies are many of the faithful heroes of the seed of the woman. Luke even traces the line back through Shem, Noah, Seth, and Adam (3:23, 36, 38). There is one story—one redemptive covenant.

Prior to Jesus' birth, Mary glorified the Lord who "has given help to Israel His servant, in remembrance of His mercy, as He spoke to our fathers, to Abraham and his offspring forever" (Luke 1:54–55). Mary not only recognized the continuity between Christ and God's previous covenant work, but also recognized Christ's work as part of the ongoing triumph of the seed of the woman over the seed of the Serpent: "His mercy is upon generation after generation toward those who fear Him. He has done mighty deeds with His arm; He has scattered those who were proud in the thoughts of their heart. He has brought down rulers from their thrones, and has exalted those who were humble" (vv. 50–52).

Similarly, Zacharias, the father of John the Baptist, sang of both God's covenant and the war between the seeds.

> Blessed be the Lord God of Israel, for He has visited us and accomplished redemption for His people, and has raised up a horn of salvation for us in the house of David His servant—as He spoke by the mouth of His holy prophets from of old—salvation from our enemies, and from the hand of all who hate us; to show mercy toward our fathers, and to remember His holy covenant, the oath which He swore to Abraham our father, to grant us that we, being delivered from the hand of our enemies, might serve Him without fear. (Luke 1:68–74)

The theology surrounding the birth of Christ is simply the theology of the covenant.

Christ Himself proclaimed His connection to God's prior covenant work when He told His listeners, "Your father Abraham rejoiced to see My day" (John 8:56). He also explained that even faithful Gentiles would "recline at the table with Abraham, and Isaac, and Jacob" (Matt. 8:11; Luke 13:28). However, He rebuked unfaithful Jews who imagined that a mere biological connection to Abraham guaranteed their redemption (Matt. 3:9), a truth present in the Abrahamic covenant itself.

In His parable about Lazarus and the rich man, Christ told about a deceased rich man descending in torment far from the comfort of Abraham. When the rich man fears for the well-being of his rebellious brothers and cries out to father Abraham for help, the patriarch interestingly points to Moses and the prophets as their only hope. He concludes that if the man's brothers will "not listen to Moses and the Prophets, neither will they be persuaded if someone rises from the dead" (Luke 16:31). Jesus knew that His work was an outgrowth of God's covenant with Abraham, and indeed that His work could not be understood apart from its covenantal moorings.

Christ stressed His continuity with Moses by explaining that He did not come "to abolish the Law or the Prophets . . . but to fulfill" (Matt. 5:17). Moreover, He upheld the Mosaic covenantal commandments (Matt. 8:4; Mark 7:10; 10:3; Luke 5:14), and even met with Moses in His transfiguration before the apostles (Matt. 17:3). After His resurrection, He discoursed with two disciples on the road to Emmaus, and "beginning with Moses and with all the prophets, He explained to them the things concerning Himself in all the Scriptures" (Luke 24:27). Then He did the same thing for all the disciples as He "opened their minds to understand the Scriptures" (Luke 24:44–45). Christ knew that His work was an outgrowth of God's covenant work with Moses.

Christ was predicted to receive the throne of David (Luke 1:31–33), and He rode into Jerusalem on a donkey in fulfillment of Zechariah's prophecy of the Davidic king (Zech. 9:9). The crowd, recognizing this fulfillment, cried out, "Hosanna to the Son of David; blessed is He who comes in the name of the Lord" (Matt. 21:9). Shortly after that, Jesus asked the Pharisees to explain how David could speak in Psalm 110 of his descendant, the Messiah, with a divine title: "If David then calls him 'Lord,' how is He his son?" (Matt. 22:45). Christ knew that His work was an outgrowth of God's covenant with David, as well as the covenants made with Abraham and Moses.

Christ's apostles clearly understood the covenantal continuity between Jesus and Abraham, Moses, and David. At the start of the apostolic church, Peter taught,

> It is you who are the sons of the prophets, and of the covenant which God made with your fathers, saying to Abraham, "And in

your seed all the families of the earth shall be blessed." For you
first, God raised up His Servant, and sent Him to bless you by
turning every one of you from your wicked ways. (Acts 3:25–26;
cf. Acts 7)

Peter spoke not only of Abraham, but also of Moses: "Moses said, 'The
Lord God shall raise up for you a prophet like me from your brethren; to
Him you shall give heed in everything He says to you' " (Acts 3:22; cf.
Acts 7). Peter spoke not only of Abraham and Moses, but of David as well:
"David . . . died and was buried. . . . And so, because he was a prophet, and
knew that God had sworn to Him with an oath to seat one of his descen-
dants upon his throne, he looked ahead and spoke of the resurrection of
the Christ" (Acts 2:29–30; cf. Acts 7).

FOR HIS SHEEP: THE PROMISE OF A PEOPLE

Having seen some of the general continuities between Christ's covenantal
work and all that preceded it, we next explore His specific connections
with the Abrahamic-Mosaic-Davidic promise of a people.

Redeeming His People as the Seed in General

From the start, we see that Christ would work to redeem a particular people—the seed of the woman, the seed of Abraham, as opposed to the seed
of the Serpent: "You shall call His name Jesus, for it is He who will save
His people from their sins" (Matt. 1:21). Zacharias understood the Abrahamic focus on a people when he declared that the Lord "has visited us
and accomplished redemption for His people" (Luke 1:68).
       Christ Himself taught that He was not laying down His life as a ran-
som for the seeds of the woman and the Serpent, for the sheep and the
goats; rather, as the Good Shepherd (cf. Ezek. 34:23; 37:24), He "lays down
His life for the sheep" (John 10:11). Speaking of Himself, He says in the
same context, "I am the good shepherd; and I know My own, and My own
know Me" (v. 14). Christ showed the same covenantal concern for a particular people when He prayed: "I ask on their behalf; I do not ask on
behalf of the world, but of those whom Thou hast given Me; for they are
Thine" (John 17:9).
       Just as Abraham and the prophets spoke of God's mercifully bringing
Gentiles into His covenant with Abraham, Moses, and David, so also Christ

testified to this marvelous truth: "I have other sheep, which are not of this fold; I must bring them also, and they shall hear My voice; and they shall become one flock with one shepherd" (John 10:16). Likewise, Christ prayed, "I do not ask in behalf of these alone, but for those also who believe in Me through their word" (John 17:20).

Moreover, we find not only covenantal blessings and redemption for faithful Jews and Gentiles, but also covenantal judgment on apostate Jews, who have despised the covenant, thus forfeiting their inheritance: "The kingdom of God will be taken away from you, and be given to a nation producing the fruit of it" (Matt. 21:43). Thus Christ commanded His disciples to "make disciples of all the nations" (Matt. 28:19).

The apostles also followed the prophets, counting faithful Gentiles as adopted into God's people (Hos. 1:9). In fact, they saw prophecies such as Amos's declaring the restoration of the house of David (Amos 9:11–12) as evidence that "God . . . [is] taking from among the Gentiles a people for His name" (Acts 15:14). Paul understood Isaiah's prophecy of being a "light of the nations" (Isa. 49:6) as the key to his "turning to the Gentiles" (Acts 13:46–47). Similarly, Peter followed Hosea (1:9; 2:23) in telling believing Gentiles, "You once were not a people, but now you are the people of God" (1 Peter 2:10).

The New Testament states explicitly that faithful Jews and Gentiles are now one people, the people of God. For example, in Ephesians 2:12–14, Gentiles are instructed to

> remember that you were at that time separate from Christ, excluded from the commonwealth of Israel, and strangers to the covenants of promise, having no hope and without God in the world. But now in Christ Jesus you who formerly were far off have been brought near by the blood of Christ. For He Himself is our peace, who made both groups into one, and broke down the barrier of the dividing wall.

In a similar vein, Paul argues in his letter to the Romans that the relationship between Jews and Gentiles can be pictured in terms of an olive tree. Some of the natural branches of a cultivated olive tree (representing the Jews) "were broken off . . . for their unbelief" (Rom. 11:17, 20), and branches from a wild olive tree (i.e., Gentiles) "were grafted in among them and became partaker with them of the rich root of the olive tree" (v. 17). Here, then, we have one cultivated tree representing the people of God, with some of the natural branches being broken off and new branches being grafted in. So, by the mercy of God, there are no longer two trees, but only one, made up of both faithful Jews and faithful Gentiles. In Christ, Paul wrote elsewhere, there is neither Jew nor Greek, since by belonging to Christ, we are Abraham's offspring, heirs according to the promise (Gal. 3:26–29; cf. 3:6–8, 14). The lesson seems to be hard to miss: Jews and Gentiles together now make up the people of God—the heirs of the Abrahamic promises.

This is why Old Covenant titles for God's people are often ascribed to God's New Covenant people: "Israel of God" (Gal. 6:16), "Abraham's offspring" (Gal. 3:29), "children of promise," like Isaac (Gal. 4:28), "the twelve tribes" (James 1:1; cf. Rev. 7:4), "a chosen race, a royal priesthood, a holy nation, a people for God's own possession" (1 Peter 2:9; cf. Ex. 19:6), and "the true circumcision" (Phil. 3:3; cf. Rom. 2:28–29). And, conversely, the New Testament describes the Old Covenant people as the "church" (Acts 7:38 and Heb. 2:12 KJV). As we have already seen, this is what was envisioned in the Old Covenant. The prophets knew nothing about two separate groups of God's people; instead, they prophesied of the Gentiles' being joined to the body of Israel, God's people.

Our Kinsman-Redeemer as the Seed in Particular

Just as we find continuity when it comes to the Gentiles' becoming the seed of the woman in general, so we find the same continuity when it comes to the other side of the promise of a people—the promise of the seed in particular—an individual. This individual, the Messiah or Christ, came as a king, receiving "the throne of His father David" (Luke 1:32), and was also a prophet (Matt. 10:41; 11:9; 13:57; 21:11; John 6:14; 7:40) and a priest (Mark 10:45; John 10:11, 15).

But the way Christ went about fulfilling His role as our prophet, priest, and king, was by being our kinsman-redeemer. The Westminster Shorter Catechism summarizes this point by noting that "Christ, as our Redeemer, executeth the offices of a prophet, of a priest, and of a king, both in his estate of humiliation and exaltation" (Q. 23).

Now if Christ was our kinsman-redeemer, we would expect Him to have acknowledged that fact and to have performed the work entailed by that position by ransoming slaves, marrying the widowed, avenging His brethren, and regaining a forfeited inheritance. Most magnificently, He did.

To begin with, in Luke 4:18ff. we find Christ applying to Himself the duties of the kinsman-redeemer as prophesied in Isaiah 61—releasing "the captives" and setting free "those who are downtrodden"—when He declared, "Today this Scripture has been fulfilled in your hearing" (v. 21). Let us see exactly how He fulfilled these duties.

He ransoms kin from slavery: The First Adam, as our representative, sold the whole human race into spiritual slavery. We are, in the words of Scripture, "slaves of sin" (Rom. 6:17; cf. John 8:34), which sometimes manifests itself in terms of civil and social slavery as promised (Deut. 28:32, 33, 41).

Because we have, through the First Adam, sold ourselves into slavery, we need a kinsman-redeemer to ransom us. In response, Christ came as the Last Adam (1 Cor. 15:45; cf. Rom. 5:12–19), who would "proclaim liberty to captives and freedom to prisoners" (Isa. 61:1; Luke 4:18). But in order to accomplish this covenantal work, Christ needed to become a kinsman-redeemer—first, by being a kinsman, a blood relative of those whom He would ransom, and, second, by paying the requisite ransom price (Lev. 25:47–55).

To meet the first condition, the second person of the Trinity had to be "made in the likeness of men" (Phil 2:7). In the incarnation, He became a kinsman to the race of Adam, the seed of the woman. The author of Hebrews emphasizes this crucial part of Christ's work.

> Since then the children share in flesh and blood, He Himself likewise also partook of the same, that through death He might render powerless him who had the power of death, that is, the devil; and might deliver those who through fear of death were subject to slavery all their lives. For assuredly He does not give help to angels, but He gives help to the seed of Abraham. Therefore He had to be made like His brethren in all things. (Heb. 2:14–17)

Notice how this passage uses the language of the kinsman-redeemer— "brethren," "slavery," etc. But notice also that it describes Christ as a kinsman-redeemer first and foremost for the line of Abraham. This priority explains why the New Testament refers to the Gentiles as having been adopted. Gentiles need to be adopted into the line of Abraham before Christ can serve as their kinsman-redeemer. Once adopted, though, they too have the privilege of crying "Abba, Father" (Rom. 8:15).

Christ met the second condition by paying the ransom price for our sin: He died in our stead. We know that "the wages of sin is death" (Rom. 6:23) and that "without shedding of blood there is no forgiveness" (Heb. 9:22). This penalty of death is a consequence of God's holy nature, as well as the result of God's self-maledictory oath to Abraham (Gen. 15).

Remember that the violator of that covenant agreed to die as a penalty for failing to keep its conditions (Gen. 15; 26:5). Although God never violated His covenant, Abraham's descendants violated it repeatedly. Hence, the kinsman-redeemer would have to ransom the people from slavery to sin by laying down a life not corrupted by sin, namely, His own life.

Christ explicitly stated His mission in this way: "The Son of Man did not come to be served, but to serve, and to give His life a ransom for many" (Matt. 20:28). And Paul described this ransom when he wrote, "For there is one God, and one mediator also between God and men, the man Christ Jesus, who gave Himself as a ransom for all, the testimony borne at the proper time" (1 Tim. 2:5–6). Because Christ met both conditions to be a kinsman-redeemer, He indeed can declare that the redemption promises of Isaiah 61 have been fulfilled (Luke 4:18ff.).

He marries widowed kin: As we learned from the book of Ruth, one of the broader duties of the kinsman-redeemer was to marry the widow of a deceased kinsman. Boaz, a kinsman-redeemer, declared, "I have acquired Ruth . . . the widow of Mahlon, to be my wife in order to raise up the name of the deceased on his inheritance" (Ruth 4:10). The covenantal bond between God and man can be expressed by analogy to marriage. Adam and Israel were both in covenant marriage with God, but because of their rebellion, God was alienated from them, widowing them as if He were dead. Isaiah gives us this image as part of the Suffering Servant prophecy.

> "Your descendants will possess nations. . . . You will forget the shame of your youth, and the reproach of your widowhood you will remember no more. For your husband is your Maker, whose name is the LORD of Hosts; and your [Kinsman-]Redeemer is the Holy One of Israel, who is called the God of all the earth. For the Lord has called you, like a wife forsaken and grieved in spirit, even like a wife of one's youth when she is rejected," says your God. "For a brief moment I forsook you, but with great compassion I will gather you. In an outburst of anger I hid My face from you for a moment; but with everlasting lovingkindness I will have compassion on you," says the LORD your [Kinsman-]Redeemer. (Isa. 54:3–8)

God widowed His people in judgment, but married them in mercy. Christ as our kinsman-redeemer (Rom. 3:24; Col. 1:14) is often depicted in a marriage relationship with His bride, the church (Matt. 9:15; 25:1ff.; John 3:29; Eph. 5): "Let us rejoice and be glad and give the glory to Him, for the marriage of the Lamb has come and His bride has made herself ready" (Rev. 19:7; cf. 21:2). Notice how the work of the kinsman-redeemer leaves no room for boasting. As people who were intentionally widowed in Adam and in Israel, we were no prize bride, but Christ mercifully redeemed and married us, making all things new, making His bride "adorned with gold and silver, . . . exceedingly beautiful and advanced to royalty" (Ezek. 16:13).

He avenges kin against their enemies: As the great Puritan Thomas Boston explains, the kinsman-redeemer

> was to avenge the blood of his slain kinsman on the slayer. . . . Our kinsman-redeemer saw all his poor kindred slain men. And the devil was the murderer. . . . He had ministered poison to them in the loins of their first parent; yea, he had smitten them to death. But no avenger of their blood could be found, till the second Adam, as their kinsman-redeemer did in the second covenant undertake the avenging of it.[1]

In cases of cold-blooded murder (Deut. 19:11), God commanded the elders of the city to "deliver him [the murderer] into the hand of the avenger [lit. kinsman-redeemer] of blood, that he may die. You shall not pity him, but you shall purge the blood of the innocent from Israel, that it may go well with you" (Deut. 19:12–13; cf. Num. 35:16–21, 31).

From the beginning to our own time, the enemies of God have maimed and slain God's people ruthlessly. In sheer numbers, the enemy-slayer has been most prominent in the form of the State—Assyria, Babylon, Rome, Mary Tudor, Charles II, Louis XIV—and for this, we are promised that the Lord "will avenge the blood of His servants, and will render vengeance on His adversaries, and will atone for His land and His people" (Deut. 32:43; cf. Job 19:23ff.; Prov. 23:11; Isa. 47:1, 4; Jer. 50:4).

In the book of Revelation, the slaughtered cry out, "How long, O Lord, holy and true, wilt Thou refrain from judging and avenging our blood on those who dwell on the earth?" (Rev. 6:10). And as our kinsman-redeemer promises, "Shall not God bring about justice for His elect, who cry to Him day and night . . . ? I tell you that He will bring about justice for them speedily" (Luke 18:7–8). We are forbidden to avenge ourselves (Rom. 12:19), but we are assured that our kinsman-redeemer will accomplish that task for us and for His namesake.

Although Christ avenges His people, even more importantly He has already triumphed over the Serpent himself: "When He had disarmed the rulers and authorities, He made a public display of them, having triumphed over them" (Col. 2:15; cf. Matt. 12:29). And that work will continue "until He has put all His enemies under His feet" (1 Cor. 15:26; cf. Rev. 19:11–21). In the meantime, even amidst tragedy and suffering, we are to "overcome evil with good" (Rom. 12:21), and be comforted that "death is swallowed up in victory," so that our "toil is not in vain in the Lord" (1 Cor. 15:54, 58).

INHERITING THE EARTH: THE PROMISE OF A LAND

Our great kinsman-redeemer not only ransomed us when we were slaves, married us when we were widowed, and avenged us as His brethren, but He also regained our forfeited inheritance. This demonstrated yet another continuity with God's covenant work, since our inheritance is tied up with the promise of a land.

As we have seen, the promise of a land was a promise of inheritance, but it was an inheritance we lost. As irresponsible relatives, we, in Adam and in unfaithful Israel, rebelled and lost the promised inheritance. Since "his nearest kinsman is to come and buy back what his relative has sold" (Lev. 25:25; cf. Jer. 32:6–11; Ruth 4:1–8), the Last Adam has given Himself to win back what the First Adam sold. The First Adam was promised eternal life for his faithful obedience, but he despised the promise. This required the Last Adam to remain perfectly faithful to the Father so He could thereby secure the promise whereby those who follow Christ "inherit eternal life" (Matt. 19:29).

Our inheritance of eternal life is a common theme in the New Testament, although we usually miss its covenantal basis. Peter tells us that we have obtained "an inheritance which is imperishable and undefiled, . . . reserved in heaven" (1 Peter 1:4). Paul explains that "we have obtained an inheritance, having been predestined according to His purpose" (Eph. 1:11; cf. Titus 3:7).

Although eternal life is sufficient in itself, God has granted His people even more of an inheritance. Abraham, Moses, and David were promised a land of their own, and the prophets revealed that this would include more than the mere token of land for ancient Israel—they were promised the earth, the land "from sea to sea, and from the river to the ends of the earth" (Ps. 72:8; cf. Ps. 2:8; Dan. 2:35). But the people despised the inheritance and turned to other gods. So, as promised, "Those blessed by Him will inherit the land; but those cursed by Him will be cut off "

(Ps. 37:22; Deut. 28:63). God disinherited Israel (Jer. 12:7–9, 15).

Our kinsman-redeemer restored the eternal inheritance of land to us, although the self-maledictory oath to Abraham needed to be satisfied. We find this redemption/inheritance language at Hebrews 9:15 (cf. Gal. 3:29–4:7): "He is the mediator of a new covenant, in order that since a death has taken place for the redemption of the transgressions that were committed under the first covenant, those who have been called may receive the promise of the eternal inheritance."

Did Christ and the apostles ever suggest that God's people will inherit the earth? Most certainly. Following the language of the Old Testament prophets, Christ declared, "Blessed are the meek, for they shall inherit the earth" (Matt. 5:5 NKJV; Ps. 37:29). Even more, our Davidic king did not merely claim authority over Palestine, but instead claimed that He has "All authority . . . in heaven and on earth" (Matt. 28:18).

Similarly, Paul did not hesitate to describe Abraham as "heir of the world" (Rom. 4:13). Even Abraham knew that the Lord was giving his seed the whole world, and not just some token land in Palestine. The writer of Hebrews tells us that Abraham was looking for much more: "He was looking for the city which has foundations, whose architect and builder is God" (Heb. 11:10). Moreover, Paul exhorts children to obey the Mosaic command to "honor your father and mother" so "that you may live long on the earth" (Eph. 6:3), even though the promise made to Moses was that obedient children would live long in "the land which the LORD your God gives you" (Ex. 20:12; Deut. 5:16). Thus, the "land" was but a token of the whole "earth" that God's people would eventually inherit. In all, then, the New Testament promises the people of God the inheritance of "a new heaven and a new earth" (Rev. 21:1).

Thus, the Abrahamic-Mosaic-Davidic promises of a land and a people are fully fulfilled in Christ (2 Cor. 1:20). Now, through Christ, all the families of the earth are being, and will be, blessed. As promised, the Gentiles have been adopted into the "Israel of God" (Gal. 6:16) and are now "Abraham's offspring, heirs according to promise" (Gal. 3:29).

All this comes to pass because the promised prophet, priest, and king, our kinsman-redeemer, the Last Adam, has won back what the First Adam renounced:

In the First Adam, we enslaved ourselves, but the Last Adam, our kinsman-redeemer, has liberated us from our captivity to sin.

In the First Adam, we played the harlot and widowed ourselves, but the Last Adam, our kinsman-redeemer, has removed our grief as widows and made us fruitful again.

In the First Adam, we were maimed and slain by the enemy, but the Last Adam, our kinsman-redeemer, wipes away all our tears and will crush all His enemies under His feet.

In the First Adam, we despoiled our inheritance and despised God's promises, but the Last Adam, our kinsman-redeemer, has regained the world and earned eternal life.

DWELLING IN US: THE SUMMARY PROMISE OF THE COVENANT

The summary promise of the covenant is one of close fellowship, a "living together" with God. In Israel, God dwelt with His people first in the tabernacle and then in the temple. There the Lord manifested Himself right in the midst of His people, though separated by walls, curtains, and ceremonies.

Under the New Covenant, the promise of union and communion has been fulfilled far more gloriously. First, God Himself pitched His tent among us in the incarnation of Jesus Christ (John 1:14). Christ was Immanuel—"God with us"—and dwelt among His people in a manner not realized in the Old Covenant (Matt. 1:23). And after Christ's departure, God indwells His people by pouring out His Spirit on them, making them His temple of dwelling (1 Cor. 3:16; 6:19; Eph. 2:21).

As He indwells His people, He signifies continuity with the Abrahamic-Mosaic-Davidic covenant by reiterating the now familiar summary promise, "I will be their God, and they shall be My people" (2 Cor. 6:16; Heb. 8:10; John 10:14).

THE UNFOLDING MYSTERY: AN EXPANDED UNDERSTANDING OF THE COVENANT

In each of the previous stages in the Covenant of Redemption, the Lord revealed more and more about His purposes. Each stage amplified the covenant in beautiful ways, but these older developments were all merely anticipatory. The reality was Christ.

In Christ, the Covenant of Redemption took on such a reality and finality that we greatly understate the truth to describe it as merely another amplification. The New Covenant is new, after all, and different from the preceding stages of the covenant in very significant ways. Although there is only one Covenant of Redemption, one stage of that covenant (the Old Covenant) is a shadow, and the other stage (the New Covenant) is the reality.

A More Glorious Covenant

Although we have already seen the many continuities linking the Old and New Covenants, we also find many differences between them. These differences make the New Covenant superior to the Old Covenant. Of the many differences, three stand out in particular.

The power and the glory: Certainly, one of the most prominent differences between the Old and New Covenants is the empowering work of the Holy Spirit. Although we read of Old Covenant believers being filled with God's Spirit, it was not of the same magnificent degree among all believers that we find in the New Covenant. Moreover, the New Testament cites this relative lack of the Spirit, this lack of power to keep the covenant, as the failing point of the Old Covenant people (Heb. 8:7–13).

But the New Covenant's outpouring of the Spirit of God is no surprise. It has its roots in the Old Covenant prophets. Joel prophesied that God would pour out His Spirit "on all mankind . . . in those days" (Joel 2:28–29). Other prophets did so as well: "I will pour out My Spirit on your offspring, and My blessing on your descendar.ʿs" (Isa. 44:3); "I will give you a new heart and put a new spirit within you. . . . And I will put My Spirit within you and cause you to walk in My statutes, and you will be careful to observe My ordinances" (Ezek. 36:26–27); "I will make a new covenant. . . . I will put My law within them, and on their heart I will write it" (Jer. 31:31–33).

In these passages, we find that God's Spirit would enable and empower New Covenant believers to obey God's commands faithfully in a way that He did not empower Old Covenant believers. The Lord declared through Ezekiel that His indwelling Spirit would "cause [them] to walk in My statutes," and, through Jeremiah, that "I will put My law within them." The Spirit, through Paul, teaches us that "what the Law could not do, weak as it was through the flesh, God did . . . in order that the requirement of the Law might be fulfilled in us" (Rom. 8:3–4). Hence, New Covenant believers are empowered to "keep His commandments; and His commandments are not burdensome" (1 John 5:3). The contrast between the Old and New Covenants on this point is so stark that Paul can use it to describe the Old Covenant as "the ministry of condemnation" (2 Cor. 3:9) and the New Covenant as the "new covenant . . . of the Spirit" and "the ministry of the Spirit" (2 Cor. 3:6, 8).

Once and for all: The Old and New Covenants also differ sharply in regard to the effectiveness of their respective sacrifices. The Old Covenant sacrificial system, in all its bloody detail, relentlessly drove home the truth that sin inescapably demands death (Lev. 17:11). Furthermore, the sacrificial system with its bloodshed for sins in all areas of life showed people the depth and pervasiveness of their sin.

Yet, for all the sacrifices and bloody ceremonies, the system was a lesson, a schoolmaster or "tutor to lead us to Christ" (Gal. 3:24). It was not the real thing. The Old Covenant ceremonial system was a system of pictures, helpful with communication, but impotent in paying the penalty for sin: "The Law, since it has only a shadow of the good things to come and not the very form of things, can never by the same sacrifices year by year, which they offer continually, make perfect those who draw near" (Heb. 10:1; cf. v. 4; Gal. 4:1ff.).

In contrast to the types and shadows and ineffective sacrifices of the Old Covenant, the New Covenant sacrificial system is Christ, the Lamb of God, who, as our substitutionary sacrifice, "through His own blood . . . entered the holy place once for all, having obtained eternal redemption" (Heb. 9:12). The shadows of the Old Covenant sacrificial system are now obsolete (Heb. 8:13), since the reality, Christ, has been "offered once to bear the sins of many" (Heb. 9:28). Therefore, "there is no longer any offering for sin" (Heb. 10:18). Believers in both Old and New Covenants were and are saved by the same sacrifice of Christ, "once for all." Old Covenant believers looked forward in faithful obedience to Christ (Acts 10:43; Heb. 11:24–26; Isa. 28:16; Luke 24:44–47; John 5:39), and New Covenant believers look back in faithful obedience to Christ.

The water and the wine: The Old and New Covenants differ in a third way as well, namely, in terms of their covenant ordinances or sacraments. Circumcision and the Passover were the two primary covenant rites in the Old Covenant, but the New Covenant teaches us that these bloody ceremonies have been replaced by the bloodless rites of baptism and the Lord's Supper. But since these topics are covered in chapter 14 of this book, we pause here only to note that there are both continuities and discontinuities between the sacraments of the Old and New Covenants.

Not One Jot or Tittle

Scripture reveals great continuities and discontinuities between the Old and New Covenants, between anticipation and fulfillment in the Covenant of Redemption. But where do God's Old Covenant moral laws, like the Ten Commandments, fit into all this? Are they a pattern for New Covenant believers or are they abolished?

The answer to this question involves the biblical notion of sanctification, which will be discussed in more detail in chapter 17. Sanctification sometimes refers to the setting apart of someone or something for a special purpose (John 10:30; 17:19; Gen. 2:3; Ex. 29:43), while at other times it refers to a setting apart or cleansing from sin (John 17:7; 1 Cor. 6:11; Eph. 1:4; 5:26; 1 Thess. 5:23). The notion is applied in both senses to believers as objects of the Spirit's work. Christians are definitively sanctified—set apart from uncleanness—when they are converted (Rom. 6:4–5, 11; 1 Cor. 6:11; 2 Cor. 5:17). Yet, the Spirit also progressively sanctifies believers—progressively separating them more and more from their inbred sin and making them more like the Lord: "I will be their God, and they shall be My people. . . . Therefore, having these promises, . . . let us cleanse ourselves from all defilement of flesh and spirit, perfecting holiness in the fear of God" (2 Cor. 6:16; 7:1). Notice the connection between the promises of the covenant and growing in holiness. This sanctification permeates the whole person: "May the God of peace Himself sanctify you entirely; and may your spirit and soul and body be preserved complete, without blame at the coming of our Lord Jesus Christ" (1 Thess. 5:23; cf. John 17:7; Rom. 8:13; 2 Cor. 3:18; 2 Peter 3:18).

But in order for us to seek, by the Spirit's help, to conform ourselves to God's holiness—"You shall be holy, for I am holy" (1 Peter 1:16)—we need to understand the nature and makeup of God's holiness. Where does God show us how to imitate His holiness? What is our pattern of righteousness? We find an answer in the prophecies foretelling the New Covenant. For example, Jeremiah proclaimed that, unlike the Old Covenant, the New Covenant believers would be enabled to keep the Lord's eternal expression of His holiness, the law of God: "When I will make a new covenant . . . I will put My law within them, and on their heart I will write it; and I will be their God, and they shall be My people" (Jer. 31:31–33). One central feature of the New Covenant would be that God's people would have His pattern of righteousness embedded in them in a way that was unavailable before (Heb. 8:7ff.).

Similarly, the Lord promised through Ezekiel that, in the New Covenant,

> I will sprinkle clean water on you. . . . I will give you a new heart
> and put a new spirit within you; and I will remove the heart of

stone from your flesh and give you a heart of flesh. And I will put My spirit within you and cause you to walk in My statutes, and you will be careful to observe My ordinances. (Ezek. 36:25–27; cf. 11:19)

The Old Covenant believers lacked the Spirit in the way it has been given to us, and so they failed to keep the covenant commandments (Heb. 8:8). New Covenant believers have been filled and renewed by God's Spirit so that they can imitate God's holiness by keeping His commandments.

This promise of faithful obedience is confirmed in the New Covenant writings: "He condemned sin in the flesh, in order that the requirement of the Law might be fulfilled in us, who do not walk according to the flesh, but according to the Spirit" (Rom. 8:3–4; cf. Heb. 8:7ff.). Moreover, we learn that the New Covenant still upholds God's law as our pattern for holiness: "The Law is holy, and the commandment is holy and righteous and good" (Rom. 7:12). The law, then, is not something to be despised; it is to be esteemed. Far from casting off the law for faith, "we establish the Law" (Rom. 3:31). Even more, in his letter to Timothy, Paul teaches that "we know that the Law is good, if one uses it lawfully" (1 Tim. 1:8). Throughout the New Covenant Scriptures, the authors cite God's law to teach righteousness (Acts 25:11; 1 Cor. 6:14; 14:34; 1 Tim. 5:18; James 2:9).

But what about love? We know that love is the greatest virtue in Christian living (1 Cor. 13:13), but is this love somehow opposed to the law, as many imagine? To the contrary, "love . . . is the fulfillment of the law" (Rom. 13:10): "For he who loves his neighbor has fulfilled the law. For this, 'You shall not commit adultery, you shall not murder, you shall not steal, you shall not covet,' and if there is any other commandment, it is summed up in this saying, 'You shall love your neighbor as yourself' " (Rom. 13:8–9).

If we love others, then we treat them from the heart in accordance with God's law, respecting their person and property in our acts and thoughts. Similarly, the apostle John upholds God's law as the pattern of New Covenant righteousness by teaching that sin is "lawlessness" (1 John 3:4) and that love is expressed through God's law: "By this we know that we love the children of God, when we love God and observe His commandments. For this is the love of God, that we keep His commandments; and His commandments are not burdensome" (1 John 5:2–3). John reiterates this point in his second letter: "This is love, that we walk according to His commandments" (2 John 6). And, in the Revelation given through John, faithful believers are described as "those who obey God's commandments" (Rev. 12:17 NIV) and "the saints who obey God's commandments and remain faithful to Jesus" (Rev. 14:12 NIV).

Christ Himself obeyed the law (John 8:46; 15:10) and rebuked those who distorted God's commandments (Mark 7:16). He upheld the details of God's law (Matt. 15:4). Moreover, when asked for the two greatest commandments (Matt. 22:36), Christ simply repeated verbatim the laws that teach us to love God with all our being (Deut. 6:5) and to love our neighbors as ourselves (Lev. 19:18). These two great commandments summarize—they do not replace—all of God's commandments: "On these two commandments depend the whole Law and the Prophets" (Matt. 22:40; cf. 7:12). Furthermore, Christ twice denied that He had come to do away with the law (Matt. 5:17), and He warned that violators of the law and those who teach others to ignore God's commandments "shall be called least in the kingdom of heaven" (Matt. 5:19), but "whoever keeps and teaches them, he shall be called great in the kingdom of heaven" (Matt. 5:19).

But what about the relationship between God's law and His grace? Many have pointed to passages such as "You are not under law, but under grace" (Rom. 6:14) to try to deny that Christians ought to keep God's commandments today. Only a little reflection, however, shows that such passages cannot mean what some say they mean. These passages do away with works-righteousness as a means of justification; they do not do away with God's law as a pattern of sanctification. If we were "not under law" in the way some people claim, then we would be permitted to lie, steal, and blaspheme. Moreover, if these passages meant what some say they mean, Christ would contradict the apostles and the apostles would contradict themselves, sometimes in the same letter. Yet we know this cannot be the case. Instead of reading these passages as some read them, we need to read them in context. By so doing, we see that sometimes the writer is working with several senses of "law," or with ceremonial laws (e.g., Gal. 3:24–25) that have been fulfilled and set aside in Christ. In the end, we find that God's commandments are our pattern for sanctification and living in love for God and our neighbors.

Instead of evading God's commandments, we ought to share John's attitude that they "are not burdensome" (1 John 5:3) and David's meditation that "every one of Thy righteous ordinances is everlasting" (Ps. 119:160), his "meditation all the day" (Ps. 119:97) that was "sweeter than honey to my mouth" (Ps. 119:103). Psalm 119 is a glorious meditation on the beauty of God's law, a meditation that ought to be shared by God's people in both the Old and New Covenants, since the pattern of righteousness has remained the same throughout, although now we have been empowered by God's Spirit to obey His eternal covenantal commandments faithfully in all areas of our lives. As the Heidelberg Catechism explains, "In this life even the holiest have only a small beginning of this obedience. Nevertheless, with earnest purpose they do begin to live not only according to some but to all the commandments of God" (Q. 114).

Before the Foundation of the World

To close out our discussion of God's past covenantal work, we need to consider its very foundation. To this point, we have considered only two distinct covenants, the Covenant of Creation and the Covenant of Redemption (in its Old Covenant shadows and New Covenant reality). The New Covenant, however, reveals that there is something even more profound standing behind these two covenants: a covenant between the Father, the Son, and the Spirit—a Covenant in the Godhead—"before the foundation of the world" (John 17:24; cf. Eph. 1:4; Rev. 13:8; 17:8).

In the Covenant in the Godhead—traditionally known as the covenant of redemption (or the pact of salvation, the eternal covenant, or the counsel of peace)—the triune God in eternity set His love upon His people and determined that the Son would covenantally submit to the Father and take upon Himself "the form of a bond-servant" (Phil. 2:7), becoming "obedient to the point of death" (v. 8), to redeem a people for Himself and commune with them through the Spirit, who "abides with you, and will be in you" (John 14:17).

On the basis of this eternal covenant, the Lord condescended to covenant, after Creation, with Adam (the Covenant of Creation). Adam broke that covenant, but it was finally fulfilled by the Last Adam (1 Cor. 15:45–47), Jesus Christ, as the mediator of the Covenant of Redemption.

J. I. Packer maintains that the biblical basis for the Covenant in the Godhead is "pervasive, arresting, and inescapable: Jesus' own words force on thoughtful readers recognition of the covenant economy as foundational to all thought about the reality of God's saving grace."[2] Indeed, all the characteristics of a divine covenant are present in the Covenant in the Godhead.

1. *A mutually binding relationship between the Lord and His servant:* "I will be a Father to Him, and He shall be a Son to Me" (Heb. 1:5). "I will surely give the nations as Thine inheritance" (Ps. 2:8; cf. Rev. 2:27); "Sit at My right hand, until I make Thine enemies a footstool for Thy feet" (Ps. 110:1). "I manifested Thy name to the men whom Thou gavest Me out of

the world" (John 17:6). "Just as My Father has granted Me a kingdom, I grant you" (Luke 22:29; cf. Rev. 11:15).

2. *Sovereign administration:* "I love the Father, and as the Father gave Me commandment, even so I do" (John 14:31). "For this reason the Father loves Me, because I lay down My life . . . on My own initiative. I have authority to lay it down, and I have authority to take it up again. This commandment I received from My Father (John 10:17–18).

3. *Conditions:*

Commandments: "I have kept My Father's commandments, and abide in His love" (John 15:10; cf. 4:32–34; 5:30; 7:16–18; 12:49–50; 17:4; 19:30). Christ "has been tempted in all things as we are, yet without sin" (Heb. 4:15). "Which one of you convicts Me of sin?" (John 8:46). ". . . as of a lamb unblemished and spotless, the blood of Christ" (1 Peter 1:19).

Sanctions (blessings and curses): Christ "for the joy set before Him endured the cross, despising the shame, and has sat down at the right hand of the throne of God" (Heb. 12:2). "He humbled Himself by becoming obedient to the point of death, even death on a cross. Therefore also God highly exalted Him, and bestowed on Him the name which is above every name, that at the name of Jesus every knee should bow" (Phil. 2:8–9). "All authority has been given to Me in heaven and on earth" (Matt. 28:18). "Christ . . . ha[s] become a curse for us" (Gal. 3:13). "Worthy is the Lamb that was slain to receive power and riches and wisdom and might and honor and glory and blessing" (Rev. 5:12). ". . . through the obedience of the One [Christ] the many will be made righteous" (Rom. 5:19; cf. Heb. 5:8–9).

4. *Promises of union and communion:*

> And now, glorify Thou Me together with Thyself, Father, with the glory which I ever had with Thee before the world was. . . . even as Thou, Father, art in Me, and I in Thee, that they also may be in Us; that the world may believe that Thou didst send Me. . . . We are one; I in them, and Thou in Me, that they may be perfected in unity. . . . Thou didst love Me before the foundation of the world. (John 17:5, 21–24)

"Then comes the end, when He [Christ] delivers up the kingdom to the God and Father. . . . And when all things are subjected to Him, then the Son Himself also will be subjected to the One who subjected all things to Him, that God may be all in all" (1 Cor. 15:24, 28). "I saw no temple in it, for the Lord God, the Almighty, and the Lamb, are its temple" (Rev. 21:22).

Given this broader and more eternal viewpoint, we can make better sense of such claims as, "The promises were spoken to Abraham and to his seed. He does not say, 'And to seeds,' as referring to many, but rather to one, 'And to your seed,' that is Christ" (Gal. 3:16). In other words, the Father promised a people and a land to Christ—"I will surely give the nations as Thine inheritance" (Ps. 2:8)—and we see this covenant between the Father and the Son determined "before the foundation of the world" (John 17:24; cf. Eph. 1:4).

A GLANCE BACK AND AHEAD

With all of the links of the intricate covenantal chain now before us, what does the whole look like? Consider the following summary of God's work in the past:

Prior to the foundation of the world, God, whose ways are higher than our ways as the heavens are above the earth, determined to be in union and communion with a people by means of a covenantal relationship. Having supreme dominion over all creation and history, the triune God determined to accomplish this communion by having the Son covenantally submit to the Father to redeem a people by the agency of the Spirit (the Covenant in the Godhead). Following Creation, the Lord graciously entered into a covenant with Adam (the Covenant of Creation), who served as a representative of the whole human race. God promised him eternal union and communion on the condition of faithful obedience.

Adam, however, rebelled against this covenant, subjecting himself and all his posterity to the curse and wrath of God. Yet, immediately after the Fall, the Lord continued to display His grace, and on the basis of the Covenant in the Godhead, began to establish a second covenant (the Covenant of Redemption), by means of which He would secure a faithful people for Himself. Our first parents were promised a descendant who would crush the deceiving Serpent, whose people would be in constant hostility with the people of the promised conqueror until the culmination of redemption.

This hostility soon erupted forcefully, and the Lord judged the rebellion by a devastating flood. He saved only a single family, through whom the coming conqueror would be born. The Lord made a covenant with Noah and all creation, promising not to destroy the creation again, thereby preserving a path for the coming Redeemer.

Soon thereafter, the Lord called Abraham out from among all the peoples of the earth, as the chosen vessel through whom He would redeem a people for Himself. The Lord covenanted with Abraham, setting forth stipulations, promises, and sanctions. Most notably, the Lord promised him a glorious land and glorious descendants, including kings, through whom all the families of the earth would be blessed. The Lord promised to be the God of Abraham and his descendants, and also promised that they would be His people. Yet, at the same time, the Lord would not bless all of Abraham's physical descendants—only the chosen covenantal line of Isaac and Jacob.

As promised, Abraham's descendants cried out under Egyptian slavery, and God remembered His covenant with Abraham. On the basis of that covenantal promise of a land and a people, the Lord called Moses to lead Abraham's descendants out of Egyptian slavery and into the land promised to Abraham. The Lord renewed the Abrahamic covenant with the nation of Israel, providing greater revelation of His covenantal stipulations, promises, and sanctions of union and communion, promising to be their God as they would be His people. From this point on, Israel's history proceeded according to God's promises of inheritance for covenant keeping and sanctions for covenant breaking. During that time, Israel struggled to find any semblance of rest, peace, and stability.

Once again, the Lord confirmed His promises to Abraham, as expanded through Moses, and thereby moved history toward His goal by calling out David to renew the covenant. The Lord promised David all that the failing, faithless, and weary Israel desired: peace and stability, and, even more, an eternal Davidic kingdom, in which the Lord would be their God, and they would be His people. David glorified God for His faithfulness to the Abrahamic promise to preserve a land and a people. But David passed away, as did his son Solomon, and the kingdom was torn asunder. God exiled most of the former Israelite nation for violating His covenant, and only a remnant remained faithful.

Later, all of Israel, the covenant breakers and the remnant, were exiled, but in their exile the Lord remembered His covenant with Abraham, Moses, and David. He prophesied of the fulfillment of these glorious promises of a land and a people. The promise that Abraham would bring blessing upon all nations was trumpeted repeatedly in prophecies of an eternal kingdom of worldwide scope, whose people would enter a "new" covenant in which the Spirit would be poured out, enabling them (as was not previously the case) to be faithful to the Lord's covenant. The prophets not only pointed to countless descendants of Abraham, but also to a unique servant-conqueror, who, as a king, would make His enemies His footstool, and who, as a priest, would redeem His people from their sin by taking upon Himself the curses of the covenant.

The years passed, with apparently only partial fulfillment of the covenantal prophesies. But then, in the fullness of time, God confirmed His covenant by incarnating the Christ, the God-man, to fill the eternal throne as promised to David, to be the unblemished Lamb of God as pictured in the Mosaic ceremonies, to secure a people and world promised to Abraham, to overcome in an earth preserved from destruction as promised to Noah, and to be without sin in faithful satisfaction of the covenant with Adam. Christ, the sacrificial Lamb, yet triumphant Lion, called His people out from every tongue and tribe and nation in order to fulfill the covenantal promise to bless all families and nations. And when all His enemies are made His footstool by the power of the Spirit, He will fulfill the Covenant in the Godhead, and God will dwell with His holy people in complete union and communion forever.

STUDY QUESTIONS

1. What are some of the titles the New Testament writers ascribe to God's people in the New Covenant era (see Rom. 2:28–29; Gal. 3:29; 4:28; 6:16; Phil. 3:3; James 1:1; 1 Peter 2:9; Rev. 7:4)? How does the New Testament refer to God's people in the Old Covenant era in Acts 7:38 and Hebrews 2:12? What do these passages teach us about the people of God in the Old and New Covenant eras?
2. Explain the three ways in which the New Covenant is more glorious than the Old Covenant.
3. What covenant do we learn more about in John 17:24 (cf. Eph. 1:4; Rev. 13:8; 17:8)? What are some of the other names by which it has been known? Explain how all aspects of a divine covenant are present in this covenant.

Notes

1. Thomas Boston, *A View of the Covenant of Grace from the Sacred Records* (1720; reprint, East Sussex: Focus Christian Ministries Trust, 1990), 43.
2. J. I. Packer, "Introduction" to Herman Witsius, *The Economy of the Covenants Between God and Man: Comprehending a Complete Body of Divinity* (1882; reprint, Escondido, Calif.: Den Dulk Christian Foundation, 1990). In contrast, O. Palmer Robertson, in *Christ of the Covenants*, rejects the notion of a Cove-

nant in the Godhead: "A sense of artificiality flavors the effort to structure in covenantal terms the mysteries of God's eternal counsels. Scripture simply does not say much on the pre-Creation shape of the decrees of God. To speak concretely of an intertrinitarian "covenant" with terms and conditions between Father and Son mutually endorsed before the foundation of the world is to extend the bounds of scriptural evidence beyond propriety" (p. 54). Robertson, however, has precluded a pre-Creation covenant by adopting a narrow definition of a covenant as a "bond in blood," which would also, if consistently applied, preclude the Covenant of Creation from being a covenant: "At the point of covenantal inauguration, the parties of the covenant are committed to one another by a formalizing process of blood-shedding" (p. 14). Moreover, given the minimal references in the text to follow, the "terms and conditions" which Robertson sees as "beyond propriety" appear hard to miss, or, as Packer notes, they are "pervasive, arresting, and inescapable."

ELEVEN

NO END IN SIGHT?

G od's covenant work began with several simple mosaic pieces in Eden and slowly expanded, adding more and more texture, depth, and beauty through Abraham, Moses, David, and the prophets. When the mosaic was completed in Christ, it was so beautifully detailed that we could meditate on it forever. All the pieces formed one mosaic, one story, one Covenant of Redemption, as God secured union and communion with His people.

Throughout this survey of God's covenant work, three themes have stood out prominently: the antithesis between the seed of the woman and the seed of the Serpent, the promises of a land and a people, and the effectual work of the covenant prophet, priest, and king—the kinsman-redeemer. These three themes will continue to stand out as we turn our attention to the future development of God's covenant work, although they will be ordered differently in accordance with varying scriptural emphases. While treatments of the covenant often stop with God's covenant work in the past, Scripture has much to say about His covenant work in the future. Let us see what Scripture says about how the covenant will develop in the future.

THE WAR CONTINUES: ALIENATION AND ENMITY

Looking Ahead

The antithesis between the seed of the woman and the seed of the Serpent, between Christian and non-Christian seeds, will most assuredly extend into the future. Christ teaches us that both "wheat" and "tares" will grow alongside one another until the end of time, struggling against one another (Matt. 13:24ff.). This enduring battle may grow more or less intense over the years, although, as the church matures, the two sides will become more clearly differentiated.

Scripture does not indicate that this antithesis will fade away. The division imposed in Eden does not recede into the background; rather, it ultimately reaches its starkest and most final development. As always, this part of redemptive history depends upon God's ongoing covenant work. In this particular case, the culmination of the antithesis between the seed of the woman and the seed of the Serpent is a direct result of the kinsman-redeemer's work of fully and finally avenging His kin. In this chapter, we will examine the culmination of the kinsman-redeemer's avenging obligations, keeping in mind that the enemies of God continue to oppose the kinsman-redeemer as laid out in the discussion of God's past covenant work; namely, they are enslaved, alienated, vengeful, and disinherited. Moreover, the culmination of the antithesis concerns only those unbelievers who continue their rebellion against the gracious Lord of the covenant; the rest will have been regenerated by God's Spirit on the basis of the ransom paid by their kinsman-redeemer.

As we have seen, in the Mosaic expression of the Covenant of Redemption, Moses declared that the Lord "will avenge the blood of His servants, and will render vengeance on His adversaries, and will atone for His land and His people" (Deut. 32:43; cf. 19:12–13; Num. 35:16–21, 31; Job 19:23ff.; Prov. 23:11; Isa. 47:1, 4; Jer. 50:4). This has been true throughout the ages, and will be in the ages to come. We know that the seed of the Serpent is made up of God's adversaries, and, in particular, our "adversary, the devil" (1 Peter 5:8). So we should expect that Christ will avenge His people against all their enemies, and especially will completely destroy the Serpent himself: "The Son of God appeared for this purpose, that He might destroy the works of the devil" (1 John 3:8). We saw in a previous chapter that Christ decisively defeated Satan at the Cross, triumphing over him openly (Col. 2:15) and binding him (Matt. 12:25–29). His final destruction, however, is yet to come.

Setting the Stage

Before looking at the culmination of Christ's avenging work against the seed of the Serpent, we need to set the stage by seeing what events lead up to Christ's culminating work.

Although there is much disagreement among Christians regarding the end-time events, most of those disagreements arise outside of the covenantal view of Scripture. Most of them arise in what we will call the popular end-times view, which, leaving room for some disagreements, proceeds as follows:

- The future will get worse and worse.
- At some secret point, Christ will rapture the church off the earth, judging the saved in heaven (the first judgment).
- Following the Rapture, there will be a seven-year period known as the Great Tribulation.
- During this Tribulation, a uniquely evil person, the Antichrist, will arise and persecute Israel and converts.
- At the end of the seven years, several armies will collide in the great Battle of Armageddon.
- During this battle, Christ's second coming (actually, the third coming) will occur, in which He physically slaughters His foes at Armageddon.
- Christ then holds another (now second) judgment, the Judgment of Nations.
- Christ resurrects all (and only) believers to live on earth (the first resurrection).
- Christ then institutes a one-thousand-year reign on earth from Jerusalem.
- At the end of the thousand years, there is a final rebellion, which Christ puts down.
- Christ then resurrects the unbelieving dead (the second resurrection).
- He then judges them (the third judgment) at the Great White Throne of judgment.
- Unbelievers are sent to hell; believers go to heaven.

That is the currently popular view among evangelicals. In contrast to it, those embracing covenant theology, with some room for variation, basically agree that:

- The covenant keeps developing.
- At the end of it, Christ's second coming occurs.
- At that time, He resurrects all the dead at once, both believers and unbelievers.

- He holds a general judgment of believers and unbelievers at the same time.
- He casts unbelievers into hell, and welcomes believers into heaven.

How are we to judge between these two very different structures of end-time events? Instead of turning to the newspaper to interpret Scripture, we must allow Scripture to interpret itself. When we do, we find that Scripture rules out the popular end-times view and supports the covenantal view.

The arguments for a secret Rapture before Christ's final coming generally depend either on falsely absolutized promises of protection (e.g., Rev. 3:10; Luke 21:36; Rom. 5:9; cf. John 16:33; 17:15; 2 Tim. 3:12) or on mistaken inferences from passages describing the final coming and judgment (1 Thess. 5:9; 1 Cor. 15:51–52; Matt. 24:40).

The case for a seven-year Great Tribulation is based solely on an alleged gap of years in the prophecy of Daniel 9:20–27. The main reason advocates give for this gap is that Christ could not effectually and decisively redeem His people (as described in Dan. 9:24) before the Second Coming. The work of the kinsman-redeemer described in chapter 12 of this book and the discussion of Christ's atonement in chapter 5 show that the premise upon which this gap theory rests is sorely mistaken. Christ has accomplished all that was promised in Daniel 9:20–27.

Scripture repeatedly speaks of one general resurrection of believers and unbelievers, not of two or three, as the popular end-times view claims. Christ declares, "All who are in the tombs shall hear His voice, and shall come forth; those who did the good deeds, to a resurrection of life, those who committed the evil deeds to a resurrection of judgment" (John 5:28–29). Similarly, Paul explains that "there shall certainly be a resurrection of both the righteous and the wicked" (Acts 24:15; cf. Dan. 12:1–2; John 11:24; 2 Tim. 2:18; Matt. 13:30, 37–43, 47–50; 1 Cor. 15:26). With only one physical resurrection, there is no room to squeeze in a thousand-year kingdom, as the popular end-times view maintains.

Scripture repeatedly speaks of one final judgment of believers and unbelievers concurrently. The Day of Judgment is described as one day or period of time (Rom. 2:5–7; John 5:29; 12:48; Acts 17:31; 2 Tim. 4:1; 1 John 4:17; 2 Thess. 1:7–10), with both believers and unbelievers present (Matt. 25; Rev. 20:11–15). In all, Scripture speaks of these final events of Christ's return, the resurrection of the dead, and the Last Judgment as one unified drama, with no room for a thousand-year intermission. The millennium of Revelation 20 must be understood differently than it is popularly understood today.

Thus, despite its widespread acceptance in this century, the popular end-times view is clearly at odds with Scripture (and more historical Protestant views). As described above, the scriptural outline of end-time events is rather straightforward and simple: at the end of covenant development, Christ returns, resurrects all, judges all, and ushers in the final state of both believers and unbelievers.

What's Final Is Final

With this structure in mind, we can better grasp the culmination of the antithesis between the seed of the woman and the seed of the Serpent. The two seeds war against each other to the very end. Christ, the avenger, comes in final judgment against those who love their rebellion and sin, separating them from God and the seed of the woman forever. The seed of the Serpent ends up in hell—total, final, and comprehensive alienation from God.

Notice the final antithesis between the seeds in the many descriptions of the Last Judgment. On that final day Christ "will separate them from one another, as the shepherd separates the sheep from the goats; and He will put the sheep on His right, and the goats on the left" (Matt. 25:32–33). To the seed of the woman, Christ will declare, "Come, you who are blessed of My Father, inherit the kingdom" (v. 34), but to the seed of the Serpent He will declare, "Depart from Me, accursed ones, into the eternal fire which has been prepared for the devil and his angels" (v. 41). The result is eternal antithesis (Rev. 20:11–15).

Similarly, the apostle Paul highlights the final antithesis when he informs the Thessalonians that

> the Lord Jesus shall be revealed from heaven . . . dealing out retribution to those who do not know God and to those who do not obey the gospel of our Lord Jesus. And these will pay the penalty of eternal destruction, away from the presence of the Lord and from the glory of His power, when He comes to be glorified in His saints on that day, and to be marveled at among all who have believed. (2 Thess. 1:7–10)

Once again, we find final and eternal antithesis.

Since many of us have heard these descriptions of final judgment over and over, we tend to miss their intriguing aspects. Why, for example, do we always read of Christ's presiding over the final judgment? Surely, the Holy Spirit or especially God the Father could preside there. Why has Christ been given the "authority to execute judgment" (John 5:27)?

The answer lies in His role as our kinsman-redeemer. With the final judgment and hell as the destiny of the seed of the Serpent, Christ has indeed kept the promise that "He will avenge the blood of His servants, and will render vengeance on His adversaries, and will atone for His land and His people" (Deut. 32:43). Christ, in His avenging duties as our kins-man-redeemer, finally and completely vindicates His name and His people, avenging their slaughter by bloody tyrants and silencing their adversaries forever. Christ's people no longer need to cry out, "How long, O Lord, holy and true, wilt Thou refrain from judging and avenging our blood . . . ?" (Rev. 6:10). The holy kinsman-avenger will faithfully and justly accomplish His covenantal duty.

In considering Christ's avenging work, we need to keep in mind that non-Christians hate God and His authority and rebelliously suppress their knowledge of Him (Rom. 1:18ff.). Although non-Christians suppress their knowledge of God, all the while showing their dependence upon Him in their day-to-day activities, this knowledge will leave them with no excuse on the Day of Judgment (Rom. 1:19–20). In other words, there are no lost tribesmen in the jungle who have never received enough revelation about God. All people without exception will be accountable for the knowledge that their Creator and Judge has revealed to them and in them. So, when the Day of Judgment finally arrives, no one will claim that they just did not know enough to believe in God. No one has an excuse for rebelling against God. And as we stand there in fear, we will confess that every condemning sentence He passes is holy and just.

Hell's final and horrible alienation from God is only a small part of His future covenant work, important as it is. Although God's Covenant of Redemption will ultimately serve as the basis for imposing the sentence of eternal alienation from God, this just vindication does not compare to the glories of union and communion, the glories of the promise of a land and a people, awaiting God's people as the seed of the woman.

THE PEACE CONTINUES: UNION AND COMMUNION

The covenantal blessings awaiting God's people involve His promise to Abraham of a people and a land. Christ secures these promises by fulfilling the three remaining duties of the kinsman-redeemer: ransoming a people from slavery, marrying the widowed, and regaining their lost inheritance.

The Promise of a People

From the very first statement of the promise of a people, the Lord showed us its broad scope. In promising the gospel to Abraham (Gal. 3:8), the Lord told him very explicitly that the covenant blessings would flow to "all the families of the earth" (Gen. 12:3) and "all the nations of the earth" (Gen. 26:4). Since other family lines and other nationalities already existed in Abraham's time, these passages indicate that the blessings of the covenant would flow to those outside Abraham's biological line (cf. Rom. 9:6ff.). As we have seen, this inclusion of the Gentiles was foretold by the Old Covenant prophets and confirmed by Christ and the apostles.

While we have previously examined the promise that the Gentiles would be added to God's people, we have not considered the extent of that blessing, that is, whether it would extend to a small remnant of Jewish and Gentile families or to the vast majority of families throughout the ages. Again, the promise to Abraham tells us what to expect—through Abraham, all the families of the earth would be blessed! This language does not suggest small remnants or narrow groups of nationalities; it suggests the widest possible scope. And this worldwide blessing of families is taught elsewhere in Scripture, especially in the Prophets. Since we have not yet seen the fulfillment of this glorious promise in the vast majority of families and nationalities, we are to expect its fulfillment in the future.

But we should not expect this glorious fulfillment just in heaven, the final state. The contexts of the passages reviewed in the following pages do not focus on heaven, since they refer to the existence of enemies and the effects of sin, all of which will be absent in heaven. So, if these blessings do not apply to heaven, what is their time frame? Where do they fit in the unfolding drama of redemptive history? Although some see them describing a future millennial kingdom set up after Christ's return, we have already seen that the biblical understanding of the final resurrection and judgment rule out any such literal thousand-year kingdom.

If these passages do not speak about blessings in heaven and cannot be squeezed into a millennial kingdom, then they must refer to events that take place prior to Christ's second coming. In other words, God's future covenant work will fulfill the promises to Abraham by establishing a world-encompassing devotion to Christ, a worldwide covenant community living in holiness and peace. As you will see, sin and enemies and death will remain, but they will be so diminished that Christ will be faithfully worshiped in all corners of the earth.

Let us examine some of these passages describing God's future covenant work and consider how the promise of a people is developed in light of the kinsman-redeemer's duties to ransom from slavery and marry the widowed.

The great passage from Isaiah regarding the kinsman-redeemer, as we have already noted, is Isaiah 61:1, 6, 8–9, 11.

> The Spirit of the Lord God is upon me, because the Lord has anointed me to bring good news to the afflicted; He has sent me to bind up the brokenhearted, to proclaim liberty to captives, and freedom to prisoners. . . . You will eat the wealth of nations, and in their riches you will boast. . . . I will make an everlasting covenant with them. *Then their offspring will be known among the nations, and their descendants in the midst of the peoples. . . . So the Lord God will cause righteousness and praise to spring up before all the nations.*

Here the kinsman-redeemer not only frees His enslaved brethren, but also causes righteousness and praise to arise among "all the nations," using the language of the Abrahamic promise.

Isaiah 61 is not alone. Consider the following passages, which speak of a future worldwide faithfulness among the nations:

> *All the ends of the earth will remember and turn to the Lord, and all the families of the nations will worship before Thee.* (Ps. 22:27)

> *So the nations will fear the name of the Lord, and all the kings of the earth Thy glory.* . . . From heaven the Lord gazed upon the earth, to hear the groaning of the prisoner; to set free those who were doomed to death; that men may tell of the name of the Lord in Zion, and His praise in Jerusalem; *when the peoples are gathered together, and the kingdoms, to serve the Lord.* (Ps. 102:15, 19–22)

> I will also make you a light of the nations so that My salvation may reach to the end of the earth. (Isa. 49:6)

> *Enlarge the place of your tent; stretch out the curtains of your dwellings, spare not; lengthen your cords, and strengthen your pegs. For you will spread abroad to the right and to the left. And your descendants will possess nations, and they will resettle the desolate cities. . . . The re-*

proach of your widowhood you will remember no more. For your hus-band is your Maker, whose name is the LORD *of hosts; and your Re-deemer is the Holy One of Israel.* (Isa. 54:2–5)

Be joyful with Jerusalem and rejoice for her, . . . for thus says the LORD, *"Behold, I extend peace to her like a river, and the glory of the nations like an overflowing stream."* (Isa. 66:10, 12)

"I will make a new covenant with the house of Israel and with the house of Judah. . . . I will be their God, and they shall be My people. *And they shall not teach again, each man his neighbor and each man his brother, saying, 'Know the* LORD,' *for they shall all know Me, from the least of them to the greatest of them,"* declares the Lord, "for I will forgive their iniquity, and their sin I will remember no more." (Jer. 31:31, 33, 34)

My servant David will be king over them, . . . and they will walk in My ordinances, . . . and they shall live on the land that I gave to Jacob My servant . . . ; they will live on it, they, and their sons, and their sons' sons, forever; . . . I will make a covenant of peace with them. . . . *And the nations will know that I am the* LORD *who sanctifies Israel, when My sanctuary is in their midst forever.* (Ezek. 37:24, 26, 28)

In that day I will raise up the fallen booth of David, . . . *that they may possess the remnant of Edom and all the nations who are called by My name.* (Amos 9:11–12)

And many nations will join themselves to the LORD in that day and will become My people. Then I will dwell in your midst. (Zech. 2:11)

So many peoples and mighty nations will come to seek the LORD *of* hosts in Jerusalem and to entreat the favor of the LORD. (Zech. 8:22)

For from the rising of the sun, even to its setting, My name will be great among the nations, and in *every place* incense is going to be offered to My name, and a grain offering that is pure; *for My name will be great among the nations.* (Mal. 1:11)

All authority has been given to Me in heaven and on earth. Go therefore and *make disciples of all the nations.* (Matt. 28:18–19)

We will see this same point made repeatedly in the promise of a land, but of particular note here is the place of ethnic Israel in the midst of the future fulfillment of the Abrahamic promise of a people. We know that faithful first-century Jews, such as the apostles and others, had inherited the Abrahamic promises in the New Covenant, along with the Gentiles whom the kinsman-redeemer adopted into the seed of Abraham (Gal. 3:29). After all, the promises were given "to the Jew first" and then to the Gentiles, even though the Gentiles—spiritual Jews—soon outnumbered ethnic Jews. But that transition did not signify the end of God's mercy to ethnic Israel.

In reflecting on the place of ethnic Jews in the future of God's covenant work, the apostle Paul reveals that not all ethnic Israel has been cast off forever: "They [ethnic Israel] did not stumble so as to fall, did they? May it never be! But by their transgression salvation has come to the Gentiles, to make them jealous" (Rom. 11:11). Even more specifically, we learn, "A partial hardness has happened to Israel until the fulness of the Gentiles has come in; and thus all Israel will be saved" (Rom. 11:25–26). The apostle reveals that Israel rejects the New Covenant only temporarily, until the "fulness of the Gentiles" has received the promise, a point still future. But at that point—perhaps when most of the Gentile world will have embraced the promises of Abraham, Isaac, Jacob, Moses, and David—the faith of the Gentiles will provoke ethnic Israel to a holy jealousy for their heritage (Rom. 11:11), and thus "all Israel will be saved" (Rom. 11:26), being regenerated by God's Spirit.

Scripture reveals not only a worldwide discipling of the nations, but also a glorious and precious future for ethnic Israel, whom the Lord has not abandoned (Rom. 11:28–29). Hence, the Jewish community has always held a special place in Reformed thinking when the future of the covenant has been clearly understood. Although rebellious Gentiles and Jews will perish, the Lord will revive an overwhelming majority of Gentiles—spiritual Jews—and such an overwhelming majority of ethnic Jews that He can speak of "all Israel" being redeemed. John Murray notes on this score that "there awaits the Gentiles . . . gospel blessing far surpassing anything experienced during the period of Israel's apostasy, and [it] will be occasioned by the conversion of Israel on a scale commensurate with that of their earlier disobedience."[1]

The Promise of a Land

The Lord promised Abraham and his seed not only an innumerable people, "all the families of the earth," but also a land. The initial land had specified borders, but Abraham understood that that was only a token of a more glorious inheritance, "for he was looking for the city which has foundations, whose architect and builder is God" (Heb. 11:10; cf. Rom. 4:13). Again, this promise of a land is more fully developed by the prophets, who beautifully describe its worldwide scope with rich imagery. This imagery includes such features as the Lord's mountain, a mighty city, a pure temple, and, most prominently, a triumphant kingdom. Consider two well-known prophecies depicting the glorious future state of the covenant prior to the Second Coming:

> In the last days, the mountain of the house of the LORD will be established as the chief of the mountains, and will be raised above the hills; and *all the nations* will stream to it. And many peoples will come and say, "Come let us go up to the mountain of the LORD, to the house of the God of Jacob; that He may teach us concerning His ways, and that we may walk in His paths." . . . And they will hammer their swords into plowshares, and their spears into pruning hooks. Nation will not lift up sword against nation, and never again will they learn war. (Isa. 2:2–4)

> The wolf will dwell with the lamb, and the leopard will lie down with the kid. . . . Also the cow and the bear will graze; their young will lie down together; and the lion will eat straw like the ox. . . . They will not hurt or destroy in all My holy mountain, *for the earth will be full of the knowledge of the LORD as the waters cover the sea. Then it will come about in that day that the nations will resort to the root of Jesse, who will stand as a signal for the peoples; and His resting place will be glorious.* (Isa. 11:6–10)

These passages not only depict the Abrahamic blessing to all the nations and families of the earth, but also symbolize some of the powerful cultural effects of a world devoted to covenant faithfulness to Christ. Righteousness and a thirst for the knowledge of God prevail, whereas the blight of death and destruction and danger have faded. This is the glorious culmination of the kinsman-redeemer's work.

Even more explicitly, Scripture pictures God's kingdom triumphing peacefully throughout the earth. From the very start, the Lord promised Abraham that his descendants would include kings (Gen. 17: 6, 16) and that they would "possess the gate" of their enemy's kingdoms (Gen. 22:17; 24:60). As we saw, the Lord also promised Abraham's kingly descendant, David, an eternal kingdom (2 Sam. 7:16) that would be characterized by peace, security, and permanence (2 Sam. 7:9–10). This imagery of the triumphant kingdom receives glorious elaboration in the Psalms and Prophets.

> "He said to Me, 'Thou art My Son, today I have begotten Thee. Ask of Me, and *I will surely give the nations as Thine inheritance, and the very ends of the earth as Thy possession. Thou shalt break them with a rod of iron, Thou shalt shatter them like earthenware.'*" . . . *Now therefore, O kings, show discernment; take warning, O judges of the earth.* . . . *Do homage to the Son, lest He become angry, and you perish in the way.* (Ps. 2:7–12)

> *All the families* of the nations will worship before Thee. For the kingdom is the LORD'S, and *He rules over the nations.* (Ps. 22:27–28)

> May he also rule *from sea to sea, and from the river to the ends of the earth.* Let the nomads of the desert bow before him; and his enemies lick the dust. . . . And let all kings bow down before him, *all nations* serve him. . . . And may the whole *earth* be filled with His glory. (Ps. 72:8–9, 11, 19)

> The LORD says to my Lord: "Sit at My right hand, until I make *Thine enemies a footstool* for Thy feet." (Ps. 110:1)

> For a child will be born to us, a son will be given to us; and the government will rest on His shoulders; and His name will be called Wonderful Counselor, Mighty God, Eternal Father, Prince of Peace. *There will be no end to the increase of His government or of peace,* on the throne of David and over his kingdom, to establish it and to uphold it with justice and righteousness from then on and forevermore. (Isa. 9:6–7)

> The stone that struck the statue became a great mountain and *filled the whole earth.* . . . And in the days of those kings the God of heaven will set up a kingdom which will never be destroyed, and that kingdom will not be left for another people; it will crush and put an end to all these kingdoms, but it will itself endure forever. Inasmuch as you saw that a stone was cut out of the mountain without hands and that it crushed the iron, the bronze, the clay, the silver, and the gold, the great God has made known to the king what will take place in the future; so the dream is true, and its interpretation is trustworthy. (Dan. 2:35, 44–45)

I kept looking in the night visions, and behold, with the clouds of heaven one like a Son of Man was coming, and He came up to the Ancient of Days and was presented before Him. And to Him was given dominion, glory and a kingdom, that *all the peoples, nations, and men of every language might serve Him. His dominion is an everlasting dominion which will not pass away; and His kingdom is one which will not be destroyed.* (Dan. 7:13–14)

And I will cut off the chariot from Ephraim, and the horse from Jerusalem; and the bow of war will be cut off. And He will speak peace to the nations; and His dominion will be from sea to sea, and from the River to the ends of the earth. (Zech. 9:10)

In the New Covenant literature, we receive even further revelation concerning the nature of this worldwide kingdom of peace. Christ not only claimed to be the king—"I am a king. For this I have been born, and for this I have come into the world" (John 18:37; cf. Luke 23:2–3; Matt. 27:11)—and fulfilled kingly descriptions (John 12:15), but also preached the "gospel of the kingdom" (Matt. 4:23), announcing that the kingdom of God was at hand: "The time is fulfilled, and the kingdom of God is at hand; repent and believe in the gospel" (Mark 1:15). Christ not only announced the coming of the kingdom, but also declared that it was established at that time (Matt. 12:28) and existing in their very midst (Luke 18:20–21)—though to be fully perfected in the future (Matt. 6:10). Given the overwhelming Old Covenant imagery of God's kingdom, Christ's listeners could not have mistaken the Davidic imagery.

But what is the nature of this divine kingdom? We know that it is not a kingdom of violence or coercion, like non-Christian kingdoms: "My kingdom is not of this world. If My kingdom were of this world, then My servants would be fighting, that I might not be delivered up to the Jews; but as it is, My kingdom is not of this realm" (John 18:36; cf. Matt. 26:52; John 6:15). That is, His kingdom does not originate from or imitate the kingdoms of the Serpent's seed. Common kingdoms and states are inherently violent institutions, and are therefore inherently inferior institutions, being tied as they are to the post-Fall world. In contrast, Christ is the "Prince of Peace" (Isa. 9:6) who conquers by the Word of God and the Spirit (Rev. 19:15; cf. Heb. 4:12; Jer. 23:29), not by physical violence or ballot-box coercion. Given its spiritual nature, Christ's kingdom is much more powerful than worldly kingdoms, since it transforms people from the inside out by means of God's Word, which cannot fail to accomplish its goals (Isa. 55:11).

Christ's kingdom exhibits its spiritual nature in other ways, as well. For example, in order to enter Christ's kingdom, a person does not need carnal citizenship; he needs to be reborn spiritually (John 3:3; cf. Matt. 18:24–25). The authority of this kingdom—symbolized by possession of its keys (Isa. 22:22)—is held by Christ's church (Matt. 16:19; 18:18), not some coercive agency. We are exhorted to seek the kingdom whose righteousness is synonymous with God's righteousness: "Seek first His kingdom and His righteousness" (Matt. 6:33). Moreover, in faithful covenantal form, Christ's kingdom includes not only faithful believers but also their children, of whom Christ Himself declares that "the kingdom of heaven belongs to such as these" (Matt. 19:14).

While the kingdom of Christ is spiritual, this spirituality does not preclude it from exerting influence in a given culture. In fact, the worldwide cultural righteousness, peace, and faithfulness described by the prophetic passages above will be the results of Christ's spiritual kingdom transforming God's enemies into His friends. Moreover, Christ Himself describes the victory of the kingdom of God by depicting it as a mustard seed that starts small but develops into the largest plant (Matt. 13:31–32), and as leaven that slowly spreads through all parts of the dough (Matt. 13:33). Even in His kingdom parable of the wheat and the tares, we see the Abrahamic promise of an innumerable people, for God's people are described as the wheat *field*, the prevailing crop, whereas unbelievers are described as interspersed weeds, far less in number than the wheat (Matt. 13:24ff.).

Furthermore, Christ Himself holds "all" authority in heaven and on earth (Matt. 28:18) and promises that "the gates of hell shall not prevail against [the church]" (Matt. 16:19 KJV). This is not just a defensive promise for the church, but also a peacefully offensive promise. The King tells us that the gates of the enemies will not be able to stand up against the gospel of the kingdom; as promised to Abraham (Gen. 22:17), we will possess the very gates of our enemies. And for this ultimate goal—that God's kingdom would be realized "on earth as it is in heaven"—we are taught to pray (Matt. 6:10).

Christ's apostles teach us these same truths about His kingdom. At Pentecost they declared that Christ was the king inheriting David's throne (Acts 2:25ff.), "waiting from that time onward until His enemies be made a footstool for His feet" (Heb. 10:13), having been seated at God's right hand, "far above all rule and authority and power and dominion" (Eph.

1:19–22). By means of Christ, the Father has "delivered us from the domain of darkness, and transferred us to the kingdom of His beloved Son" (Col. 1:13). Thus, like Christ, the apostles preached "the kingdom of God" (Acts 28:31).

The apostles also understood that the kingdom was powerfully spiritual and life-transforming: "The kingdom of God is not eating and drinking, but righteousness and peace and joy in the Holy Spirit" (Rom. 14:17). Paul instructs us along similar lines that, "though we walk in the flesh, we do not war according to the flesh, for the weapons of our warfare are not of the flesh, but divinely powerful for the destruction of fortresses" (2 Cor. 10:3–4; cf. Col. 2:15; 1 John 3:8).

Although the apostles recognized that Christ had established His kingdom (Col. 1:13), and that "we receive a kingdom which cannot be shaken" (Heb. 12:28; Rev. 11:15), they also recognized that the kingdom's full and glorious state was still future (Heb. 2:8), though prior to the Second Coming:

> For as in Adam all die, so also in Christ all shall be made alive. But each in his own order: Christ the first fruits, after that those who are Christ's at His coming, then comes the end, when He delivers up the kingdom to the God and Father, when He has abolished all rule and all authority and power. For He must reign until He has put all His enemies under His feet. The last enemy that will be abolished is death. (1 Cor. 15:22–26)

In this passage, we see Christ delivering a glorious kingdom in which He reigned until He had subdued all His enemies. Notice that by this glorious point, all of Christ's enemies will have either been transformed or avenged, for the only enemy remaining prior to the final state will be death, and then that too will be finally conquered in heaven. What a glorious vision of peaceful, spiritual triumph for Christ's kingdom, a triumph by the "King of kings" (Rev. 19:16) through the subduing and awesome power of His word, the gospel (Rev. 19:15). Such a scene inspired those sitting before God's throne to declare, "The kingdom of the world has become the kingdom of our Lord, and of His Christ; and He will reign forever and ever" (Rev. 11:15).

As the kingdom of God develops, the covenant promise of a land is fulfilled, from its humble beginnings to its awe-inspiring peaceful triumph throughout the world. To God alone belongs the glory! And He is greatly to be praised!

UP FROM EDEN: THE INTENT TO RESTORE UNION AND COMMUNION

One more aspect of God's beautiful covenant remains to be considered, namely, the path from Eden to the new heavens and new earth, especially as presented in the book of Revelation.

God created Adam and Eve in covenantal union and communion with Himself, giving them stewardship of the earth, and promising them eternal life if they would obey Him. After their rebellion—and ours in them—the Lord banished the human race from Eden and left us in corruption and despair, our union and communion with Him severed. Despite the resulting alienation and enmity, the Lord set about to redeem a people for His own glory by means of a redemptive covenant.

At various points in the development of the Covenant of Redemption, the Lord showed us His intent to restore Eden. Through Isaiah, the Lord declared,

> "Look to Abraham your father, and to Sarah who gave birth to you in pain; when he was one I called him, then I blessed and multiplied him." Indeed the LORD will comfort Zion; He will comfort all her waste places. And her wilderness *He will make like Eden*, and her desert like the garden of the LORD; joy and gladness will be found in her, thanksgiving and sound of a melody. (Isa. 51:2–3)

We find similar language describing the restoration of Eden in Ezekiel.

> "I will give you a new heart and put a new spirit within you; . . . And you will live in the land that I gave to your forefathers; so you will be My people, and I will be your God. . . ." Thus says the Lord GOD, "On the day that I cleanse you from all your iniquities, I will cause the cities to be inhabited, and the waste places will be rebuilt. . . . And they will say, '*This desolate land has become like the garden of Eden.*'" (Ezek. 36:26–36; cf. Joel 2:3)

Beginning from the depth of the initial curse, God developed His covenant from the promise of victory given to Adam, the promise of preservation given to Noah, and the promise of the salvation of the world given to Abraham, Israel, and David, to the glorious work of the kinsman-redeemer, Christ. As prophet, priest, and king, Christ ransomed His people from slavery, married them as widows, regained their inheritance, and avenged them—the seed of the woman—by crushing the seed of the Serpent. By doing so, Christ's gospel of the kingdom will peacefully conquer the world, completely fulfilling the Abrahamic promises. As the Last Adam, Christ faithfully obeys the covenant, gathering a people for eternal union and communion with God in His fullness. This path from union and communion lost to union and communion regained is beautifully depicted at the end of the book of Revelation, using so much of the rich covenantal imagery first used in Genesis.

Although Revelation 21–22 deserves a full reading to grasp its deep beauty, let us consider here some of its prominent imagery. The passage begins, "And I saw a new heaven and a new earth; for the first heaven and the first earth passed away" (Rev. 21:1). Although many see this as a description of the final state, its Old Covenant context requires us to understand it differently. The description of "a new heaven and a new earth" is taken from Isaiah's prophecy concerning the triumph of the covenantal promises (Isa. 65:17ff.). In that context, we see a glorious picture of the success of the covenant through faithful rejoicing (v. 18), the end of weeping (v. 19), long life (v. 20), and secure and fruitful labor (v. 21ff.). But death is still present (v. 20), so it is not a description of the final state, heaven. This should not be surprising. In other places, Scripture uses such powerfully contrasting language to describe radical spiritual changes without suggesting changes in the physical world (e.g., Isa. 13:9–10; 34:4; Ezek. 32:7–8; Amos 8:9; Matt. 24:29; Heb. 12:26). So when we read of the new heavens and the new earth, we should think of the culmination of the covenant on earth, as depicted in Isaiah, blending with images of the final state in the background.

Revelation 21 continues, "And I saw the holy city, new Jerusalem, . . . made ready as a bride adorned for her husband" (v. 2). Here we read of the holy city sought by Abraham (Heb. 11:10), a city made by God. As we have seen, this image is used in the Prophets to depict the fulfillment of the Abrahamic promise of a people and a land (Isa. 2:11). Moreover, the common covenantal image of a bride is used to depict God's people, thus giving us a rich image—both city and bride—of God's people descending from heaven.

The passage continues, "And I heard a loud voice from the throne saying, 'Behold, the tabernacle of God is among men, and He shall dwell among them, and they shall be His people, and God Himself shall be among them' " (Rev. 21:3). The Lord dwelt closely with His people in Eden, but only at a distance after that, even in the tabernacle and later the temple.

In Christ's incarnation, and in the indwelling and sanctification of His people through the ages, especially in the latter glorious years, the central promise of union and communion is realized more than ever.

Further along John writes, "And he carried me away in the Spirit to a great and high mountain, and showed me the holy city, Jerusalem, coming down out of heaven from God, having the glory of God. Her brilliance was like a very costly stone, as a stone of crystal-clear jasper" (Rev. 21:10–11). At this point in the chapter, the Lord uses the image of a great mountain and city again, as was common in the Old Covenant prophecies of future glory (cf. Heb. 12:22–23). So once more God's people are depicted with familiar Old Covenant imagery.

John describes the Holy City: "It had a great high wall, with twelve gates, and at the gates twelve angels; and names were written on them, which are those of the twelve tribes of the sons of Israel. . . . And the wall of the city had twelve foundation stones, and on them were the twelve names of the twelve apostles of the Lamb" (Rev. 21:12–14). This image depicts the covenantal unity between the Old and New Covenants, as the Abrahamic line and the New Covenant apostles constitute parts of the same structure, the same people of the one covenant (cf. Heb. 3:2–6; Eph. 2:20).

The description of the city continues, "The foundation stones of the city wall were adorned with every kind of precious stone. . . . And I saw no temple in it, for the Lord God, the Almighty, and the Lamb, are its Temple" (Rev. 21:19, 22). Like Eden, the city of God is depicted as being jeweled with precious stones. And the city has no temple, for the Old Covenant temple was just a shadow of union and communion. But Christ is the real temple (John 2:21), the real dwelling of God with His people.

John adds, "And the nations shall walk by its light, and the kings of the earth shall bring their glory into it" (Rev. 21:24). In fulfillment of the Abrahamic promise, here we see the city (the people) of God extending the blessings of faithful obedience to all nations and kings as depicted in Isaiah chapters 2 and 11 and elsewhere.

John's vision continues in Revelation 22.

> And he showed me a river of the water of life, clear as crystal, coming from the throne of God and of the Lamb, in the middle of its street. And on either side of the river was the tree of life. . . . And there shall no longer be any curse; and the throne of God and of the Lamb shall be in it, and His bond-servants shall serve him;

and they shall see His face, and His name shall be on their foreheads. . . . [A]nd they shall reign forever and ever. (vv. 1–5)

Here we see another link to Eden—the river that flows from the throne of
God and of the Lamb (Gen. 2:10; cf. Ezek. 47). And we also see the Tree
of Life, which the Lord denied to Adam after the Fall, but which the Lamb
of God restored to His people through the inheritance of eternal life. Furthermore, we see that the curse imposed at the Fall will be lifted. As Christ's
kingdom spreads throughout the world, sin and the curse progressively recede as He conquers His enemies, until He completely removes the curse
at the end.

The final portion of this passage shows God's people in covenant
with Him as servants, wearing His mark of ownership on their foreheads,
thus truly in union and communion with their covenant Lord.

The images of God's people as described at the end of Revelation
give us an overview of God's completed covenant work, the completed
mosaic, the completed intricate chain that started before Eden and culmi-
nates in the fulfillment of the promise of a land and a people. This glorious
redemption of the vast majority of people in history and the restoration of
the whole world by the Spirit of God gives us a far deeper understanding of
Christ's claim that "God so loved *the world,* that He gave His only begot-
ten Son, that whoever believes in Him should not perish, but have eternal
life. For God did not send the Son into the world to judge the world; but
that *the world should be saved* through Him" (John 3:16–17). This goal will
most assuredly be realized because the Lord Himself has promised, "I will
be exalted among the *nations,* I will be exalted in the *earth*" (Ps. 46:10).
And for this great covenant work, past, present, and future, all God's people joyfully bow and confess as one: "To Him who sits on the throne, and
to the Lamb, be blessing and honor and glory and dominion forever and
ever" (Rev. 5:13). Amen.

STUDY QUESTIONS

1. Explain the structure of the popular end-times view. How does the covenantal view contrast with the popular millennial view? What are some
of the biblical difficulties with the popular millennial view? Which view
do you hold and why? Is it ever right to believe something just because
it is popular? What is our standard for determining what is true and
what is false?

2. How do the descriptions of the Last Judgment point to a final antithesis between the seed of the woman and the seed of the Serpent (see Matt. 25:32–34; Rev. 20:11–15)? Why has Christ been given "authority to execute judgment" (see Deut. 32:43; John 5:29; Rev. 6:10)? Will anyone have an excuse for unbelief on the Day of Judgment according to Romans 1:18–20? Do these truths motivate you to proclaim the gospel to the enemies of Christ?

3. When God promised Abraham that all the families of the earth would be blessed, did He thereby imply that believing families would constitute a numerical minority or majority? How do Pss. 22:16–19, 26–27; 102:15, 19–22; Isa. 49:6; 54:2–5, 13; 61:9, 11; 66:10, 12; Jer. 31:31–34; Ezek. 37:24, 26, 28; Amos 9:11–12; Zech. 8:22; Mal. 1:11; Matt. 28:19 amplify this promise to Abraham? Do these prophesies refer to heaven? Why not? What specific hope do these prophesies offer you?

Notes

1. John Murray, *The Epistle to the Romans* (Grand Rapids: Eerdmans, 1965), 79.

PART THREE

BACK TO THE CHURCH

Roger Wagner

INTRODUCTION

We have seen that the Reformed faith starts and stops with the sovereign and gracious God who has revealed Himself in Scripture. Equally important to the Reformed faith, as we have also seen, is the way in which this sovereign and gracious God deals with His people and their offspring by entering into a covenantal relationship with them.

The sovereignty of God and His covenantal dealings with His people, in turn, shape what the Reformed faith says about the church. God calls us into a covenantal relationship not only with Himself, but also with one another in the church.

In this part of the book, we will examine how God calls us out of the world together as His church, commands us to worship Him in spirit and in truth, gives us the water and the wine as means of growing in His grace, and provides us with the oversight of elders who rule and teach in accordance with Holy Scripture.

Today, when many people think of the church as an optional feature of their Christian lives, we need to get back to basics—back to the church. [D. G. H.]

TWELVE

JOINING THE FOLD

For many people, the word *church* conjures up visions of gothic cathedrals, New England meetinghouses, spires and pulpits and pews—things having to do with buildings. According to Scripture, though, the church is not a place but a people. The church, to be a bit more precise, is the community of God's covenant people.

Contrary to the modern assumption that the church burst on the scene at Pentecost, the Bible teaches that the church has existed as long as God has been redeeming His people. Under the Old Covenant, the church was manifest as a family (e.g., the patriarchal families of Abraham, Isaac, and Jacob), a people (Deut. 6:7–8), and a nation (Ex. 19:5). It was associated in a particular way with the living presence of God, symbolized by the tabernacle and later by the temple, where God caused His name—His very presence—to dwell (Deut. 12:5–8; 1 Kings 8:29; Ezra 6:12).

With the coming of Christ and the New Covenant, the international character of the church, implicit from the beginning (Gen. 12:3; cf. 28:14; Acts 3:25; Gal. 3:8), became more clearly and fully revealed with the ingrafting of the Gentiles (Gal. 3:14; Eph. 3:4–6). Paul encouraged his Gentile converts by writing, "You are no longer foreigners and aliens, but fellow citizens with God's people and members of God's household" (Eph. 2:19). The time had come, about which Jesus had spoken to the woman at the well:

> Believe me, woman, a time is coming when you will worship the
> Father neither on this mountain nor in Jerusalem. You Samari-

143

tans worship what you do not know; we worship what we do know, for salvation is from the Jews. Yet a time is coming and has now come when the true worshipers will worship the Father in spirit and truth, for they are the kind of worshipers the Father seeks. God is spirit, and his worshipers must worship in spirit and in truth. (John 4:21–24)

No longer was the location of worship as important as it had been before (Deut. 12). With the coming of the glorious fullness of the New Covenant, the *manner* of true worship became paramount. The New Covenant church, like that of the Old Covenant, is described in terms of its special relationship to God (1 Tim. 3:15). Like their forefathers, the members of the New Testament church, whom Peter addressed as "strangers in the world, scattered throughout Pontus, Galatia, Cappadocia, Asia and Bithynia" (1 Peter 1:1), were just as much "a chosen people, a royal priesthood, a holy nation, a people belonging to God" (1 Peter 2:9) as the saints of old had been.

Thus, there is one church—the people of God—which God has redeemed "from every tribe and language and people and nation" (Rev. 5:9) by the shedding of Christ's precious blood. That church, bought with the dear price of Christ's precious blood, ought to draw our keen attention and elicit our deepest affection so that, along with Timothy Dwight, we can sing,

> I love thy kingdom, Lord
> The house of thine abode,
> The church our blest Redeemer saved
> With his own precious blood.
>
> For her my tears shall fall,
> For her my prayers ascend;
> To her my cares and toils be giv'n,
> Till toils and cares shall end.
>
> Beyond my highest joy
> I prize her heav'nly ways,
> Her sweet communion, solemn vows,
> Her hymns of love and praise.[1]

While such ecclesiastical sentiments are not found exclusively in Reformed churches, they nonetheless characterize true Reformed piety and worship.

MEMBERS ONE OF ANOTHER

Many Christians recognize that God sheds His redeeming grace abroad in the hearts of His people when He brings them into a covenantal relationship with Himself in conversion. What they sometimes fail to recognize, however, is that Christ simultaneously brings us to Himself *and to His church* by the same sovereign acts of calling and regeneration.

Note how Paul addresses the Corinthian church: "To the *church* of God in Corinth, to *those sanctified in Christ Jesus and called to be holy*, together with all those everywhere who call on the name of our Lord Jesus Christ—their Lord and ours" (1 Cor. 1:2). In this passage, the apostle speaks of "the church of God" as those who have been "sanctified in Christ Jesus and called to be holy." The Greek term translated "church" in the New Testament is *ekklesia*, which, like the Hebrew term *qahal*, literally refers to an assembly of those who have been "called out" of a larger body for a particular purpose. The church, therefore, is the assembly of those who have been *called out* of the world by the preaching of the gospel and *called together* to worship and serve God through faith and obedience to Jesus Christ.

Church membership is understood in terms of holiness, to which men and women are called through the faithful preaching of the Word and the sovereign working of the Holy Spirit. For this reason, the members of the church are consistently addressed as "saints" or "holy ones" (Rom. 1:1; Eph. 1:1; Phil. 1:1).

Individual church members are holy because of what Christ, by His death and resurrection, has done for the church as a whole: "Christ loved the church and gave himself up for her to make her holy, cleansing her by the washing with water through the word" (Eph. 5:25–26). Paul speaks of the church here in the singular, stressing her corporate unity. The cleansing provided by Christ was, first of all, for the sake of the church in her corporate identity as His bride, but also, by extension, for each individual believer who is called by the Holy Spirit into communion with the church.

Although this point can be and has been misunderstood, *as individuals we experience the saving blessings of the gospel as we are united with the church.* This is so not because those benefits are mediated by the church as the channel of God's grace, but rather because those benefits are mediated by Christ, through the Holy Spirit, directly to the church of which we are members.

Paul emphasizes that blessings come to the individual believer as a result of the provisions that God has made for the whole church. For example, Paul says to the Corinthians,

The body is a unit, though it is made up of many parts; and though all its parts are many, they form one body. So it is with Christ. For we were all baptized by one Spirit into one body—whether Jews or Greeks, slave or free—and we were all given the one Spirit to drink. Now the body is not made up of one part but of many. (1 Cor. 12:12–14)

Or consider his words to the Ephesians: "There is one body and one Spirit—just as you were called to one hope when you were called—one Lord, one faith, one baptism; one God and Father of all, who is over all and through all and in all" (Eph. 4:4–6).

This part-to-whole dynamic is not only characteristic of God's working with His people at any given period of history, but also true over time. According to Paul, the Gentiles enjoyed the blessings of salvation in Christ at a comparatively late stage in redemptive history because they had been incorporated into that church which had its "root" in the patriarchs and, with them, in the ancient blessings of the covenant that God promised to Abraham.

If the *root* is holy, so are the branches. If some of the branches have been broken off, and you, though a wild olive shoot, have been *grafted in* among the others and now *share in the nourishing sap from the olive root,* do not boast over those branches. If you do, consider this: You do not support the root, but *the root supports you.* . . . After all, if you were cut out of an olive tree that is wild by nature, and contrary to nature were *grafted into* a cultivated olive tree, how much more readily will these, the natural branches, be *grafted into* their own olive tree! (Rom. 11:16–18, 24)

This branch-to-root metaphor emphasizes the central importance of the single source of blessing (the root) upon which each individual beneficiary (branch) depends. Jesus used the same metaphor in describing the believer's relationship to Him as the true vine.

I am the true vine, and my Father is the gardener. . . . I am the vine; you are the branches. If a man remains in me and I in him, he will bear much fruit; apart from me you can do nothing. If anyone does not remain in me, he is like a branch that is thrown away and withers; such branches are picked up, thrown into the fire and burned. (John 15:1, 5–6)

If we combine the branch-to-root and branch-to-vine metaphors, we can see that the believer must abide in the church in a manner parallel to the way he abides in Christ, and that the blessings of the gospel flow to the believer as a member of the church.

I stress this point because too many Christians today think that their relationship to Christ has little or nothing to do with their relationship to the church. To them the church is peripheral, at best. They may become church members, but that is considered an additional or optional feature of their Christian experience. If they leave the church, or fail to fulfill the terms of their membership, they do not see that as compromising their standing as Christians in any way. According to this view, "being a Christian" and "being a church member" are completely separate matters.

The Bible, by contrast, speaks of the intimate connection between the believer and the church. Luke tells us, for instance, that individuals who responded to the apostolic preaching of the Good News became Christians and were added to the church as part of the same experience of conversion: "Those who accepted [Peter's] message [on the Day of Pentecost] were baptized, and about three thousand were added to their number that day" (Acts 2:41). Whose number? The church's.

Right after the Ascension, the apostles in Jerusalem were joined by Mary (Jesus' mother), some other women, Jesus' brothers, and other believers (a total of about one hundred and twenty people). "They all joined together constantly in prayer" in an upstairs room where the apostles were staying (Acts 1:12–14). Later, as the church continued to grow, Luke tells us, "Every day they continued to meet together in the temple courts. They broke bread in their homes and ate together with glad and sincere hearts, praising God and enjoying the favor of all the people. And the Lord added to their number daily those who were being saved" (Acts 2:46–47).

Take careful note of the pattern—the church is assembled, the gospel is preached to the surrounding multitude, those who believe the message are "called out," responding to the gospel by repenting and receiving baptism. In this way, men and women move from the world to the church and thus to Christ. As Peter says, God has "called you out of darkness into his wonderful light" (1 Peter 2:9).

One becomes a Christian and a church member at the same time, and by the same means! Indeed, according to Scripture, becoming a Christian is ordinarily synonymous with becoming a member of the church.

THERE'S NO PLACE LIKE HOME

Several years ago I was talking about evangelism to a fellow minister when I said that one cannot become a Christian only in the privacy of one's own living room. He was somewhat taken aback by the statement, and asked what I meant. He was especially concerned in light of the many door-to-door evangelism programs that have been developed to help people become Christians in the privacy of their own homes.

Of course, I was not saying that the New Testament frowns on door-to-door evangelism. My point was that when the New Testament speaks of "becoming a Christian," it has much more in view than many contemporary evangelicals suppose. Specifically, becoming a Christian involves more than just believing the gospel and receiving Christ (though both are essential first steps). It must include a definitive act of "coming out" in response to the call of the gospel. According to the biblical pattern, those who come out in this way are to receive baptism and consequently identify with the church, participate in the worship and service of the covenant community, and submit to its leadership. Genuine converts, in other words, will come out of the world. They will stand up and be counted with God's people.

COME OUT, COME OUT, WHEREVER YOU ARE

"But," you may protest, "what about the 'invisible church'? The relationship between conversion and church membership that you have been stressing has nothing to do with the invisible church that we join when we are converted."

True, the concept of the invisible church does highlight some important biblical features about the nature of the church, but it cannot be understood properly apart from the related notion of the visible church. Indeed, the whole distinction between the visible and invisible church may be misleading, and has sometimes proved to be more dangerous than helpful.

The idea of the invisible church is a theological construct that seeks to express some truths about the church as viewed from God's omniscient perspective. A classic expression of this concept is found in the Westminster Confession of Faith: "The catholic or universal church, which is invisible, consists of the whole number of the elect, that have been, are, or shall be gathered into one, under Christ the Head thereof; and is the spouse, the body, the fullness of him that filleth all in all" (25.1).

The confession emphasizes what God knows about the church: He alone knows the exact number and identity of the elect; He alone looks upon the heart and therefore knows infallibly those who are His own; He alone looks upon the church without being limited by time and space. God knows the church and her membership in ways no finite human being can ever expect to know her.

So far so good, since the characteristics of the church indicated by the phrase *invisible church* are thoroughly biblical. But then a problem arises. Many give this theological construct a life all of its own! Many Christians imagine that the invisible church has an existence distinct, if not separate, from the visible church—the church in the world as we know it. After separating the invisible from the visible in this way, many then take the next step by imagining that their relationship to Christ and His invisible church has little, if any, bearing on their relationship to the visible church in which they are to worship and to whose leadership they are to submit.

This kind of reasoning led John Murray to conclude that the "distinction between the church visible and the church invisible is not well-grounded in terms of Scripture."[2] To substantiate this conclusion, Murray argues that

> even in those passages in which the concept of the "church invisible" might appear to be present, the case is rather that there is no evidence for the notion of the "church" as an invisible entity distinct from the church visible. As noted earlier, there are those aspects pertaining to the church that may be characterized as invisible. But it is to "the church" those aspects pertain, and "the church" in the New Testament never appears as an invisible entity and therefore may never be defined in terms of invisibility.[3]

Having examined the ways the construct of the invisible church is misleading, Murray goes on to discuss briefly the ways in which this distinction has affected the life of the church. To Murray, this distinction has led believers to suppress their "corporate responsibility" within the church. As a result, believers have sometimes failed to maintain the purity and proper unity of the church because they have mistakenly attributed those characteristics only to the invisible church.

Some contemporary evangelicals also press this distinction between the visible and the invisible church into service to justify other abuses as well. By imagining that they need only be members of the invisible church, they neglect to worship on the Lord's Day, participate in the sacraments, submit to the biblical authority of church leaders, or heed the discipline of the church. Murray long ago asked those so inclined where in the New Testament they could find an invisible church where they could fellowship concretely and practically the way they are commanded to do so in Scripture. No one has ever answered Murray's question. And no one ever will.

THE CHURCH BEFORE A WATCHING WORLD

One of the most distressing difficulties facing church leaders who seek to be faithful to their biblical charge over their flock (1 Peter 5:2) is trying to keep track of "invisible sheep" who insist on remaining disassociated with the visible church in favor of being enfolded in the invisible church.

In a culture like that of contemporary America, where some significant cultural influences of Christianity remain, even where there may be little or no vital faith left, the dividing line between the church and the world can easily be blurred since it is possible for individuals to involve themselves with the church only to the degree they find convenient. The oft-heard charge that "the church is full of hypocrites" is no doubt partially justified by the fact that in our culture, people think that they can be called to Christ without being decisively called out of the world.

Many today consider church discipline and submission to the authoritative ministry of the overseers in the church more or less optional, even though both are essential to maintaining sound doctrine and holy living (2 Tim. 4:2–4; Titus 2:15; Heb. 13:17). It comes as no surprise, then, that the church is unable to maintain the consistent holiness that must adorn her profession in the eyes of a watching world if the charge of hypocrisy is to be avoided.

In overtly and pervasively pagan lands like those often encountered by foreign missionaries, the call to Christ often entails an obvious and profound breach with the surrounding culture. Embracing Christ in such cultures requires embracing the church as well, for the new convert becomes a cultural alien almost immediately. Facing the rejection of family and neighbors, he must seek the fellowship of the body of Christ. His identity in Christ carries with it an identification with the church.

While such converts often encounter vicious persecution, their conversion to Christ and His church more closely approximates the New Testament pattern than does that of the average American convert. In "post-Christian" American culture, by contrast, we are fooled into thinking that it is possible (at least to some degree) to live in fellowship with Christ apart from His church. Thus, the biblical call to make a radical breach with the world when we come to Christ grates on us (e.g., Matt. 6:24; James 4:4; 1 John 2:15). We think it is too extreme.

In our culture, we need to stress the importance of the visible church, with its worship, sacraments, officers, and discipline more than ever. The Reformed faith, with its unique doctrine of the church, should open the eyes of all who name the name of Christ. Murray once wrote that the church is

> that visible entity that exists and functions in accord with the institution of Christ as its Head, the church that is the body of Christ indwelt and directed by the Holy Spirit, consisting of those sanctified in Christ Jesus and called to be saints, manifested in the congregations of the faithful, and finally the church glorious, holy and without blemish.[4]

Oh, that we would all become responsible members of congregations of the faithful! If only we would see that "joining the church"—the visible community of God's people—is not an optional second step after conversion. To come to Christ is to come to His church.

The church is the sphere of God's covenant blessing. God extends His saving grace to the church and to individual believers within the fellowship of the church. He does so not by means of a mediatorial priesthood acting as the channel of His grace, but by the means He has appointed—worshiping His name by hearing His Word, offering prayer and praise, receiving the sacraments, and receiving both oversight and discipline.

In the chapters that follow, we will examine these precious means by which God sovereignly extends His grace to us as we gather together with His covenant people.

STUDY QUESTIONS

1. Are we brought to Christ and then, at some subsequent point in time, to His church? Support your answer from Scripture.
2. Can believers really experience the saving blessings of the gospel as

they unite themselves to the church? Does this mean that such blessings are dispensed by the church or the priesthood as a channel of God's grace? What does it mean?

3. Describe the distinction between the "visible" and the "invisible" church. In what ways is this distinction helpful? In what ways might it be harmful? Where in the New Testament are believers commanded to fellowship concretely and practically with the invisible church? How about with the visible church? In what ways do you need to assume your responsibility to the corporate body of believers in a visible church?

Notes

1. "I Love Thy Kingdom, Lord," *Trinity Hymnal* (Philadelphia: Great Commission Publications, 1990), 353.
2. John Murray, "The Church—Its Identity, Functions, and Resources," *Collected Writings*, 4 vols. (Edinburgh: Banner of Truth, 1976), 1:231–32.
3. Ibid., 234.
4. Ibid., 236.

THIRTEEN

IN SPIRIT AND IN TRUTH

In Psalm 100 the people of God receive their highest calling from the Lord—the call to worship.

> Shout for joy to the LORD, all the earth. Worship the LORD with gladness; come before him with joyful songs. Know that the LORD is God. It is he who made us, and we are his; we are his people, the sheep of his pasture. Enter his gates with thanksgiving and his courts with praise; give thanks to him and praise his name. For the LORD is good and his love endures forever; his faithfulness continues through all generations.

Every Christian enjoys the high privilege and responsibility of worshiping the Lord. Page after page in Scripture emphasizes the importance of worship in the lives of God's people. From the days of Enosh "men began to call on the name of the LORD" (Gen. 4:26). The chosen people of God are called to worship: "Ascribe to the LORD the glory due his name; worship the LORD in the splendor of his holiness" (Ps. 29:2). All the earth is called to worship the Lord in light of His universal sovereignty and His mighty deeds: "Sing to the LORD a new song; sing to the LORD, all the earth" (Ps. 96:1). "All the nations you have made will come and worship before you, O LORD; they will bring glory to your name" (Ps. 86:9).

The hope fostered by the Old Covenant includes the gathering of the nations from the ends of the earth to worship the Lord: "In the last days the mountain of the LORD's temple will be established as chief among the mountains; it will be raised above the hills, and all nations will stream to it. Many peoples will come and say, 'Come, let us go up to the mountain of the LORD, to the house of the God of Jacob. He will teach us his ways, so that we may walk in his paths' " (Isa. 2:2–4).

At that time, even the ancient enemies of Israel will become faithful worshipers of God: "In that day there will be a highway from Egypt to Assyria. The Assyrians will go to Egypt and the Egyptians to Assyria. The Egyptians and Assyrians will worship together" (Isa. 19:23). In fulfillment of this expectation, the book of Revelation describes the praises offered by the diverse multitudes of the earth joined with the worship of the hosts of heaven, glorifying God for the gracious salvation He has brought through His Son.

> After this I looked and there before me was a great multitude that no one could count, from every nation, tribe, people and language, standing before the throne and in front of the Lamb. They were wearing white robes and were holding palm branches in their hands. And they cried out in a loud voice: "Salvation belongs to our God, who sits on the throne, and to the Lamb." All the angels were standing around the throne and around the elders and the four living creatures. They fell down on their faces before the throne and worshiped God, saying: "Amen! Praise and glory and wisdom and thanks and honor and power and strength be to our God for ever and ever. Amen!" (Rev. 7:9–12)

From cover to cover, Scripture calls us as God's people to worship Him, and tells us that it is a privilege we will enjoy for ever and ever.

A RICH HERITAGE

The Reformers well understood the biblical emphasis upon worship, particularly corporate worship, and sought to free it from medieval accretions and superstitions. In particular, they sought to restore worship to its simple glory, since worship occurs when God meets with His people as they solemnly assemble together in His name.

Although American evangelicals, in some sense, are heirs of the Reformation, in our century they have sadly neglected their rich Reformation heritage with regard to worship. Indeed, the contemporary church has too often neglected the whole subject of worship to her detriment. As Ronald Allen and Gordon Borror have correctly pointed out,

> We who are identified with evangelical Christianity are hard put to demonstrate any serious concern for worship in this century. As scholars we have failed to study worship, or give attention to the theology of worship. Principles of biblical worship are not sought as the foundation of local church practice. Most of our evangelical seminaries have not even offered full courses in worship.[1]

Robert Rayburn calls attention to the same deficiency among even some Bible-believing churches when he writes that the

> worship of God is at once the true believer's most important activity and at the same time it is one of the most tragically neglected activities in the average evangelical church today. . . . There remains . . . among sincere believers today a woeful ignorance concerning the significance of true worship and the means of attaining the blessing of rich, rewarding corporate worship.[2]

While some signs have pointed to a revived interest in the subject of worship and the biblical principles that should guide our worship, if the evangelical community is to be true to its Reformation heritage, it still has a lot of lost ground to recover.

Over against much of modern evangelicalism, the Reformed tradition has consistently maintained a serious concern for the biblical principles of worship since the sixteenth century. The Westminster Confession of Faith devotes an entire chapter to the subject of religious worship and the Lord's Day.[3] In addition, the Westminster Assembly produced a directory for the public worship of God, which sets forth detailed instructions on many elements in worship. Other Reformed churches have produced similar handbooks to guide both public and private worship. These documents attest to the importance that Reformed churches have placed on the theology and practice of worship. And they will pay great spiritual dividends to those who invest in studying them.

THE GLORY AND JOY OF TRUE WORSHIP

If, as the Reformed faith teaches, man's chief goal in all of life is to glorify God and to enjoy Him forever (Westminster Shorter Catechism, Q. 1; cf.

1 Cor. 10:31), then certainly worship, man's highest calling, his most blessed work, should be guided and directed by this principle. Glorifying God should be the highest purpose of our worship, and enjoying Him, its deepest benefit.

Because the Reformed faith strongly emphasizes the sovereignty of God, Reformed churches have traditionally emphasized the centrality of God in corporate worship. In light of the man-centered and so-called "need"-oriented concerns that have set the agenda for worship in many American evangelical churches today, it is vital that we rediscover together the glorious biblical truth that worship, from beginning to end, should center on God. Thus, God's people have one central task in worship: bringing honor and glory to God in response to their growing understanding of His mercy and grace in Christ. Only then will we truly grow in grace in worship and find our true needs—as He has defined them—to be fully satisfied. Only then will we truly glorify and enjoy Him in worship.

God's call to worship is a call to praise and adore the Creator of the heavens and the earth, the gracious Redeemer of His people.

> Come, let us sing for joy to the LORD; let us shout aloud to the Rock of our salvation. Let us come before him with thanksgiving and extol him with music and song. For the LORD is the great God, the great King above all gods. In his hand are the depths of the earth, and the mountain peaks belong to him. The sea is his, for he made it, and his hands formed the dry land. Come, let us bow down in worship, let us kneel before the LORD our Maker; for he is our God and we are the people of his pasture, the flock under his care. (Ps. 95:1–7)

> Ascribe to the LORD, O mighty ones, ascribe to the LORD glory and strength. Ascribe to the LORD the glory due his name; worship the LORD in the splendor of his holiness. . . . The LORD sits enthroned over the flood; the LORD is enthroned as King forever. The LORD gives strength to his people; the LORD blesses his people with peace. (Ps. 29:1–2, 10–11)

Man's every meditation on the heavens above, the world around him, and even upon his own existence and nature, should lead his thoughts Godward in wonder and thanksgiving: "The heavens declare the glory of God; the skies proclaim the work of his hands" (Ps. 19:1). "How many are your works, O LORD! In wisdom you made them all; the earth is full of your creatures" (Ps. 104:24). "I praise you because I am fearfully and wonderfully made; your works are wonderful, I know that full well. . . . How precious to me are your thoughts, O God! How vast is the sum of them! (Ps. 139:14, 17). In worship, as in all of life, man's highest purpose is to glorify God.

But worship is also the setting in which we can most fully enjoy God's presence. It is true that God walks with His people through every experience of life, but we often do not sense His presence as we should. In corporate worship we have the best opportunity to know and feel the blessed presence of God. That anticipated joy was behind the psalmist's eagerness to attend the worship of God: "How lovely is your dwelling place, O LORD Almighty! My soul yearns, even faints, for the courts of the LORD; my heart and my flesh cry out for the living God. . . . Blessed are those who dwell in your house; they are ever praising you" (Ps. 84:1–2, 4). To enter the courts of the Lord was to enjoy blessed union and communion with the faithful covenant kinsman-Redeemer of Israel.

When the believer contemplates all the bitter and disappointing complexities of life within this fallen and cursed world, he finds his consolation in the reality of worship. It is "in the sanctuary" that he remembers that what is most important in life—the enjoyment of God—can never be taken from him.

> When I tried to understand [why the wicked prosper and the righteous suffer], it was oppressive to me till I entered the sanctuary of God; then I understood their final destiny. . . . When my heart was grieved and my spirit embittered, I was senseless and ignorant; I was a brute beast before you. Yet I am always with you; you hold me by my right hand. You guide me with your counsel, and afterward you will take me into glory. Whom have I in heaven but you? And earth has nothing I desire besides you. My flesh and my heart may fail, but God is the strength of my heart and my portion forever. Those who are far from you will perish; you destroy all who are unfaithful to you. But as for me, it is good to be near God. I have made the Sovereign LORD my refuge; I will tell of all your deeds. (Ps. 73:16–17, 21–28)

Worship, when understood biblically, is not simply an obligation but also a tremendous privilege. On the one hand, it is the highest duty of the creature toward his Creator. On the other, it is the greatest blessing the redeemed sinner receives from his gracious Lord and Savior. What draws us to worship, then, is both loving devotion and eager anticipation of the gift of God's mercy: "One thing I ask of the LORD, this is what I seek: that I may dwell in the house of the LORD all the days of my life, to gaze upon the beauty of the LORD and to seek him in his temple" (Ps. 27:4).

Many American evangelicals today have lost sight of this biblical balance, however. A very understandable and laudable concern for evangelism has come to dominate their thinking about the nature of worship. Meeting man's self-perceived "needs" has taken precedence over bringing worship and praise to God. In doing so, man's true need has been trivialized. In its worst form, this man-centered emphasis sets an agenda for worship governed not by Scripture, but by human priorities. Sermons that set forth the realities of "righteousness, self-control and the judgment to come" are considered too threatening to the non-believer's self-esteem—after all, one such sermon certainly "turned off" Felix (Acts 24:25)! These biblical themes are thus abandoned in favor of what is thought to be a more "positive approach."

Another consequence of such a man-centered focus in worship is the conviction that worship must be scaled-down and simplified for the sake of the unbelieving and "unchurched" visitor for whom the forms and content of worship may be difficult to understand. Preaching may even give way altogether to other forms of communication, such as video or multimedia presentations and dramatic skits, on the assumption that contemporary members of the "TV generation" will not respond well to a "talking head." The "sound bite" replaces the reasoned discourse of apostolic days (cf. Act 17:2, 7; 18:4) as the source of spiritual instruction.

While we should always be concerned to evangelize and build bridges to our contemporary culture, we must see that when those concerns dominate our corporate worship, we almost always fail to do an adequate job evangelizing or offering meaningful worship to God. Evangelism may take place incidentally as a result of God-centered worship (1 Cor 14:24–25), and certainly the people of God will be built up in the process of worship (v. 12; Eph. 4:12). But those concerns must never be allowed to diminish or eclipse the God-centered character of true biblical worship. We will only properly enjoy the blessings of God promised in Scripture if we first give glory to God as commanded by the Scriptures.

The Westminster Confession of Faith stresses this point when it declares, "Religious worship is to be given to God, the Father, Son, and Holy Ghost; and to him alone; not to angels, saints, or any other creature: and, since the fall, not without a Mediator; nor in the mediation of any other but Christ alone" (21.2). Seen in this way, worship is the response of the

Christian to the glory and grace of God, which is revealed uniquely in the midst of their assemblies when God's Word is faithfully preached and His sacraments are rightly observed. Our response in worship takes the form of praying, singing praises, and giving offerings.

ACCESS DENIED AND GRANTED

God is not only the central focus of worship, but also the only one who grants access into His presence in worship. From the beginning, it has been God who has come to us—who has made Himself available by voluntarily condescending to us—and opened a way of access for us to fellowship with Him and offer worship to Him. As creatures, we owe our Creator worship and service, but He alone has the authority to set the terms by which we do so. This He does by means of His Word, the Holy Scriptures.

But the worship of God has been hindered by the entrance of sin into the world. Since the fall of Adam, sinners have been excluded from the presence of God: "So the LORD God banished him from the Garden of Eden to work the ground from which he had been taken. After he drove the man out, he placed on the east side of the Garden of Eden cherubim and a flaming sword flashing back and forth to guard the way to the tree of life" (Gen. 3:23–24). For sinners, true fellowship and worship are now blocked by the angel's flaming sword of judgment. Death—the curse of God upon man's sin—has now intervened. Because of their sin, sinners everywhere are excluded from worshiping God.

Oblivious to this fact, unbelievers often wrongly assume that access into the presence of God can be found anywhere. They also assume that they themselves must devise a system of religious observances and ceremonies to enter into His presence. Their idols, their sacrifices, and their superstitions are all efforts to unlock the door—efforts that are all doomed to failure from the outset.

Since mankind has rejected the true knowledge of God, he is unable to worship Him properly and fellowship with Him. True worship must be mediated by Christ (or, in times past, by His Old Covenant precursors like the Levitical priests). It must also conform to the express dictates of His Word; merely avoiding overt idolatry is not enough.

Since the Fall, sinners can only be restored to the true worship of God if God Himself intervenes and redeems them. When the true worshiper of God entered the Old Covenant sanctuary (the tabernacle or later the temple), he was confronted with the bronze laver and the altar of burnt offerings. The laver and the altar served as visual reminders that God had to provide for man's salvation in order for him even to be permitted to enter into the presence of the Lord.

When Jesus appeared upon the earth in the fullness of time, He declared Himself to be "the way and the truth and the life." He claimed to be the exclusive mediator between God and man: "No one comes to the Father except through me" (John 14:6; cf. 10:7; 1 Tim. 2:5). True worship, then, must involve the mediation of Christ. By His death, Jesus made the ultimate satisfaction for the judgment of God against sin (Heb. 9:11–14, 23–28), and, as a result, believers can again draw near to God in fellowship and worship.

> Therefore, brothers, since we have confidence to enter the Most Holy Place by the blood of Jesus, by a new and living way opened for us through the curtain, that is, his body, and since we have a great priest over the house of God, let us draw near to God with a sincere heart in full assurance of faith, having our hearts sprinkled to cleanse us from a guilty conscience and having our bodies washed with pure water. (Heb. 10:19–22)

By faith in Jesus Christ, men and women can gain access into the presence of God again, overcoming the barrier presented by their sin.

RULES AND REGULATIONS

Once the barrier of sin has been overcome by faith in Christ, and the forgiveness that flows from it, one question still remains: What constitutes acceptable worship? Jesus discussed this very question with the Samaritan woman at the well.

> Believe me, woman, a time is coming when you will worship the Father neither on this mountain nor in Jerusalem. You Samaritans worship what you do not know; we worship what we do know, for salvation is from the Jews. Yet a time is coming and has now come when the true worshipers will worship the Father in spirit and truth, for they are the kind of worshipers the Father seeks. God is spirit, and his worshipers must worship in spirit and in truth. (John 4:21–24)

As we noted earlier, Jesus makes it clear that with His coming, the place of worship (e.g., on Mt. Zion in Jerusalem or on Mt. Gerazim) is no longer relevant. The paramount question now is how true worship should be offered. Jesus accused the Samaritans of worshiping in ignorance, while the Jews followed the biblical pattern (at least formally). Worship that is acceptable to God must be offered "in spirit and truth."

Since sin continues to be a problem, even for believers, we must not trust either our traditions or our instincts to lead us into proper worship. If our worship is to be acceptable and pleasing to God, we must rather look to the Word of the Spirit in Scripture to direct our efforts. God's Word is truth (John 17:17), and from it alone can we learn what constitutes true worship.

For this reason, the Westminster Confession states that "the acceptable way of worshiping the true God is instituted by himself, and so limited by his own revealed will, that he may not be worshiped . . . any other way not prescribed in the Holy Scripture" (21.1). This statement has come to be known as "the regulative principle of worship," since it regulates or governs the type of worship we may offer to God. Phrased somewhat differently, the regulative principle of worship provides that *whatever is not prescribed in Scripture is thereby prohibited in worship.* Or, put positively, we can only do in worship what Scripture prescribes.

This principle for regulating our worship is important (especially in our day and age) because we believers frequently assume that our personal preferences or tastes are a sufficient guide to knowing what will please God in worship. We also have a tendency to believe that what has been traditionally offered to God in worship is acceptable to Him. Or we believe that as long as we are sincere in worship, God will be pleased, regardless of the forms our worship takes,[4] apparently forgetting that one can be sincerely wrong.

Those who offer worship contrary to Scripture are playing with fire—literally. In Leviticus 10, we read of Aaron's sons, Nadab and Abihu, who offered "strange incense" or "unauthorized fire" to the Lord.

> Aaron's sons Nadab and Abihu took their censers, put fire in them and added incense; and they offered *unauthorized* fire before the Lord, *contrary to his command.* So fire came out from the presence of the Lord and consumed them, and they died before the Lord. Moses then said to Aaron, "This is what the Lord spoke of when he said: 'Among those who approach me I will show myself holy; in the sight of all the people I will be honored.' " (vv. 1–3)

Notice that Nadab and Abihu were not offering worship to false gods, but to the Lord. They were not private citizens, but priests—sons of Aaron. We have no reason to suspect that they were insincere or had evil motives in approaching the Lord. They were even coming to the proper place— the sanctuary. But the sacrifices they brought were not commanded, and the Lord struck them down with fire because they failed to honor Him; they failed to obey His commandments concerning worship. In short, they offered "worship" in a way God never commanded.

Nadab and Abihu are not alone. Generations later, the well-intentioned Uzzah had a similar experience: "When they came to the threshing floor of Nacon, Uzzah reached out and took hold of the ark of God, because the oxen stumbled. The LORD's anger burned against Uzzah because of his irreverent act; therefore God struck him down and he died there beside the ark of God" (2 Sam. 6:6–7). Why was Uzzah's act judged irreverent? After all, he was simply trying to keep the ark from falling and being damaged. What could be a more sincere expression of devotion to the Lord? But Uzzah was not a priest, and thus was not permitted to touch the ark—for any reason. When he did, he died.

Was God overreacting when He struck Nadab and Abihu and Uzzah? We may be inclined to think so, but that is because we are not nearly as zealous for the holy name of the Lord as He Himself is. Our indifference to the concerns of proper worship is perhaps an indication of how shallow twentieth-century spirituality has become. What we need, more than ever, is to focus on God and to realize that He has granted us access into His presence. Then we need to worship Him only as He has commanded.

Exactly how has God commanded us to worship Him? In particular, what should our worship comprise? God has commanded things like calling the congregation to worship and offering benedictions (Num. 6:21–27; Rom. 1:7; 15:33; 1 Cor. 1:3; 16:23–24; 2 Cor. 13:14), praying (Acts 2:42; Eph. 5:20; Phil. 4:6; 1 Thess. 5:17), reading the Word of God (2 Thess. 3:14; 1 Cor. 14:37; Col. 4:16; 2 Peter 3:15), preaching and teaching the Word of God (Acts 2:42; 20:7–12; 1 Cor. 14:26; 2 Tim. 4:2), administering the sacraments (Matt. 28:19; Luke 22:14–20; Acts 2:42; 1 Cor. 11:17–34), singing praises (Exod. 15:1; Ps. 7:17; 96:1; Eph. 5:19; Col. 3:16), and giving and receiving tithes and offerings to support God's work and the poor (1 Cor. 9:3–12; 1 Cor. 16:1–2).[5]

Believers should appreciate the "antiphonal" character of public worship: God speaks and His people respond.[6] God addresses His church with the call to worship, the reading and preaching of the Word, the words of institution for the sacraments, and the benediction. His people respond by praying (e.g., confessing their sins, petitioning God for help, etc.), praising and thanking, participating in the sacraments, and bringing their offerings. Frequently our verbal responses are given expression in singing.[7] When thoughtfully and properly done, singing in worship should accomplish several functions. Sometimes our singing is praying ("Come, My Soul, Thy Suit Prepare"). Sometimes it declares the mighty acts of God as reminders of His grace ("O God, Our Help in Ages Past"). Sometimes our songs praise Him directly ("Praise to the Lord, The Almighty"). And sometimes our singing exhorts and instructs us ("Trust and Obey"). Thus, congregational singing can be used in connection with several of the elements of worship we have mentioned.

A MATTER OF CHARACTER

Just as the Reformed faith calls believers to worship God only as He has commanded in Scripture, so it also calls them to return to true worship. What, then, is the character of true worship?

First, true worship must be offered with holy boldness and confidence—an aggressiveness born of faith (Heb. 10:19–25). If you are going to worship properly, you must know who you are in Christ, what He has done for you by redeeming you, and what you intend to do as you approach Him in worship. Your worship must be characterized by vitality and understanding.

Second, true worship must center on the atoning work of Christ. As sinners, we need cleansing. Without the forgiveness of our sins, we would be unable to approach God in the majesty of His glorious holiness. Jesus has provided His own blood to cleanse us, and our worship must accordingly have much to say about confessing our sin, repenting of it, and seeking God's pardon.

Admittedly, many consider this emphasis on sin "too negative." Pastors and evangelists, armed with the latest church-growth studies, would rather emphasize the "positive" side of worship. They want people to know how glad the church is to have the worshiper present, and, by implication, how glad God is, too. Confrontations over sin and judgment—either in the sermon or anywhere else in the service—are considered bad form. They will "turn people off" and drive them away, we are told.

Yet, as we have already seen, God denies sinners access to Him on account of their sin and His judgment against it. If we nonetheless encourage sinners to approach Him without a profound sense of their sin and the forgiveness and reconciliation that Christ alone has provided through the Cross, then we have not really done them any favors. Indeed, only as the knowledge of our sinfulness humbles us more and more before the presence of God, and causes us to embrace the cross of Christ with deeper confidence, will we experience the cleansing and liberation that alone can issue in true joy and peace with God. It may seem paradoxical to many, but deep and lasting comfort comes not from ignoring or minimizing the problem of sin in the worshiper's life, but by confronting it in all its depth by an even deeper appreciation of the definitiveness of the atonement and the forgiveness it brings (cf. Ps 32:1–5).

Third, because worship takes the Cross seriously, it is also a time of joyful celebration. The message of the gospel of Christ is that "where sin increased, grace increased all the more, so that, just as sin reigned in death, so also grace might reign through righteousness to bring eternal life through Jesus Christ our Lord" (Rom. 5:20–21)—and that is cause for celebration! While we must emphasize a return to a more serious realization of the problem of sin in contemporary worship (for that is where the current imbalance lies), we must not forget that the knowledge of sin is not an end in itself. Rather, our knowledge of sin should convict us and lead us to repent our sin (2 Cor. 7:9–10) so that joy might come to our hearts through faith. True worship, then, will give expression to the full range of human emotions as we contemplate all the biblical realities—sin, righteousness, judgment, forgiveness, adoption into God's family, new life in the Spirit, and the hope of glory.

Fourth, worship that is truly God-centered must be edifying and challenging. Hebrews 10 calls us to "consider how we may spur one another on toward love and good deeds" (v. 24). I am always a little amused to hear how often Christians talk about wanting to feel "comfortable" in church and prefer the kinds of worship services that will make them feel that way. Although God repeatedly offers true comfort to His worshipers (e.g., Ps. 71:21; 119:50, 76; Isa. 40:1), that comfort is often not the same thing as "feeling comfortable" (cf. Joel 2:25). Genuine comfort arises not in the absence of discomfort, but in the triumph of God's mercy over our troubles. True worship, according to Scripture, is anything but "comfortable"! We read in Hebrews,

> But you have come to Mount Zion, to the heavenly Jerusalem, the city of the living God. You have come to thousands upon thousands of angels in joyful assembly, to the church of the firstborn,

whose names are written in heaven. You have come to God, the judge of all men, to the spirits of righteous men made perfect, to Jesus the mediator of a new covenant, and to the sprinkled blood that speaks a better word than the blood of Abel. See to it that you do not refuse him who speaks. If they did not escape when they refused him who warned them on earth, how much less will we, if we turn away from him who warns us from heaven? . . . Therefore, since we are receiving a kingdom that cannot be shaken, let us be thankful, and so worship God acceptably with reverence and awe, for our "God is a consuming fire." (Heb. 12:22–25, 29)

Does that sound like a place of "comfort"? If the church is worshiping as it should, Paul tells us what the reaction of the sinner in the service will be: "If an unbeliever or someone who does not understand comes in while everybody is prophesying, he will be convinced by all that he is a sinner and will be judged by all, and the secrets of his heart will be laid bare. So he will fall down and worship God, exclaiming, 'God is really among you!' " (1 Cor. 14:24–25). This is what God expects of our worship services. We should expect nothing less.

Finally, true worship should not only be offered with boldness and confidence, centered on the atoning work of Christ, celebrated with true joy, and rendered so as to challenge and edify us; it should also be seen as an obligation incumbent upon God's people. For this reason, believers should not neglect to participate in public worship. "Let us not give up meeting together, as some are in the habit of doing, but let us encourage one another—and all the more as you see the Day approaching" (Heb. 10:25). Notice that taking church attendance lightly is not a modern invention!

Worshiping God is more important than most anything else we can do as Christians. Sadly, some think they know what they need better than the Lord, even on His day. Additional sleep, an exquisite brunch, "family time," playing or watching sports, traveling—all take precedence over worship in the lives of many Christians today. Yet the Lord declares,

Observe the Sabbath day by keeping it holy, as the LORD your God has commanded you. Six days you shall labor and do all your work, but the seventh day is a Sabbath to the LORD your God. On it you shall not do any work, neither you, nor your son or daughter, nor your manservant or maidservant, nor your ox, your donkey or any

of your animals, nor the alien within your gates, so that your manservant and maidservant may rest, as you do. Remember that you
were slaves in Egypt and that the LORD your God brought you out
of there with a mighty hand and an outstretched arm. Therefore
the LORD your God has commanded you to observe the Sabbath
day. (Deut. 5:12–15)

"If you keep your feet from breaking the Sabbath and from doing
as you please on my holy day, if you call the Sabbath a delight and
the Lord's holy day honorable, and if you honor it by not going
your own way and not doing as you please or speaking idle words,
then you will find your joy in the LORD, and I will cause you to ride
on the heights of the land and to feast on the inheritance of your
father Jacob." The mouth of the LORD has spoken. (Isa. 58:13–14)

We cannot take time here to discuss at length the principle and practice of honoring the Lord's Day, which is itself a subject of much disagreement among evangelicals. But notice, at least in passing, that the command
to honor the Sabbath did not originate with the Mosaic law. Nor is it
based solely on a creation ordinance set forth by God our Creator ("For in
six days the LORD made the heavens and the earth, the sea, and all that is
in them, but he rested on the seventh day. *Therefore* the LORD blessed the
Sabbath day and made it holy" [Ex. 20:11].). It is also rooted in the *redemptive accomplishment* of God our Savior ("Remember that you were slaves in
Egypt and that *the LORD your God brought you out of there* with a mighty
hand and an outstretched arm" [Deut. 5:15].).

The Sabbath is the great memorial day of redemption for the people
of God. In the Old Covenant, it looked back to the Exodus, while in the
New Covenant it looks back to the greater "exodus" (or "departure," Luke
9:31) accomplished in the death, and especially the resurrection, of Christ
(hence the change of days from the last to the first of the week). But, at
the same time, the weekly Sabbath or Lord's Day also looks forward to that
eternal "Sabbath-rest" which yet remains for the people of God (Heb. 4:9).[8]

The Lord's Day, then, constitutes a celebration of God's redemption—centering on the Cross of Christ and His resurrection—which
comes to explicit focus in the formal worship of God. When God has
made this "mini-jubilee" available to us as His people at the cost of His
own Son's life, and has graciously invited us into His presence for worship, we sin grievously by neglecting that high privilege and refusing
that gracious invitation.

STANDING THE HEAT

While some Christians neglect to worship the Lord on His appointed day of worship, still others neglect the means He has appointed for communicating His Word to His people. Perhaps nowhere is the modern church's drift from its Reformed moorings more evident than when it comes to preaching. Somewhere along the line, the pulpit stopped occupying the central role it once assumed in Protestant worship.

Today, many consider preaching to be an outmoded and largely irrelevant method of communicating to contemporary men and women. Churches are turning to drama and multimedia presentations as a supplement to, or substitute for, preaching as the means of conveying God's message. They imagine that the truth of God's Word can be better conveyed by other media and methods.

In the 1960s, Marshall McLuhan claimed that "the medium is the message," and pled for "cooler" methods of communication. Preaching, as traditionally understood and practiced, is very "hot." When McLuhan's ideas about communication began to influence the church, preaching came to be considered unsuitable for reaching our post-modern culture. Sadly, what has happened is that the new methods have affected the ancient message as well. Whether a weakening of the church's commitment to the biblical message makes the church more amenable to changes in methodology, or vice versa, is uncertain. But one thing is certain: modern communication methods and the modern "gospel" go hand in hand. And that connection is not accidental.

Indeed, preaching is hot communication precisely because the biblical message is a hot message. There is nothing subtle or cool about the gospel message that Jesus preached: " 'The time has come,' he said. 'The kingdom of God is near. Repent and believe the good news!' " (Mark 1:15).

Nor was Peter's message on the Day of Pentecost characterized by cool sophistication and indirection when he accused some of his hearers of wickedly putting the Lord and Christ to death by nailing Him to the cross (Acts 2:22–24, 32–36). And Stephen had never read McLuhan or his ecclesiastical followers, else he never would have said to the Sanhedrin, "You stiff-necked people, with uncircumcised hearts and ears! . . . You always resist the Holy Spirit!" (Acts 7:51).

The problem is not that preaching has become out-of-date in the late twentieth century. Rather, it is that pastors and church leaders have lost sight of the confrontational character of the biblical message. They have focused instead on the positive, "person-affirming" features of the

Bible, which they believe can be communicated better, with greater sub-
tlety, sometimes by other means, such as dramatic skits.

And even when pastors preach, what they serve up to the people of
God on a weekly basis often leads to malnourishment. Often the flock
does not realize that it could and should have better feeding from its shepherds. For all the jokes about church members being too critical of their
preachers, the opposite is probably more characteristic of the true state of
affairs in the church. By and large, congregations are very tolerant—sometimes because they are gracious and patient, sometimes because they lack
the biblical discernment to determine the quality of the preaching they
are hearing, and sometimes for both reasons.

The "Berean ideal" is still the standard for listening to sermons. The
noble-minded Bereans "received the message with great eagerness and examined the Scriptures every day to see if what Paul said was true" (Acts
17:11). God's people should be like the Bereans. They should eagerly receive the Word of God that is preached to them, and wisely discern the
biblical accuracy of what they are receiving. If they do, they will grow and
flourish as they drink deeply each week of the "pure spiritual milk" of God's
Word (1 Peter 2:2).[9] Bold, faithful, "apostolic" preaching from the pulpit
and eager, wise, discerning attentiveness from the pew deserve another try
today!

Preaching with Purpose

What, specifically, should biblical preaching accomplish in the life of the
church in general, and in its worship services in particular? Some preachers lay particular emphasis on the evangelistic purpose of preaching. They
believe that preaching should be aimed specifically at man's need of salvation, and should set forth the salvation accomplished in Christ.

Other preachers stress the importance of discipleship. To them,
preaching should teach believers how to live in accordance with God's
will, since the Bible has a word of direction for every area of life.

Still other preachers believe that preaching should set forth the
"worldview" dimensions of the Bible and the Christian faith. They think
preaching should seek to explain and apply every word that proceeds from
the mouth of God. Believers who sit under the preaching of God's Word
can be assured that God has given them a revelation that enables them to
make sense of all thought through the whole system of biblical truth.

Which view is correct? Paul's sermon to the Ephesian elders, recorded for us in Acts 20, helps us answer that question. He uses three parallel phrases in this message to describe his ministry among the Christians of Ephesus.

First, Paul says that in his ministry he was preaching "anything that would be helpful" (v. 20). This draws our attention to the discipleship aspect of his instruction. Paul was not interested in empty theories. He was concerned to instruct the churches in the practical implications of the message of Christ. Elsewhere in his writings he explains that Scripture teaches, rebukes, corrects, and trains in righteousness, so that believers will be "thoroughly equipped for every good work" (2 Tim. 3:17).

At the same time, Paul describes his preaching as "declar[ing] to both Jews and Greeks that they must turn to God in repentance and have faith in our Lord Jesus" (Acts 20:21). Here he affirms the evangelistic focus of his proclamation of the Word. The particular call of the gospel was an important element in his preaching, just as it had been in the preaching of Jesus (cf. Mark 1:14–15).

Paul, however, does not let the evangelistic "call" of the gospel narrow his view of the overall purpose of his preaching. On the contrary, the apostle goes on to say that he did not hesitate "to proclaim to [them] the whole will [counsel] of God" (Acts 20:27). He knew that all Scripture is profitable, and that the faith once for all delivered to the saints forms a system (cf. 2 Tim. 1:13: "the pattern of sound teaching"). The Christian is called upon to "demolish arguments and every pretension that sets itself up against the knowledge of God" and to "take captive every thought to make it obedient to Christ" (2 Cor. 10:5). Through his preaching and teaching, Paul introduced his hearers to the broad scope of biblical instruction, to the "systematic theology" of the Bible.[10]

These were the purposes Paul had for his public preaching ministry and for his more private instruction "from house to house" (Acts 20:20). This made up his task of "testifying to the gospel of God's grace" (v. 24). He had a broad and rich conception of preaching.

While Paul and the other New Testament preachers had a sense of the breadth of their preaching task, they never lost sight of its particular focus and purpose. If preachers today would share this devotion to declare what Scripture declares, adopt the broad, threefold purpose that Paul outlined for his own ministry, and imitate his bold method of presenting that truth, preaching would again become the vital heartbeat of the church's worship, fellowship, and service, as it was in years gone by.

May God grant the church in our day the same fruits of revival and reformation that He brought to our fathers through the faithful preachers of old!

Study Questions

1. What is the one task that God's people have in worship? Do you consider this your task as you approach God in worship?
2. Why do believers need to seek the guidance of Scripture as they worship the Lord? What role, if any, should personal preferences, tradition, or sincerity have in shaping our worship? What should be our standard for determining whether worship is acceptable to God (see John 4:21–24; John 17:17)? In what ways is your worship consistent with this standard? In what ways might it be inconsistent? How can you make it more consistent?
3. What should the threefold purpose of preaching be, as illustrated in Acts 20:20–21, 27? Should any one of these three purposes be allowed to eclipse or preclude the others? Which one receives undue emphasis in the preaching you feed on? Which ones need to receive more emphasis and why?

Notes

1. Ronald Allen and Gordon Borror, *Worship: Rediscovering the Missing Jewel* (Portland, Oreg.: Multnomah, 1982), 9.
2. Robert G. Rayburn, *O Come, Let Us Worship* (Grand Rapids: Baker, 1980), 11.
3. The general subject of worship is also treated in the Westminster Larger and Shorter Catechism questions concerning the second and fourth commandments, the ministry of the Word, the sacraments, and prayer. Other Reformed confessions, like the Heidelberg Catechism, deal with the same subjects.
4. Today, evangelicals frequently downplay or denounce forms in favor of attitudes. Iconoclasm is often considered a virtue among us. But God is not willing to trade forms for attitude. He wants both. While an empty use of forms is sinful (e.g., Hos. 6:6, "For I desire mercy, not sacrifice, and acknowledgment of God rather than burnt offerings"; cf. Matt. 9:13), so also, as we shall see, is a sincere abuse of biblical forms of worship.
5. Westminster Confession of Faith, 31.3–6.
6. Cf. G. Van Dooren, *The Beauty of Reformed Liturgy* (Winnipeg: Premier Publishing, 1980).
7. For this reason a carefully compiled and theologically sound hymnal and/or praise book is one of the most important and valuable worship "tools" any church can have. Sadly, more than a few churches today neglect this valuable worship tool, opting instead for songs that are less than biblical. Yet, few in the pews pay any attention because the tunes are so melodious. A profound concern over the *content* of sung praise has also led to considerable debate

within Reformed circles through the years over just what songs should be sung in corporate worship. Some have argued that only canonical songs (e.g., the Psalms) should be used, while others believe that post-biblical hymns may also be sung in worship, so long as they are tested and approved by the Scriptures and sound theological principles.

8. In the context of Heb. 4, the Holy Spirit warns us not to fail, through unbelief or disobedience, to enter into the rest that God has prepared for us: "There remains, then, a Sabbath-rest for the people of God; for anyone who enters God's rest also rests from his own work, just as God did from his. Let us, therefore, make every effort to enter that rest, so that no one will fall by following their example of disobedience" (vv. 9–11).

9. Two brief but helpful books by Jay E. Adams discuss the matters of discernment and listening to preaching: *A Call to Discernment* (Eugene, Oreg.: Harvest House, 1987), and *A Consumer's Guide to Preaching* (Wheaton, Ill.: Victor, 1991).

10. Cf. B. B. Warfield, "The Indispensableness of Systematic Theology to the Preacher," *Selected Shorter Writings*, 2 vols. (Phillipsburg, N.J.: Presbyterian and Reformed, 1973), 2:280–88.

FOURTEEN

THE WATER AND THE WINE

While the sacraments of baptism and the Lord's Supper have been hotly debated throughout the centuries, one thing cannot be debated: they cannot be rightly understood apart from the covenant and the spiritual reality of the nearness of God that grows out of the covenant.

According to Scripture, God's redeeming love for His people in Christ is expressed in the covenant, at the center of which is the supreme blessing of God's presence with His people: "My dwelling place will be with them; I will be their God, and they will be my people" (Ezek. 37:27). As we saw in Part Two of this book, God's people enjoy an abiding relationship of union and communion with Him.

This relationship of union and communion—the nearness of God— was expressed in various ways in the Old Covenant: theophany, tabernacle, and temple; priesthood, prayer, and the Passover Lamb. Then, in the fullness of time, God manifested His redeeming presence in His incarnate Son, Jesus Christ. When Jesus "pitched His tent" among us (see John 1:14), the abiding reality of the nearness of God had come. All that preceded Him were but types and shadows. Jesus is Immanuel—God with us.

And yet, even the incarnation of God the Son was not the final way God manifested His nearness to His people. After the resurrection and ascension of Christ, God manifested His nearness anew in the abiding presence of the Holy Spirit: "But I tell you the truth: It is for your good that I am going away. Unless I go away, the Counselor will not come to you; but if I go, I will send him to you" (John 16:7). The Spirit is sent by the Father in the name of the Son (John 14:26), so that He is indeed "the Spirit of Christ" (Rom. 8:9) and "the Spirit of the Lord" (2 Cor. 3:17–18). The Last Adam, with His resurrection and ascension, "became . . . a life-giving spirit" (1 Cor. 15:45).

Thus, the Spirit who indwells God's covenant people is God's ulti-mate expression of the covenant blessing of His nearness in this world. The Spirit is the One who brings about our union and communion with God our Savior, and He does so by indwelling us and by means of the ministry of the Word and the sacraments.

In the pages that follow, we will briefly examine how the Holy Spirit uses the sacraments to confirm and edify us as God's people.

What the Sacraments Are All About

Perhaps there is no better place to begin a study of the sacraments than to understand exactly what the term *sacrament* means. According to the Westminster Confession, 27.1, the sacraments are

> holy signs and seals of the covenant of grace, immediately insti-tuted by God, to represent Christ, and his benefits; and to confirm our interest in him: as also, to put a visible difference between those that belong unto the church, and the rest of the world; and solemnly to engage them to the service of God in Christ, accord-ing to his Word.

From this definition, we learn several important truths about the sacra-ments.

Signs and Seals

To begin with, the sacraments are signs and seals. As signs, they represent something, and that something is Christ Himself. Since the blessings of Christ's saving work are never enjoyed apart from union and communion with Him (John 15:4–5), the sacraments, in representing Christ, also show forth the redemptive benefits that the believer possesses in Him.

As signs, the sacraments involve external physical elements (water, in the case of baptism, and both bread and wine, in the case of the Lord's Supper). They also involve actions that derive their meaning by referring to an inward, invisible working of God's grace.

God graciously gives the church the sacraments as divinely authorized "illustrations" or pictures of the gospel, which help us to understand intangible truths in a tangible way. Calvin taught that because we are like children in our understanding of God's ways, and because He deeply desires to have us benefit fully from the riches of His redeeming grace, He stooped to our weakness by communicating the gospel to us with clarity and simplicity in the Scriptures. But then beyond that, knowing that we are but dust, He has also reinforced His message of grace to our senses by giving us the sacraments.[1]

While the sacraments are signs, the Reformed faith holds that they are more than signs—more than mere memorials. They are also seals, which is to say that a sacramental union or spiritual relationship exists between the external elements and the inner reality that they signify. This is just another way of saying that the Holy Spirit actually uses the sacraments to convey grace to the believing recipient.

The power of this grace, however, is not inherent in the sacrament itself (as Rome teaches), but in the Holy Spirit. It is the Holy Spirit who applies the grace signified in the sacrament to the believer, much as He conveys converting, renewing, and transforming grace in and through God's Word. This parallel between the Holy Spirit's ministry through the written Word and the "visible words" of the sacraments is crucial to the Reformed understanding of the sacraments. The sacraments are thus made effective to bless the one who participates in them through faith.

Marked Men

In addition to being signs and seals, the sacraments are also marks of identity, which "put a visible difference between those that belong unto the church, and the rest of the world."

Often, the significance of the sacraments as marks of identity is more clearly appreciated in a missionary setting than in our own Western culture. In our nominally Christian societies, one may profess allegiance to Christ and the church without suffering immediate or serious consequences such as losing one's life or being cut off from one's family, culture, or society. In our culture, then, the sacramental marks of that allegiance (in particular, baptism) do not necessarily carry a great deal of weight in the minds of many professing believers.

In a culture dominated by a non-Christian religion such as Buddhism or Islam, by contrast, a convert to Christianity may think long and hard about receiving baptism, since that sacrament in particular will forever mark the convert as one identified with Christ and His church, and may cause serious consequences to follow. This pattern is actually much closer to the situation in the New Testament. For people to draw near to God by faith in Christ and receive baptism (Acts 2:38) was to become instant "aliens" and "strangers" in the first-century Roman Empire (1 Peter 1:1; 2:11; cf. Heb. 11:13). As church history illustrates, the costs of such a step were often quite high. Thus, the sacraments have a very important role to play in identifying the people of God and separating them from the world.

Privileges and Responsibilities

Finally, the sacraments lay upon God's people His claim to their love and loyalty. Like every covenant privilege, the sacraments carry a corresponding obligation or responsibility. In the words of the Westminster Confession, they "solemnly . . . engage [believers] to the service of God in Christ, according to his Word." As signs and seals of our calling in Christ, the sacraments bear ongoing, objective witness to the command to "live a life worthy of the calling [we] have received" (Eph. 4:1). Knowing that we have been baptized "into the name" of the triune God whose name we bear by virtue of baptism, should instill in us a deep desire to be faithful and obedient to Him who loved us and redeemed us. Likewise, the table of the Lord should challenge us to take up our cross daily, deny ourselves, and follow Him as the One who was crucified in our stead. When properly used, therefore, the sacraments should motivate us to grow and mature in holiness.

WHAT THE CHURCH NEEDS NOW

At the time of the Reformation, the Roman Catholic Church taught that the sacraments were the indispensable means of conveying saving grace to the believer through the mediation of an earthly priesthood.[2] Since then, some Protestants have reacted so strongly to Rome's view, that they have gone to the opposite extreme by placing little or no emphasis upon the sacraments, especially the Lord's Supper. Those who have overreacted in this way need to understand that God gave the sacraments to His church to edify her. And He is not in the habit of giving the church superfluities. The sacraments are necessities—not in the way defined by Rome, to be sure, but rather, as part of God's plan to build up His church.

In our zeal to avoid a false sacramentalism, we do not want to forget that Christ is "the living bread that came down from heaven," such that anyone who eats of it will live forever. For the one who partakes of Christ's flesh and blood remains in Christ, has eternal life, and will be raised up at the Last Day (John 6:50–56). To ignore or downplay the sacraments is to empty our Savior's words of their meaning. If He is the Bread of Life, we need to feed on Him.

As we learn to feed on Him, we must also put the sacraments in their proper place. Calvin and his followers thus spoke of the sacraments as secondary, not in the sense of importance, but in the sense that they depend upon the Word for their meaning.[3] Because the Reformed faith puts the sacraments in their proper place, it rejects the separation of the sacraments from the ministry of the Word, which had become common under Rome during the Reformation era. Contrary to this separation, the Reformed faith maintains that the Lord's Supper and baptism should always be accompanied by the faithful proclamation of the Word.

Given our need to feed our faith with the truth of God's Word (1 Peter 2:2–3), what a blessing it is when the "audible word" is accompanied regularly and frequently by the "visible word" set forth in the sacraments! May God give us grace to feed fully upon all the delicacies with which He has spread the table of worship before us!

In this connection, we should again note the central role of the church in the life of God's people. The sacraments are not given by God to individual Christians *per se*. They are given to the church. Like citizenship certificates, the sacraments are the "identity papers" of the people of God. While it is true that the believer must be set apart from the world by the holy character of his life, it is equally true and necessary that he or she be marked with the God-appointed signs of the church.

Yet, in many circles, the sacraments are seen as essentially private privileges, and are thus enjoyed apart from the authoritative oversight of the church and her leaders. It is not uncommon, for example, to see non-ordained persons administering the Lord's Supper in private gatherings of believers. To see how this practice is mistaken, think about how one becomes a citizen of the United States. One does not become a citizen simply because he desires to do so. The privilege of becoming a citizen must be conferred by those with the authority to act on behalf of the federal government. Once certain qualifications and procedures are followed, these duly constituted authorities grant the privilege of citizenship to those who apply for it.

In a similar way, Jesus has entrusted the sacraments (along with the "keys" of admission, Matt. 16:19) to His undershepherds, the elders of the church. They alone are vested with the authority and charged with the responsibility to admit men and women to, and exclude them from, joining the body of Christ and participating in the sacraments, based on their profession of faith and holiness of life. A believer may not be admitted automatically to baptism or the Lord's Supper simply because of the desire to do so, even if those desires are borne of true faith. Such desires should rather bring the believer to the elders of the church, who have been given authority by Christ to nurture and discipline those under their care within the church. And, as we will see in succeeding chapters, the sacraments are but one aspect of the nurture and discipline entrusted to the church.

FROM CIRCUMCISION TO BAPTISM

Both the Old Covenant and the New have sacraments that mark the introduction of a person into the sphere of covenantal blessing. In the Old Covenant it was circumcision, whereas in the New Covenant it is baptism.

Abraham and his male children were to receive the covenant sign of baptism as an indication that they belonged to the Lord in the bonds of covenant love and faithfulness.

> "I will establish my covenant as an everlasting covenant between me and you and your descendants after you for the generations to come, to be your God and the God of your descendants after you." . . . Then God said to Abraham, "As for you, you must keep my covenant, you and your descendants after you for the generations to come. This is my covenant with you and your descendants after you, the covenant you are to keep: Every male among you shall be circumcised. You are to undergo circumcision, and it will be the sign of the covenant between me and you. . . . My covenant in your flesh is to be an everlasting covenant. Any uncircumcised male, who has not been circumcised in the flesh, will be cut off from his people; he has broken my covenant." (Gen. 17:7, 9–11, 13–14)

Circumcision was a sign and seal of the covenant of grace that God made with Abraham and his descendants. Thus, it is called "the covenant of circumcision" by Stephen in Acts 7:8. Circumcision signified and sealed the realities of covenantal blessing in the forgiveness of sins and acceptance with God (i.e., "a seal of the righteousness that he had by faith," Rom. 4:11), in the inward renewal of the heart (i.e., the circumcision of the heart, Deut. 30:6; cf. 10:12–13, 16), and in the hope of the coming fulfillment of the "New Covenant" (Jer. 31:31–34; 32:40; cf. Ezek. 36:25–28).

Circumcision was also a mark of citizenship, of inclusion in the commonwealth of Israel (cf. Eph. 2:12). As such, it identified the people of God and distinguished them from the world. It laid the foundation for the covenantal nurture and discipline of Abraham's descendants (Gen. 17:9; 18:19).

This Old Covenant sacrament finds its counterpart—indeed, its very fulfillment—in the "circumcision of Christ," which is identified as the New Covenant sacrament of baptism.

> In him *you were also circumcised*, in the putting off of the sinful nature, not with a circumcision done by the hands of men but *with the circumcision done by Christ, having been buried with him in baptism* and raised with him through your faith in the power of God, who raised him from the dead. When you were dead in your sins and in the uncircumcision of your sinful nature, God made you alive with Christ. He forgave us all our sins, having canceled the written code, with its regulations, that was against us and that stood opposed to us; he took it away, nailing it to the cross. (Col. 2:11–14)

This correspondence between the sacraments of the old and new administrations of the covenant of grace provides the framework for the Reformed understanding of Christian baptism.

First of all, baptism signifies the union and communion of believers with the triune God in the bonds of the covenant. The blessed promise of God's presence, which was at the heart of the covenant from the beginning and which echoes throughout the Old Testament, was "I will walk among you and be your God, and you will be my people" (Lev. 26:12; cf. Ezek. 36:28). The children of Israel were chosen by the Lord to be His "treasured possession" (Deut. 7:6), and, though judgment might intervene, days were coming when He would again gather them and make them His own (cf. Mal. 3:17). That hope was realized with the coming of Christ, who gathers the sheep of God from Israel and from the nations, and makes them His own: "I am the good shepherd; I know my sheep and my sheep know me—just as the Father knows me and I know the Father—and I lay down my life for the sheep. I have other sheep that are not of this sheep pen. I must bring them also. They too will listen to my voice, and there shall be one flock and one shepherd" (John 10:14–16).

Against this backdrop, Jesus commands the apostles: "Therefore go and make disciples of all nations, baptizing them in the name of the Father and of the Son and of the Holy Spirit, and teaching them to obey everything I have commanded you. And surely I am with you always, to the very end of the age" (Matt. 28:19–20). Baptism "into the name of " (to be identified with) the triune God marks the people of God as those who are His by means of the special relationship of the covenant, and thereby distinguishes them from the world.

In particular, Christian baptism symbolizes our union with Christ, the mediator of the covenant: "Or don't you know that all of us who were baptized into Christ Jesus were baptized into his death?" (Rom. 6:3). And "all of you who were baptized into Christ have clothed yourselves with Christ" (Gal. 3:27). Union with Christ, of course, entails union with the Father and the Holy Spirit (cf. John 14:16–23; 17:20–23).

As union with Christ enables us to participate in the benefits of salvation purchased by Christ, so baptism, as the sign and seal of our union with Christ, signifies and seals the redemptive blessings we enjoy as believers, namely, the pardoning of, and cleansing from, our sin through the sprinkling of the blood of Jesus (Acts 2:38; 22:16; 1 Cor. 6:11; 1 Peter 3:21), as well as our possession of, and renewal by, the Holy Spirit (Titus 3:5; John 3:5; Col. 2:11).

The Holy Spirit makes baptism effective, and thus it is fitting that the New Covenant age was inaugurated by the historic event of Pentecost, marking the outpouring of the Spirit on the church (Acts 2:33). This event is called the "baptism of the Holy Spirit" (Matt. 3:11; Acts 1:5; 2:17).

Now we can understand how baptism marks the transition of a convert from the world to the church, from unbelief to faith in Christ: baptism is a sign of citizenship in the kingdom of God. By baptism we become members of the church, the body of Christ (Acts 2:38, 41, 47). As members of the church, we are subject to the discipline of the Word, and receive its nurture, just as our fathers did before us from the beginning. Further, our baptism constitutes a permanent, objective call to love, faithfulness, and obedience to God's commandments.

FOR ADULTS ONLY?

Both Reformed and non-Reformed churches teach that adults who come to Christ ought to be baptized. But they often differ when it comes to whether infants ought to be baptized. Because many evangelicals who become interested in the Reformed faith find infant baptism to be a stumbling block, we will discuss it in the hope of easing difficulties that some have with this historic Reformed practice.

At the outset, we need to see that there are two mistaken reasons for baptizing infants, which should not be confused with the Reformed practice. Some churches baptize infants in the belief that baptism itself will save them. But baptism does not itself regenerate the heart or impart faith. To teach that it does is to confuse the sign with the thing signified. Baptism is the external sign of the internal working of the Holy Spirit, whose ineffable work of renewal is done when He pleases. In the words of the Westminster Confession, "The efficacy of baptism is not tied to that moment of time wherein it is administered" (28.6).

Just as we do not baptize infants to save them, so we do not baptize infants because we presume them to be saved already. We do not administer the sacraments on the basis of our presumption, but rather on the basis of the commandment of God. Because the church contains both wheat and tares (Matt. 13:24–30), some who are baptized are regenerate, whereas, sadly, others are not.[4] We cannot read the heart. We can only see the covenantal realities that are reflected in the outward life of professing believers. Baptism and its efficacy cannot be understood in abstraction from its covenantal context in the fellowship, nurture, and discipline of the church.

In contrast to these mistaken views, the Reformed faith has grounded the administration of baptism only in the commandment of God. The real question, then, is whether God has commanded the church to baptize adults only, or whether His command to baptize encompasses infants as well.

The Reformed faith answers that question by once again emphasizing the covenantal way in which God has dealt with His people. And when we turn to the covenant, we note that God administered His covenantal grace to families—"*to you and to your descendants after you*" (cf. Gen. 9:9; 17:7–10; 35:12; 48:4). Even then, though, the covenant envisioned a worldwide blessing—"I will bless those who bless you, and whoever curses you I will curse; and *all peoples on earth* will be blessed through you" (Gen. 12:3; cf. 28:14; Acts 3:25; etc.).

Against this covenantal background, it is not difficult to see that children born within the covenant, as heirs of the promise, should be baptized (Gen. 17:9–14; Acts 2:38–39; cf. Matt. 19:13–14; Acts 16:15, 33–34; 1 Cor. 1:16; 7:14). We also see that those who turn to God in repentance and faith can become heirs and should also be baptized. Ruth the Moabitess, for example, fell into this latter group: "But Ruth replied, 'Don't urge me to leave you or to turn back from you. Where you go I will go, and where you stay I will stay. Your people will be my people and your God my God. Where you die I will die, and there I will be buried. May the Lord deal with me, be it ever so severely, if anything but death separates you and me' " (Ruth 1:16–17).

Though an "outsider," Ruth found grace in the eyes of "the LORD, the God of Israel, under whose wings [she had] come to take refuge" (2:12). Committing herself to Naomi and Naomi's people, Ruth also identified herself with Naomi's God and became an heir of His covenant promises. But because she was a woman of the Old Covenant, she could not receive the sacramental sign of circumcision.

A similar event took place after the dawning of the New Covenant in the coming of Christ. Not only did the Gentile Cornelius receive the New Covenant sign of baptism, but the other members of his household did so as well (Acts 10:34–47). The household of Lydia and the household of the Philippian jailer also received baptism when Lydia and the jailer, respectively, identified themselves by faith with Christ and His apostles (Acts 16:14–15, 31–33). This was also the case with Jews who came to Christ during the apostolic age of the church. They had already received circumcision, but the transition from old to new in their case was marked by receiving baptism in the name of Christ, and their children were involved in that promise as well (Acts 2:38–39).

While we could debate whether children were present in the households mentioned above, we would really profit more if we focused on what was going on at this point in redemptive history: the Holy Spirit was grafting new branches into the ancient root of the patriarchs (Rom. 11:16–23). The conversion of a man who was formerly a stranger to the covenants of promise (Eph. 2:12) meant that covenant life was brought to his family.

The descendants of faithful Abraham were introduced to blessing— not that each and every child of Abraham was saved, but that God's grace was powerfully at work within his family through the covenant. So it is with anyone who comes to Christ. God does not unconditionally guarantee to save each and every one of our children. But He does promise to be our God and the God of our children after us. The promise of the covenant, according to Peter, is for us and for our children (Acts 2:39). And in that light God commands that children receive the sign of covenantal initiation. They are to be baptized in the New Covenant, just as they were circumcised in the Old—only now all of God's children can receive the sign.

Baptism introduces the person baptized, whether adult or child, into the disciplines of covenant life. Baptism itself, according to Christ's commission, is one part of the task of discipling the nations. The other element is teaching the baptized to observe all that Christ commanded (Matt. 28:18–20). Children (or adults) thus baptized are in Christ and are to receive the nurture and discipline that is uniquely "of the Lord" (Eph. 6:1, 4; cf. Col. 3:20–21).

Those who are baptized enjoy the privileges and undertake the responsibilities and obligations of covenant life. They are subject to the discipline of the Lord as administered in the church, of which we will have more to say later.

For now, we should be content to realize that there will be false sons and daughters. Will they all come into the church as infants or children? No. How, then, should the problem of hypocrisy be addressed? Not by restricting baptism beyond the warrant of Scripture, nor by interpreting the significance of baptism in different ways (so as to leave us with two or more baptisms), but by being faithful in teaching and discipling every baptized person in the fellowship of the church.

If we do that, we will, by God's good grace, see covenant children growing up in the Lord to become faithful, fruitful, covenant-keeping adults. We will also see a steady stream of outsiders coming to seek the blessings of being included in the community of God's people marked off from the world by baptism.

From Passover to Lord's Supper

The great redemptive event of the Old Covenant was the deliverance of Israel from Egypt under the leadership of Moses. The Exodus was commemorated annually throughout the history of Israel in the Feast of Passover (Ex. 12).

The apostle Paul reminds the Corinthians, "Christ, our Passover lamb, has been sacrificed. Therefore let us keep the Festival, not with the old yeast, the yeast of malice and wickedness, but with bread without yeast, the bread of sincerity and truth" (1 Cor. 5:7–8). The apostle is not calling for the continuance of the Old Covenant festival; rather, he is acknowledging its continuity with, and fulfillment in, the New Covenant sacrament of the Lord's Supper.

In a later chapter of the same letter, Paul goes on to expand his discussion of this sacrament.

> For I received from the Lord what I also passed on to you: The Lord Jesus, on the night he was betrayed, took bread, and when he had given thanks, he broke it and said, "This is my body, which is for you; do this in remembrance of me." In the same way, after supper he took the cup, saying, "This cup is the new covenant in my blood; do this, whenever you drink it, in remembrance of me." For whenever you eat this bread and drink this cup, you proclaim the Lord's death until he comes. (1 Cor. 11:23–26)

Jesus instituted the Lord's Supper when He celebrated the Passover with His disciples before His suffering and death (cf. Luke 22:15). During that meal, Jesus superimposed the meaning of the sacramental bread and wine—"This is my body . . . this is my blood"—upon the Old Covenant Passover lamb, unleavened bread, and wine. Christ thereby drew the disciples' attention and ours to the fact that when God redeemed and delivered Israel from Egypt, He prefigured the even greater "exodus" which He was to accomplish through Christ's death on the cross (Luke 9:28–31; cf. John 12:31–33).

IN REMEMBRANCE OF ME

The church of the New Covenant is constantly to remember that Calvary's cross is central to its life and hope. The church can do this by preaching the gospel of "Jesus Christ and Him crucified" and by celebrating the sacrament of the Lord's Supper in remembrance of Him, thus proclaiming His death until He comes.

Celebrating Christ's death does not mean perpetuating Christ's death as Rome teaches in its "Mass." Scripture forthrightly precludes Rome's practice since "Christ died for sins *once for all*, the righteous for the unrighteous, to bring you to God" (1 Peter 3:18; cf. Heb. 7:27; 9:12, 26; 10:10). Thus, while the church is not to perpetuate Christ's death, it is nonetheless perpetually to remember His death by administering the Lord's Supper.

Yet the Lord's Supper is more than a mere memorial. Unlike most evangelicals today, who, like the Anabaptists of the Reformation era, teach that the Supper is merely a memorial, adherents of the Reformed faith teach that the Lord's Supper is also a real communion between the risen Christ and the believing participant. Christ is *really present* in the Supper. He is not physically present through the changing of the substance of the elements into the actual body and blood of Christ, as Rome teaches ("transubstantiation"), nor in terms of the actual body and blood being in, with, and under the elements, as Lutheranism teaches ("consubstantiation"). Rather, He is present spiritually, through the Holy Spirit, who ministers the blessings of faith in Christ to the believer through the sacrament, even as He does through the ministry of the Word.

This is why Paul rhetorically asks the Corinthians, "Is not the cup of thanksgiving for which we give thanks a participation in the blood of Christ? And is not the bread that we break a participation in the body of Christ?" (1 Cor. 10:16). He reminds them of the reality that was signified by the Old Covenant sacrificial meals: "Consider the people of Israel: Do not those who eat the sacrifices participate in the altar?" (v. 18). Israelites who ate the postsacrificial meal participated truly in the sacrifice that was offered on the altar (e.g., Lev. 7:6, 14–15; 1 Cor. 10:18). In the same way, the Christian who partakes of the Lord's Supper by faith truly shares in the benefits of the altar of Calvary, even though he is vastly separated in time and space from that once-for-all sacrifice of Christ.

This same principle of real participation through the use of a sacrificial (sacramental) meal stands behind Paul's warning to first-century believers not to eat at sacrificial feasts associated with pagan idols and temples. Even though the pagan idols are nothing in themselves, they are "fronts" for demons, and thus to eat at the sacrificial feasts associated with the pagan temples is to identify with demons. Because such participation is a damning disloyalty to Christ, it must be rejected by the faithful, who are to participate only in the Lord's table:

> Do I mean then that a sacrifice offered to an idol is anything, or that an idol is anything? No, but the sacrifices of pagans are offered to demons, not to God, and I do not want you to be participants with demons. You cannot drink the cup of the Lord and the cup of demons too; you cannot have a part in both the Lord's table and the table of demons. (1 Cor. 10:19–21)

Thus, communion in the body and blood of the Lord means participation in the benefits secured by Christ in His atoning death. Many spiritual realities are signified and sealed by eating the bread and drinking the cup. To begin with, the Lord's Supper is a sign of our justification, that is, God's forgiveness of our sins through the shed blood of the Savior, who was made sin for us that we might become the righteousness of God in Him.

The Lord's Supper is also a sign and seal of our sanctification, our definitive separation from the world and progressive growth in holiness, accomplished by our union with Christ in His death and resurrection.

> Therefore let us keep the Festival, not with the old yeast, the yeast of malice and wickedness, but with bread without yeast, the bread of sincerity and truth. I have written you in my letter not to associate with sexually immoral people—not at all meaning the people of this world who are immoral, or the greedy and swindlers, or idolaters. In that case you would have to leave this world. But now I am writing you that you must not associate with anyone who calls himself a brother but is sexually immoral or greedy, an idolater or a slanderer, a drunkard or a swindler. With such a man do not even eat. (1 Cor. 5:8–11)

The symbol of the loaf also sets forth the communion of believers with one another in the unity of the body of Christ: "Because there is one loaf, we, who are many, are one body, for we all partake of the one loaf " (1 Cor. 10:17).

Finally, the Lord's Supper also holds before the church the great hope of the consummation of the ages. According to Jesus' own testimony, the church, by its use of the Supper, "proclaims" the Lord's death "until He comes." The bodily presence of Christ symbolized in the Supper will one day give way to the reality when He physically returns to His church at the end of history: "I am going there to prepare a place for you. And if I go and prepare a place for you, I will come back and take you to be with me that you also may be where I am" (John 14:2–3).

As often as the church celebrates this sacrament, it is reminded, comforted, and challenged afresh with the words of the angels to the disciples at the time of Jesus' ascension: "This same Jesus, who has been taken from you into heaven, will come back in the same way you have seen him go into heaven" (Acts 1:11). Thus, whenever the church gathers around the table of the Lord, the silent cry of every heart should be, "Come, Lord Jesus."

EATING AND DRINKING WORTHILY

Who may properly come to the table of the Lord? Those who have been incorporated into the body of Christ through baptism and have been brought under its nurture and discipline may properly participate. In the early church, those who participated in the breaking of bread were those "who accepted his message [and] were baptized . . . [who] devoted themselves to the apostles' teaching and to the fellowship . . . and to prayer" (Acts 2:41–42).

Since the Lord's Supper is a sign and seal of the blessings that Christ extends to those who trust in Him, one cannot rightly participate in the sacrament without saving faith. Such faith is essential to the proper use of the sacrament. It would be the worst kind of hypocrisy—and a most dangerous sort—to participate in the supper if one did not embrace the Savior in saving faith.

But true faith is not all that is required of those who would make proper use of the sacrament. In his instructions to the Corinthians concerning their observance of the Lord's Supper, Paul warns them,

> Therefore, whoever eats the bread or drinks the cup of the Lord in an unworthy manner will be guilty of sinning against the body and blood of the Lord. A man ought to examine himself before he eats of the bread and drinks of the cup. For anyone who eats and drinks without recognizing the body of the Lord eats and drinks judgment on himself. That is why many among you are weak and sick, and a number of you have fallen asleep. But if we judged ourselves, we would not come under judgment. (1 Cor. 11:27–31)

The Corinthians were not unbelievers, since Paul calls them "saints" at the beginning of the letter (1 Cor. 1:2). Yet, they were being chastened by the Lord with sickness and even death because they were not showing proper discernment when they participated in the Supper.

> When you come together, it is not the Lord's Supper you eat, for as you eat, each of you goes ahead without waiting for anybody else. One remains hungry, another gets drunk. Don't you have homes to eat and drink in? Or do you despise the church of God and humiliate those who have nothing? What shall I say to you? Shall I praise you for this? Certainly not! (vv. 20–22)

It was not so much that the Corinthians failed to understand the symbolism of the bread (i.e., as the "body of Christ" in the narrow, physical sense). Rather, they failed to appreciate the role of the Lord's Supper in the edification of the church as a whole (i.e., the "body of Christ" as the church itself).

They were treating the sacrament as if it were a common meal: "It is not the Lord's Supper you eat." They were showing a lack of consideration for one another, even, apparently, to the point of displaying party spirits. Far from a solemn and holy feast of profound spiritual significance, the Supper had been turned into an occasion for drunkenness and gluttony! For this lack of discernment, and unworthy practice, the Lord had intervened directly to chasten them.

When Paul calls upon them to examine themselves, therefore, he is not so much calling for an introspective self-examination, as he is calling for an active demonstration that will prove that they now understand what they are doing when they come to the Lord's Supper.[5] The particular form that demonstration was to take in their case is described by the apostle in verses 33–34: "So then, my brothers, when you come together to eat, wait for each other. If anyone is hungry, he should eat at home, so that when you meet together it may not result in judgment. And when I come I will give further directions."

For our part, Paul is warning that we must not only understand the significance of the sacrament itself, but also appreciate its place in the life of the church, if we are to participate in a "worthy" (i.e., appropriate) fashion. Indeed, as Protestants it is difficult to see how our thumbnail-size pieces of bread and miniature cups of wine (or grape juice) afford us an opportunity for becoming gluttonous or drunk! Nevertheless, we may so emphasize the Godward, vertical significance of the Lord's Supper that we fail to appreciate its horizontal dimensions as well. Our communion with Christ is also a communion with one another as members of His body. In this respect, the Lord's Supper (like baptism) identifies us as the people of God, distinguishes us from the world, and summons us to our responsibilities to one another as members of one body.

The requirements that we love one another (e.g., Rom. 12:10, 16; 13:8), minister the grace of God to one another (e.g., 1 Peter 4:10–11), help one another materially when necessary (e.g., Gal. 6:10; 1 Peter 4:9), and maintain with one another a holy fellowship (e.g., Heb. 3:13; 10:24–25) are pressed upon us each time we assemble around the table of the Lord. To participate in the Lord's Supper and yet fail to discharge these covenantal responsibilities to one another is to court the Lord's chastening judgment upon us and our churches.

SOME PARTING THOUGHTS

The Reformed faith calls us to appreciate anew the sacraments that God has given to us as signs and seals of His gracious covenant with us. As Calvin taught, He has given the sacraments to edify us—first, by uniting us more fully to Christ through faith and thus aiding our spiritual growth, and second, by confirming and strengthening us as we daily face adverse circumstances and temptations, and third, by spurring us on to greater faithfulness in Christian living as we come to recognize more fully our personal responsibilities to God and to each other as members of God's covenant family.

These great needs are still pressing on the church today, and thus the time is ripe for the church to rediscover what the Reformed faith has to say about the sacraments.

STUDY QUESTIONS

1. Explain the nearness of God to His covenant people (Ezek. 37:27). How did the Incarnation express this nearness, in view of passages such as John 1:14? What is God's ultimate expression of His nearness to His people (see John 16:7)? Explain how the Word and the sacraments bring us near to God. When was the last time you approached the Word and the sacraments as opportunities—privileges—to draw near to God?
2. Explain how the sacraments are more than mere signs or memorials. Who applies the grace signified in the sacraments to believers and how does He do so?
3. Explain the connection between the "audible word" and the "visible word" of the sacraments. Should the latter ever be separated from the former? Why not? What is your church's practice?

Notes

1. John Calvin, *The Institutes of the Christian Religion*, ed. John T. McNeill, trans. Lewis Ford Battles (Philadelphia: Westminster Press, 1960), 4.14.3.
2. The Roman Catholic Church has seven sacraments (baptism, confirmation, penance, the Mass, marriage, ordination, and extreme unction). Protestants,

by contrast, have accepted only two sacraments—baptism (Matt. 28:19; Acts 2:38–39; Gal. 3:27–28) and the Lord's Supper (Matt. 26:26–28; Mark 14:22–24; Luke 22:19–20; John 6:53–55; 1 Cor. 11:23–29). These two sacraments alone have the authoritative sanction of Scripture, were instituted by Christ during His earthly ministry, signify and seal the covenant of grace, and are parallel in meaning to the Old Covenant sacraments of circumcision and the Passover.

3. "The grace which is exhibited in or by the sacraments rightly used, is not conferred by any power in them; neither doth the efficacy of a sacrament depend upon the piety or intention of him that doth administer it: but upon the work of the Spirit, and *the word of institution*, which contains, together with a precept authorizing the use thereof, a promise of benefit to worthy receivers" (Westminster Confession of Faith, 27.3, emphasis added).

4. Even those who hold to adult-only baptism face the sad fact that some who are baptized as adults later manifest unbelief and rebellion. The same tragedy exists in Reformed churches, as well, since some children of the covenant, as well as adult converts, later forsake the covenant with its privileges and obligations. While this is a bitter reality, it says nothing about the propriety of baptizing infants. Baptism is a sacrament and, as such, it cannot be more than a sign and seal of an inward work of God. It cannot be a "window on the soul," guaranteeing regeneration in either the infant or the adult. Some baptized persons have faith, others do not. This is why baptism is a blessing only to those who believe. To those who do not believe and who reject God's covenant, it becomes a sign of divine curse. Those who fall into unbelief are to be disciplined and ultimately "put out of the church" if necessary (cf. Matt. 18:17; 1 Cor. 5:5), as we will see in the next chapter.

5. The Greek term translated "examine" has the sense of testing something in order to prove or demonstrate its genuineness. Paul calls the Corinthians to act in such a way as to demonstrate that they can pass God's test and be approved by Him. If they fail to repent of their abuses of the Lord's Supper, God's testing will continue to take the form of the disciplinary judgment mentioned in verses 29–30. See Gordon D. Fee, *The First Epistle to the Corinthians* (Grand Rapids: Eerdmans, 1987), 531–69.

FIFTEEN

RESPECTING YOUR ELDERS

A s the apostle Paul went through the Mediterranean world preaching the gospel and calling men and women into fellowship with Christ in His church, he and Barnabas "appointed elders for them in each church" (Acts 14:23). Because the church is the covenant people of God assembled together with their elders (or overseers) and deacons, Paul could address the Philippian church as "the saints in Christ Jesus at Philippi, together with the overseers and deacons" (Phil. 1:1).

Christ has appointed a government for His church, and He both calls and equips men to teach, rule, and show mercy in and through the local church. These functions are exercised by the continuing officers of the church—elders (who are to teach and rule) and deacons (who are to show mercy). Our particular focus in this chapter will be on what the Reformed faith has to say about the office of elder and the role of elders in the process of church discipline.

A MATTER OF FORM

Throughout church history, three major views have emerged regarding church government. Some have argued for a hierarchical form of church government, with authority vested in graded levels of individual church officers (such as priests, bishops, archbishops, etc.). This is sometimes known as the episcopal form of church government (from *episkopos*, the Greek term for "bishop").

Others have argued for a congregational form of government, in which church authority is exercised directly by independent local congregations—sometimes through elected officers as their representatives, and sometimes without any elected officers—since some congregationalist groups have rejected the very idea of an ordained ministry.

Still others have argued for a presbyterian form of church government, in which church authority is to be exercised through a plurality of representative officers, who are elected by the congregation and who function in both the local church (in sessions or consistories) and in a system of graded church courts (presbyteries, classes, or synods at the regional level, and sometimes even at the national level).

OF, BY, AND FOR THE PEOPLE

Despite significant differences on some matters of church government, most Reformed churches emphasize the biblical pattern of government by representative men, chosen by God through His people to exercise oversight in the church.[1] Since the principle of representation is central to the way God has administered His covenant among His people throughout history, once again we can see the covenantal character of Reformed theology shaping the Reformed view of the church.

Soon after Israel was delivered from Egypt, Moses became overwhelmed with the responsibility of shepherding God's people: "The next day Moses took his seat to serve as judge for the people, and they stood around him from morning till evening" (Ex. 18:13). All day the people came to him to seek God's will in settling their disputes with one another (vv. 15–16).

Moses' father-in-law, Jethro, then offered this wise counsel:

> What you are doing is not good. You and these people who come to you will only wear yourselves out. The work is too heavy for you; you cannot handle it alone. Listen now to me and I will give you some advice, and may God be with you. You must be the people's *representative* before God and bring their disputes to him. Teach them the decrees and laws, and show them the way to live and the duties they are to perform. *But select capable men from all the people*—men who fear God, trustworthy men who hate dishonest gain—*and appoint them as officials over thousands, hundreds, fifties and tens*. Have them serve as judges for the people at all times, but have them *bring every difficult case to you*; the simple cases they

can decide themselves. That will make your load lighter, because they will share it with you. If you do this and God so commands, you will be able to stand the strain, and all these people will go home satisfied. (vv. 17–23)

Jethro advised Moses to select responsible men from among the people—capable men who feared God, who were trustworthy, and who hated dishonest gain. These were to be the elders of the people, who would serve as administrators and judges for the people in settling disputes in accordance with the Word of God, which Moses taught to all the people. Throughout the pages of the Old Testament, this ministry of the local elders exists alongside the special ministries of the prophets (Ex. 19:7; Deut. 27:1), priests (Josh. 8:33), and kings (1 Sam. 8:4–5).

This brief sketch of the office of elder in the "church in the wilderness" (Acts 7:38 KJV) helps us understand the office of elder as it appears in the New Testament church.[2] New Testament elders (pastoral "overseers") are to serve as representatives of the people and are given their authority by Christ to administer the Word of God among His people by teaching and discipling them.

According to the apostolic pattern, these elders were appointed in each local church: "Paul and Barnabas *appointed elders for them in each church* and, with prayer and fasting, committed them to the Lord, in whom they had put their trust" (Acts 14:23). Paul wrote to Titus, "The reason I left you in Crete was that you might straighten out what was left unfinished and *appoint elders in every town, as I directed you*" (Titus 1:5).

Another link to the Old Covenant office of elder can be seen in 1 Timothy 3 and Titus 1, where Paul lists the qualifications for elders. Jethro had advised Moses to choose "capable men from all the people—men who fear God, trustworthy men who hate dishonest gain" (Ex. 18:21). These basic categories are filled out in Paul's instructions.

Now the overseer must be above reproach, the husband of but one wife, temperate, self-controlled, respectable, hospitable, able to teach, not given to drunkenness, not violent but gentle, not quarrelsome, not a lover of money. He must manage his own family well and see that his children obey him with proper respect. . . . He must not be a recent convert, or he may become conceited and fall under the same judgment as the devil. He must also have a good reputation with outsiders, so that he will not fall into disgrace and into the devil's trap. (1 Tim. 3:2–7)

Those who demonstrate these qualities and assume the office of elder are charged with the awesome responsibility of exercising pastoral oversight. In fact, the biblical names "elder" (*presbyteros*—"presbyter") and "overseer" (*episkopos*—"bishop") are used interchangeably to describe a single pastoral office in the church (Acts 20:17, 28; 1 Tim. 3:1; 4:14; 5:17, 19; Titus 1:5, 7; 1 Peter 5:1–2). As those who hold this pastoral office, elders are charged by God with the responsibility of teaching and leading His people as Christ's undershepherds. Paul told the Ephesian elders: "Keep watch over yourselves and all the flock of which the Holy Spirit has made you overseers. Be shepherds of the church of God, which he bought with his own blood" (Acts 20:28). And Peter adds, "Be shepherds of God's flock that is under your care, serving as overseers—not because you must, but because you are willing, as God wants you to be; not greedy for money, but eager to serve" (1 Peter 5:2).

While all elders are to shepherd the flock, some elders are to give themselves in a special way to the ministry of the Word in preaching and teaching (sometimes called "teaching elders"). But teaching elders are joined by other elders (sometimes called "ruling elders") to share collectively in exercising oversight in the church: "The elders who direct [rule] the affairs of the church well are worthy of double honor, especially those whose work is preaching and teaching" (1 Tim. 5:17). As these teaching and ruling elders deliberate together and render decisions true to Scripture, they administer Christ's own authoritative rule in the local church.[3] Christ rules the local church through His elders.

But these elders do not simply exercise their authority in the local church alone, as the important events recorded for us by Luke in Acts 15 indicate. Early in the apostolic era of the New Testament church, a critical issue arose regarding the place of newly converted Gentiles in the church: "So Paul and Barnabas were appointed, along with some other believers, to go up to Jerusalem to see the apostles and elders about this question" (Acts 15:2). Note that the apostles were joined by the elders in considering this vital issue in the life of the church. The elders are mentioned several other times by Luke in his account of the council that met in Jerusalem.

When they came to Jerusalem, they were welcomed by the church and the apostles and elders, to whom they reported everything God had done through them. . . . The apostles and elders met to consider this question. . . . Then the apostles and elders, with the whole church, decided to choose some of their own men and send them to Antioch with Paul and Barnabas. They chose Judas (called Barsabbas) and Silas, two men who were leaders among the brothers. (vv. 4, 6, 22)

On the basis of these passages of Scripture, the Reformed churches are governed by representatives chosen by the people on the basis of their godly character and spiritual gifts. They have been given authority by Christ to teach and rule in the church for the benefit and protection of His people under their care. Further, they exercise that ministry on behalf of the broader church through a system of graded courts.[4]

RULE BY THE BOOK

Related to the Reformed understanding of representative church government is the idea that Scripture regulates how elders are to govern the church. Elders exercise their authority only by ministering and declaring the Word of God (Acts 6:2, 4). No matter how godly or gifted men may be, they are not given the prerogative of legislating for the church. They may only minister God's will for His people by declaring and applying what God has already spoken in the Scriptures.

Thus, the Bible is the "constitution" of the church by defining the church's nature, form, and function. The elders are called upon to govern the church in accordance with biblical standards. God regulates all facets of the corporate life of His people in accordance with His Word. And it is the elders' responsibility to teach the church God's decrees and laws, showing the church how to live and what to do to please the Lord (Ex. 18:20).

Churches within the Reformed tradition have characteristically developed confessions of faith, creeds, and catechisms to instruct God's people in biblical truth and to be an authoritative expression of the doctrinal commitment of the church. These confessions and catechisms are always subject to the supreme authority of Scripture. These secondary standards are authoritative only to the extent that they are biblical.

Because they are biblical, these creedal statements have been given constitutional status in that the leaders of the church have been required to subscribe to them and are held accountable to them as a control on what they believe and do. In addition, statements summarizing the biblical pattern of church government, directions for worship, and procedures for exercising church discipline have also been used to make the leadership of the elders uniform throughout the broader church.[5]

Thus, the two features of Reformed church government are representative rule by elders and constitutional limitations based on biblical principles, often embodied in confessions, creeds, and catechisms. Now we can see how these principles apply to one of the most solemn responsibilities of elders: church discipline.

A MATTER OF DISCIPLINE

Since "no discipline seems pleasant at the time, but painful" (Heb. 12:11), many believers sadly reject church discipline as an element of pastoral care. From a biblical vantage point, however, believers should delight in church discipline, not only as a tremendous privilege, but also as a "means of grace." That is, along with the ministry of the Word, prayer, and the administration of the sacraments, church discipline is one of the spiritual means that God has ordained to help His people grow in holiness.

Of course, church discipline is not the only form of discipline that God has ordained for our growth in holiness. The most basic form of discipline is self-discipline or "self-control"—a fruit of the Spirit (Gal. 5:23). As such, Paul made it an important part of his presentation of the gospel (e.g., Acts 24:25), as did Peter, who taught that effective and productive Christian living requires self-discipline (2 Peter 1:5–8). Without it, we are vulnerable to many temptations and sins (Prov. 25:28; cf. 2 Tim. 3:3). In addition to self-discipline, God has given His people mutual discipline in the home, state, and church. Although God's discipline is usually mediated by human agents whom He has appointed for that task (e.g., parents, civil rulers, and elders), it can either be neglected (as in the situation mentioned in 1 Cor. 5:1–8) or ineffective, owing to its inherent limitations (e.g., the church's inability to read the heart). In such circumstances, God sometimes disciplines or intervenes directly in the lives of His people either individually or collectively to chasten them (e.g., Ananias and Sapphira in Acts 5, and the Corinthians who participated unworthily in the Lord's Supper [1 Cor. 11:27–30]).

Paul brings this discussion full circle by telling the Corinthians— and us—that "if we judged ourselves, we would not come under judgment. When we are judged by the Lord, we are being disciplined so that we will not be condemned with the world" (1 Cor. 11:31–32). The lesson here is clear: it is better to discipline yourselves, or to be disciplined by one another in the body of Christ, than to leave yourselves open to the direct discipline or intervention of the Lord.

We must always remember that discipline—whether it be self-discipline, mutual discipline, or direct discipline/intervention—is a sign that we are children of the living God. Discipline thus identifies the true children of God and distinguishes them from pretenders.

> "My son, do not make light of the Lord's discipline, and do not lose heart when he rebukes you, because the Lord disciplines those he loves, and he punishes everyone he accepts as a son." Endure hardship as discipline; God is treating you as sons. . . . If you are not disciplined (and everyone undergoes discipline), then you are illegitimate children and not true sons. (Heb. 12:5–8)

Because you are a child of God, the question is not whether the Lord will discipline you, but how He will do it, and how you will respond to it. Will you despise and reject it by abusing or neglecting it in your church? Or will you submit to it by practicing it in your church, being confident that "it produces a harvest of righteousness and peace for those who have been trained by it" (Heb. 12:11)?

If you are God's child, He loves you, and for that reason He will discipline you in order that you may share in His holiness (v. 10). Let us now consider how He designed church discipline to help us grow in His holiness.

WITH A PURPOSE

Why did God design church discipline? What are the purposes furthered by church discipline? The Westminster Confession of Faith, 30.3, answers that very question.

> Church censures are necessary, for the reclaiming and gaining of offending brethren, for deterring of others from the like offenses, for purging out of that leaven which might infect the whole lump, for vindicating the honor of Christ, and the holy profession of the gospel, and for preventing the wrath of God, which might justly fall upon the church, if they should suffer his covenant, and the seals thereof, to be profaned by notorious and obstinate offenders.

We have already discussed the direct, historical intervention of Christ in the life of His church to bring about discipline that the church cannot, or

will not, exercise herself. We will now take a brief look at the other purposes found in the Westminster Confession, and we will look at them in
reverse order.

*First, church discipline honors Christ since men will glorify God as they see
the good works of His people.* In His Sermon on the Mount, Christ taught us
that we are to "let [our] light shine before men, that they may see [our]
good deeds and praise [our] Father in heaven" (Matt. 5:16). Just as men
will praise God when they see our good works, so they will blaspheme God
when they see the shameful inconsistencies of a church whose life does
not match her profession: "You who brag about the law, do you dishonor
God by breaking the law? As it is written: 'God's name is blasphemed
among the Gentiles because of you' " (Rom. 2:23–24).

Overwhelming as it may be, the glory of God is intimately tied up
with whether the church "walks" her "talk." If she does not do so, and does
nothing about it, the world will blaspheme the name of God. But if the
church practices biblical discipline when her members stray, Christ will be
glorified. This is at least part of what Jesus had in mind when He declared,
"By this all men will know that you are my disciples, if you love one
another" (John 13:35). Christian love is not sentimental mishmash; it loves
and promotes holiness in the church and in the lives of individual believers. It is a loving holiness and a holy love. If your church, as the true bride
of Christ, really loves Him and seeks His honor, she will practice biblical
discipline to protect His name and promote His glory.

Second, church discipline purifies the church. The prophet Malachi announced the coming of the Messiah in terms of His work of purifying the
worship and fellowship of the house of God: "He will sit as a refiner and
purifier of silver; he will purify the Levites and refine them like gold and
silver. Then the LORD will have men who will bring offerings in righteousness" (Mal. 3:3).

True to that prophetic word, Jesus came into the world, and, on the
cross of Calvary, "gave himself for us to redeem us from all wickedness and
to purify for himself a people that are his very own, eager to do what is
good" (Titus 2:14). The blood-washed character of the church requires
that every Christian do his utmost to preserve and promote the purity of
the church: "Since we have these promises, dear friends, let us purify ourselves from everything that contaminates body and spirit, perfecting holiness out of reverence for God" (2 Cor. 7:1).

Christ calls us to practice discipline in our local churches for the
same reason the apostle Paul exhorted the Corinthian church to deal with
the wickedness that it had tolerated.

Don't you know that a little yeast works through the whole batch of dough? Get rid of the old yeast that you may be a new batch without yeast—as you really are. For Christ, our Passover lamb, has been sacrificed. Therefore let us keep the Festival, not with the old yeast, the yeast of malice and wickedness, but with bread without yeast, the bread of sincerity and truth. (1 Cor. 5:6–8)

If your church really loves the Cross of Christ, and the blood-bought purity that is hers in Him, she will give herself to practicing biblical discipline carefully and consistently.

Third, church discipline warns others who might succumb to similar temptations. When Korah's followers rebelled against Moses and Aaron in the wilderness—and therefore rebelled against the Lord—God judged them by causing the earth to open its mouth and swallow them. Others also died when fire devoured them. Moses' conclusion on the episode is to the point: "And they served as a warning sign" (Num. 26:9–10). The New Testament has some warning signs of its own: when God took the lives of Ananias and Sapphira in judgment, for example, "great fear" came upon all who heard of it (Acts 5:5, 11).

God warns His people to take heed to their lives by bringing His discipline upon them. If a miraculous judgment like that upon the rebellious Korahites gives warning to the church, so does the disciplinary word of Christ as ministered in the church by its leaders: "Those who sin are to be rebuked publicly, so that the others may take warning" (1 Tim. 5:20). Of course, an errant believer should not be censured publicly to satisfy a vindictive intention on the part of the elders to be "holier than thou." Those who exercise discipline are not to provoke people to fear. That is Christ's job. They are simply to be faithful to Him as they faithfully exercise church discipline.

While many debate the deterrent effects of some forms of civil punishment, there is no debate in Scripture over the fact that Christ's discipline teaches others to flee similar ensnaring offenses. If the proverb is true—"Flog a mocker, and the simple will learn prudence" (Prov. 19:25)—how much more will the child of God learn prudence and self-control as he witnesses God's discipline administered publicly within the church.

If your church is really looking for ways to "spur one another on toward love and good deeds" (Heb. 10:24), she must never forget that few ways compare to exercising biblical church discipline.

Fourth, church discipline reclaims and restores the fallen believer. While all the other purposes of discipline that we have examined are biblical and important, the desire to reclaim and restore the fallen believer is the immediate purpose for church discipline. Listen to the repeated emphasis of Scripture. Jesus said: "If your brother sins against you, go and show him his fault, just between the two of you. If he listens to you, you have won your brother over" (Matt. 18:15).

Paul says much the same thing in his letter to the churches in Galatia: "Brothers, if someone is caught in a sin, you who are spiritual should restore him gently. But watch yourself, or you also may be tempted. Carry each other's burdens, and in this way you will fulfill the law of Christ" (Gal. 6:1–2). Biblical church discipline is all about winning your brother and restoring your sister gently.

Tragically, church discipline evokes negative images in the minds of many Christians today. We will never practice discipline faithfully in our churches until we see it as a blessed instrument of God's grace in the life of the church.[6]

Today, as never before, we need to recapture a biblical sense of the necessity of practicing restorative discipline in the body of Christ.

STEP BY STEP

Now that we have a better understanding of why we are to practice church discipline, we can appreciate exactly how such discipline is to be exercised. Scripture does not leave us in the dark on this point. Christ Himself taught,

> If your brother sins against you, go and show him his fault, just between the two of you. If he listens to you, you have won your brother over. But if he will not listen, take one or two brothers along, so that "every matter may be established by the testimony of two or three witnesses." If he refuses to listen to them, tell it to the church; and if he refuses to listen even to the church, treat him as you would a pagan or a tax collector. (Matt. 18:15–17)

Notice, from the outset, that Matthew 18 is all about mutual discipline in the life of the church. We have already seen that self-discipline lies on one end of the Matthew 18 process; had the offending brother exercised self-discipline, he would never have sinned against and offended his brother. At the other end of the Matthew 18 process is the direct discipline or intervention of the Lord, which, as we have already seen, may be brought to bear when the church fails to discipline those in her midst.

The mutual discipline outlined in Matthew 18 starts with the offended party's confronting the offending party informally in private, just between the two of them. If that private confrontation proves unfruitful, the offended party is to get help by taking two or three witnesses with him. Should that confrontation fail, the offended party, together with his witnesses, is to tell the matter to the church. Then the church, through its elders, can institute formal church discipline. If the offending party refuses to listen to the church, he is to be treated as a pagan or a tax collector, that is, censured publicly and, if necessary, put out of the church. These, then, are the four steps outlined in Matthew 18, which we will now discuss in greater detail.

Just Between the Two of You

Christ taught that the early stages of the disciplinary process are to be both private and informal. When a brother or sister in the body of Christ has sinned against you, Christ commands you to go to that brother or sister privately and resolve the issue by lovingly and restoratively confronting him or her.

Most of us are all a bit reluctant to do this sort of thing. Indeed, church discipline often flounders at this first step precisely because we refuse to obey Christ's command. We offer excuse after excuse for not dealing with the situation as Christ commands: "It is too embarrassing." "I'm not a confrontational type of person." "Time will heal the wounds." "I may lose a friendship." And so on.

But let us be honest. Even if all these things were true, they would provide no reason for disobeying our Lord. To be sure, it is hard to confront a brother or sister in the right spirit. And we never can tell how he or she may respond. Jesus understands all that, and because He does, He gives us great assurance in this very passage.

For starters, He reminds us that we are "brothers" with the one who has sinned against us. As members of the same family, we should gladly give and gladly receive this restorative discipline from one another's hands. But this command also contains a blessed promise: "I will be with you" (see v. 20). This promise gives great hope to those who are willing to believe it. You will never have to do this spiritual work alone. Jesus will always walk you through it and make it a blessing for you and your brother.

In addition to assuring and comforting you, Christ also states exactly what your purpose is to be: to win your brother over (v. 15). That is why you go—not to prove your point, not to ease your hurt feelings, but to win over a fellow Christian who has fallen into sin. You go to help and to heal.

What will it take to win him over? It will take a rebuke, which sometimes comes in the form of an indictment, and at other times in the form of an appeal.[7] Both kinds of rebuke have their proper place. The "spirit of gentleness" that Paul commends (Gal. 6:1) would seem to suggest that we start with an appeal—the softer approach—which may disarm even a wrathful brother (cf. Prov. 15:1). If, however, the offender proves stubborn, an indictment—the more forceful approach—may be necessary to win him over. In either case, we must remember that we must first be clear-sighted by getting the beam out of our own eye before we approach our brother (Matt. 7:1ff.).

But why should you rebuke your brother in private? By doing so, you protect the good name of your brother. Gossip creates a spreading fire, which, once kindled, often does considerable damage to all parties as well as to the cause of Christ. Beyond not adding fuel to the fire, we are called elsewhere in Scripture to be "peacemakers," and, as such, it is our responsibility to keep the peace by solving our interpersonal problems at the interpersonal level. You may have to take the matter beyond this level if your efforts are unsuccessful, but you should never be quick to do so. If private discipline works well, it should bear its fruit quietly, with minimal disruption to the fellowship and ministry of the church.

Remember that your goal in the whole process is to restore your brother: "If he listens to you, you have won your brother over." If the offending brother heeds the loving admonitions of a fellow Christian, he will respond to the convicting work of the Spirit by repenting of his sin. Jesus does not say "if he apologizes," as if the offending brother brushes off a tiresome and embarrassing confrontation. He says "if he listens"—that is, if he takes to heart what has been said and seeks forgiveness as part of his desire to make things right in whatever ways are appropriate.

But the picture presented in Matthew 18 is even more beautiful, since winning a brother over involves turning enmity into friendship. A grudging concession is not what is called for, but rather, full reconciliation and a new and even better relationship.

Take Two or Three Witnesses

What are you to do if your brother refuses to "listen" and is not "won over"? You must first realize that refusing to listen is what moves the process of discipline along from the first step to the second step.[8] In addition to whatever the offense may have been, at this stage hardness of heart has become the offending brother's major problem.

The second step of discipline requires getting help from two or three others to turn up the spiritual "pressure" on the errant brother. These brothers and sisters that join you in seeking to win over and restore your brother function both as witnesses and confronters. As witnesses, they will hear both parties out and decide who is right and who is wrong. As confronters, they will help in trying to bring the offender to repentance. If the brother still will not heed the loving admonitions of his fellow believers, they will serve to bear witness to the continued stubbornness of the offender when he is brought before the elders of the church in the third step of discipline.

Tell It to the Church

When a matter moves from the second step (i.e., taking witnesses) to the third step (i.e., bringing the matter before the elders), it moves out of the realm of informal discipline into the realm of formal discipline. This is a serious dividing line, since it shows that a brother has been persistently unrepentant. As before, his hardness of heart continues to be his major problem.

At this point, a private matter begins to become public, because the restoration of the offender is now a matter of more direct concern to the whole church body. Sin always affects the whole body since, as members of the church, we are all interconnected as members of one another. When sin begins to infect the church body, informal discipline serves as the church's "immune system." But, just as is the case with our physical bodies, that system can become overloaded and thus unable to repel the infection adequately. When that happens, we need more help. We must bring the matter to the "physicians of the soul"—the elders of the church.

We have already discussed the role of the elders as representatives of the whole church and as pastoral ministers. Because of their role within the church, matters of discipline come to them first for judgment, counsel, and other actions appropriate to the situation. When they have discovered the facts of the case, it is their responsibility to take disciplinary action (if the offender is in fact guilty, and still refuses to repent), and to communicate that action to the church in a discreet, orderly way, with instructions to the congregation about their role in this stage of discipline.

The New Testament gives us examples of how the apostles exercised their leadership in disciplinary cases. Paul, for example, had much to say to the Corinthians about their practice of discipline or lack thereof (1

Cor. 5:3–5; 2 Cor. 2:6–10), as did the apostle John (3 John 9–14). Elders must learn from and follow the apostolic example by setting things straight in the church.

In order to set things straight, elders need to understand the situation they are facing when a brother refuses to listen to them. When a brother has become hard-hearted and stubborn, has resorted repeatedly to unrepentant self-justification, and has refused to listen to the elders, he demonstrates that his profession of faith in Christ is seriously in question. Salvation depends upon being one of Christ's sheep, and that is evidenced by hearing His voice. Refusing to hear the Shepherd through His under-shepherds, therefore, may very well indicate that the errant "brother" may not really be one of Christ's sheep. Christ minces no words on this point.

> "The man who enters by the gate is the shepherd of his sheep. The watchman opens the gate for him, and the sheep listen to his voice. He calls his own sheep by name and leads them out. When he has brought out all his own, he goes on ahead of them, and *his sheep follow him because they know his voice.* . . . I am the good shepherd; I know my sheep and my sheep know me—just as the Father knows me and I know the Father—and I lay down my life for the sheep. I have other sheep that are not of this sheep pen. I must bring them also. *They too will listen to my voice*, and there shall be one flock and one shepherd." . . . The Jews gathered around him, saying, "How long will you keep us in suspense? If you are the Christ, tell us plainly." Jesus answered, "I did tell you, but you do not believe. The miracles I do in my Father's name speak for me, but *you do not believe because you are not my sheep. My sheep listen to my voice;* I know them, and they follow me." (John 10:2–4, 14–16, 24–27)

Are you careful to hear and heed the voice of Christ as you listen to sermons week by week and receive the exhortations of your fellow believers and the leaders of the church—or are you selective in what you hear? Are you resistant to those who try to provoke you to love and good works in the body of Christ (Heb. 10:24)? You can tell a great deal about the condition of your heart and your relationship to the Lord and His church by asking yourself whether you really hear His voice.

You can now appreciate more fully why any failure to hear His voice by heeding His discipline as outlined in Matthew 18 is so serious. Now you know why He says that, in the end, the church must treat such a person as "a pagan or a tax collector" (Matt. 18:17).

Treat Him as a Pagan or a Tax Collector

Jesus makes it very clear that, if a brother or sister refuses to repent, the process of church discipline must end with a censure: "Treat him as you would a pagan or a tax collector" (Matt. 18:17).

Censures are those means of chastening which God has entrusted to His church for spiritually correcting His people and for excluding willful hypocrites from the body of Christ.

Christ has called the church through its elders to make a judgment about the profession and life of the unheeding brother. Such negative judgments are much despised in the church today, thus proving how grievously the church has set herself against the Lord Jesus Himself. When we decide that we are wiser or more "compassionate" than the Lord Jesus, we are well on the way to apostasy. For that reason, the church today needs to be called back to the biblical pattern of discipline that we have been discussing, lest she lose her identity and her holiness.

The reason for making this judgment, and communicating it to the church, is not to persecute the offender, but rather to make it possible for the members of the church to take steps to adjust their relationship to, and treatment of, the offender in light of that judgment.

There are several degrees of censure outlined in the Bible, and we will survey them briefly here. To do that, we will have to look at other New Testament passages and place them in the context of the passage in Matthew 18 that we have been studying, which speaks explicitly only of the last, and most severe, form of censure—being put out of the midst of the church and treated as an unbeliever. There are three forms of censure:

Admonition or rebuke: God's Word is designed, among other things, to admonish the believer and rebuke him when he strays from the path of obedience. Although admonitions and rebukes are part of the informal disciplinary process that we have been studying, when the matter has at last come before the church, the elders may determine that a public admonition or rebuke is in order: "Those who sin are to be rebuked publicly, so that the others may take warning" (1 Tim. 5:20).

Disassociation: Here is another term that sends shivers down the spine of modern American Christians, since they think that it resonates with "cultic" overtones. Our reaction shows how far we have strayed from Scripture on this point.

In the name of the Lord Jesus Christ, we command you, brothers, to *keep away from* every brother who is idle and does not live according to the teaching you received from us. . . . If anyone does not obey our instruction in this letter, *take special note* of him. *Do not associate with* him, in order that he may feel ashamed. (2 Thess. 3:6, 14)

I have written you in my letter *not to associate with* sexually immoral people—not at all meaning the people of this world who are immoral, or the greedy and swindlers, or idolaters. In that case you would have to leave this world. But now I am writing you that *you must not associate with* anyone who calls himself a brother but is sexually immoral or greedy, an idolater or a slanderer, a drunkard or a swindler. With such a man do not even eat. (1 Cor. 5:9–11)

These passages require that believers keep away from and do not associate with so-called believers who are living unrepentant lives. This, of course, requires that the church identify such people publicly; in the words of Paul, the church is to "take special note" of them. Then the church is to withhold from them the blessings and comforts of social contact or fellowship within the church. They are not to fellowship with us over a meal or participate with us in the Lord's Supper.

Despite this serious exclusion from the social fellowship of the body, the offender must still be treated as a brother. In this very same context, Paul writes, "Yet do not regard him as an enemy, but warn him as a brother" (2 Thess. 3:15). The purpose of this censure is to make the offender "feel ashamed" (2 Thess. 3:14). Yes, God believes in using shame as one means of bringing His children to repentance. It takes a tough love as well as a confident hope to carry out this censure effectively, but the Lord may well use this censure to bring the wayward brother at last to repentance. If you believe the Lord, you will obey Him by not shrinking away from this censure.

Putting out of the church: While many people refer to this final censure as "excommunication," excommunication more properly is to exclude an errant brother from participating in the sacrament of communion, and that takes place when we withhold fellowship from him.

In Matthew 18:17, Christ commands us that we are to treat an unheeding brother "as [we] would a pagan or a tax collector." No longer is the offender to be treated as a brother. Now he is to be treated as a pagan. No longer is such a person entitled to the blessings of covenant fellowship with Christ and His people. Now he is put out of the church.

In 1 Corinthians 5:4–7, Paul tells us a little more about putting someone out of the church.

When you are assembled in the name of our Lord Jesus and I am with you in spirit, and the power of our Lord Jesus is present, hand this man over to Satan, so that the sinful nature may be destroyed and his spirit saved on the day of the Lord. . . . Don't you know that a little yeast works through the whole batch of dough? Get rid of the old yeast that you may be a new batch without yeast.

In this passage, Paul speaks of handing the offending brother "over to Satan." This language is somewhat enigmatic, but it gives the distinct impression of a removal of the divine protection that God affords His people as members of the church. The expelled offender is now subject to affliction at the hands of the Evil One "so that the sinful nature may be destroyed."

Notice that, even at this extreme stage in the Lord's discipline, Paul holds out a true hope that the errant brother will repent and be restored: "so that the sinful nature may be destroyed and his spirit saved on the day of the Lord."

Nevertheless, there is a strong emphasis in this passage on removing the unrepentant offender from the midst of the church. This must not be overlooked or minimized. Remember, we identified several purposes that God has in disciplining His church, one of which is restoring the offender. But the other goals of discipline are also served by this step of putting the offender out of the church.

All sin offends God's holiness, but when a professing believer persists in sinning, despite the repeated efforts of his fellow saints to bring him to repentance, it is especially hateful in God's sight. Through Isaiah, the Lord declares,

The ox knows his master, the donkey his owner's manger, but Israel does not know, my people do not understand. Ah, sinful nation, a people loaded with guilt, a brood of evildoers, children given to corruption! They have forsaken the LORD; they have spurned the Holy One of Israel and turned their backs on him. Why should you be beaten anymore? Why do you persist in rebellion? Your whole head is injured, your whole heart afflicted. From the sole of your foot to the top of your head there is no soundness—only wounds and welts and open sores, not cleansed or bandaged or soothed with oil. (Isa. 1:3–6)

Flagrant sin and hypocrisy bring a shameful reproach upon the Lord God, whose name we bear as Christians. Such sinful behavior causes God's name to be blasphemed among those outside the church (cf. Rom. 2:24). For these reasons, the Lord will not tolerate such offenses in His church, and He calls for those who practice them to be put out.

Toleration of such sin also endangers the church, for others may be caused to stumble as a result of the continued disobedience of one member.

> "For the lips of a priest ought to preserve knowledge, and from his mouth men should seek instruction—because he is the messenger of the LORD Almighty. But you have turned from the way and by your teaching have caused many to stumble; you have violated the covenant with Levi," says the LORD Almighty. (Mal. 2:7–8)

What was true of the priests of the Old Covenant is true of every believer, for we are a "kingdom of priests" in Christ. The New Testament contains several warnings against the dangers of an evil example becoming a stumbling block to God's people: "Let us, therefore, make every effort to enter that rest, so that no one will *fall by following their example of disobedience*" (Heb. 4:11). "See to it that no one misses the grace of God and *that no bitter root grows up to cause trouble and defile many*. See that no one is sexually immoral, or is godless like Esau, who for a single meal sold his inheritance rights as the oldest son" (Heb. 12:15–16).

For these reasons, as well as the ongoing hope that the offender will be restored, the church is called to practice church discipline faithfully. Nothing less than the honor of Christ and the good of the church are at stake.

A BROTHER WON

Many today scoff at the very idea of practicing church discipline. "It will never work," they say. All too often, professing believers refuse to believe that discipline is useful or that it will be effective. And, sadly, they frequently receive from it just what they expect!

But that is not God's attitude. No work or word of God is without power, and church discipline, as a ministry of the Word of God, when administered by faithful elders in accordance with the dictates of Scripture, will always accomplish God's purposes for it. To kindle and strengthen our faith on this point, God gives us many encouraging promises along the way, as well as the "success story" of the recovery and restoration of the Corinthian offender whom we met in 1 Corinthians 5. In his second letter, Paul tells us the rest of the story.

> The punishment inflicted on him by the majority is sufficient for him. Now instead, you ought to forgive and comfort him, so that he will not be overwhelmed by excessive sorrow. I urge you, therefore, to reaffirm your love for him. The reason I wrote you was to see if you would stand the test and be obedient in everything. If you forgive anyone, I also forgive him. And what I have forgiven—if there was anything to forgive—I have forgiven in the sight of Christ for your sake, in order that Satan might not outwit us. For we are not unaware of his schemes. (2 Cor. 2:6–11)[9]

In light of the repentance of the offender, Paul gave three commands to the Corinthians. First, they were to forgive him (v. 7). This accords with Jesus' command that repentance be met with forgiveness: "If your brother sins, rebuke him, and if he repents, forgive him" (Luke 17:3). In the case at Corinth, it took a great deal of effort—including expulsion from the church—to bring the offender to repentance. But when at last he repented, Paul was quick to urge the whole church to forgive him. We might imagine that Paul would have called for some kind of probationary period during which the repentant offender would have to "prove himself" before he could be readmitted to the fellowship of the church. But Paul would have none of that. He commanded, "Forgive him." Second, Paul called upon the church to comfort the restored offender. Indeed, the body-life of the church was itself a comfort, but Paul wanted that encouragement to become explicit in word and deed. Third, Paul commanded the believers at Corinth to "reaffirm their love" for him (v. 8).

Behind these acts of restoration was the same divine authority that stood behind the acts of discipline and censure: "If you forgive anyone, I also will forgive him. And what I have forgiven—if there was anything to forgive—I have forgiven in the sight of Christ for your sake" (2 Cor. 2:10). Here the apostle expresses the same principle articulated by our Savior: "I tell you the truth, whatever you bind on earth will be bound in heaven, and whatever you loose on earth will be loosed in heaven" (Matt. 18:18).

Paul tells us here how to overcome the Devil (2 Cor 2:11), just as Jesus told His disciples (and us) in Matthew 18. Exercising church discipline in a faithful and orderly manner, together with forgiving and restoring repentant offenders, is the most effective means that the church has to be healed and strengthened. If we as sons and daughters of God allow

ourselves to be trained by the loving, caring, gracious discipline of the
Lord as it comes to expression in the blessed fellowship of the church, we
can rest assured that we will be blessed with the "peaceful fruit of righteousness." And what a blessing it will be! Amen.

STUDY QUESTIONS

1. What are the three major forms of church government? How are they
   similar to and/or different from one another? Which form of government characterizes your church?
2. What are the purposes of church discipline? Does your church practice
   loving and restorative discipline? In light of the purposes of church discipline, ought your church to do so? What can you do about it?
3. What are the steps outlined in Matthew 18:15–17 for dealing with a
   brother who has sinned against you? When was the last time you obeyed
   your Lord's command in this passage?

Notes

1. While Reformed churches have been historically identified with a presbyterian form of church government, there have also been Reformed congregationalists (such as the English Puritans) and Reformed episcopalians (e.g.,
   Bishop J. C. Ryle). Reformed congregationalists believe in government by
   representative elders who exercise authority on the local level, while Reformed
   episcopalians tend to be comparatively "low church."
2. This office is introduced in the New Testament without explanation, indicating that it was already a familiar institution—because of the Old Covenant
   pattern.
3. In Matt. 16:19, Christ proclaims: "I will give you the keys of the kingdom of
   heaven; whatever you bind on earth will be bound in heaven, and whatever
   you loose on earth will be loosed in heaven." Reformed theologians have historically understood that Christ, in this passage and its parallels, delegates His
   authority as Head of the church to the apostles (as the foundation of the church,
   Eph. 2:20) and also to the continuing officers of the church.
4. The presbyterian system of church government maintains that the New Testament warrants local, regional, and synodical courts, each made up of a plurality of elders who exercise their authority jointly (Acts 15; 1 Tim. 4:14).
   The higher courts of the church sustain an appellate relationship to the lower,
   so that decisions of the lower courts can be subjected to broader levels of
   advice and consent.
5. See, for example, *The Book of Church Order of the Orthodox Presbyterian Church*

(Willow Grove, Pa.: Committee on Christian Education, 1995), and *The Book of Church Order of the Presbyterian Church in America* (Atlanta: Office of the Stated Clerk of the General Assembly of the Presbyterian Church in America, 1991).

6. Even putting someone out of the church is a gracious provision of God for the whole church by preserving her holiness and health. Further, as evidenced by Paul's discipline of the Corinthian offender and its sequel (1 Cor. 5:5; 2 Cor. 2:7f.), "excommunication" may be blessed of God to bring the erring brother to repentance, even after he has had to be treated by the church like "a pagan or a tax collector" (Matt. 18:17). Thus, discipline is an important step in further sanctifying and restoring the wayward member of the church (see the discussion under the heading "A Brother Won," pp. 208–10).

7. The term used in Matt. 18:15 is *elegcho,* which means "to prosecute successfully." You make your case against the offender in such a way as to bring conviction to his heart, leading to repentance. Another term is used in Luke 17:3—*epitimao*—which has the sense of rebuking "tentatively." Here the idea is to lay the situation before your brother (or sister) as you see it, giving him the opportunity to share his perspective and volunteer his repentance in that light.

8. Repentance always ends the process of discipline, no matter what the underlying offense may have been. Stubborn unrepentance, by contrast, always intensifies discipline, regardless of the nature of the underlying offense.

9. Behind the actions of the Corinthian church that led to the repentance of the offender, there was the equally wonderful and remarkable repentance of the church itself in response to Paul's first letter (2 Cor. 7:6–12).

PART FOUR

BACK TO THE CHRISTIAN LIFE

David G. Hagopian

INTRODUCTION

As those who have been sovereignly and graciously converted and drawn into covenant with God and His people, we are called to glorify and enjoy Him in all that we do.

But the only way we can do that is to keep our gaze fixed on Christ. Because He is the Alpha and the Omega, the First and the Last, we need to trust that He who began a good work in us will perfect it until we are with Him in glory.

As we will see in the pages that follow, He is the One who was made sin for us, that we might become the righteousness of God in Him. He is the One who, by His indwelling Spirit, enables us to become progressively conformed to His image from one degree of glory to another. He is the One who has set us free from the dominion and bondage of sin and has made us free indeed. He is the One who has made us His royal priests in our respective callings. And He is the One who is to be glorified in everything we believe and do as we learn to cultivate a distinctively biblical worldview.

Apart from Him we can do nothing. But in Him we can glorify and enjoy Him because in Him we are blessed with every spiritual blessing in the heavenly places. The Christian life, then, is about Christ for us and Christ in us, our hope of glory.

In a day when many live solely for their own glory and enjoyment, we need to get back to basics—back to the Christian life. [D. G. H.]

SIXTEEN

JUST SINNERS?

What, honestly, is your chief end or primary purpose in life? Is it, as with so many Christians today, to find personal meaning, pleasure, happiness, and satisfaction—in a word, self-fulfillment? Is that really what the Christian life is all about?

Although the Christian life, if properly lived, will lead to true self-fulfillment, it is not about self-fulfillment in its own right. While the Christian life involves the impact of the gospel on man, it should not really focus on man. It should focus on God. Man's primary purpose is to glorify and enjoy God, to honor Him for who He is and what He has done. He is the One, as we have already seen, who has sovereignly and graciously converted us, drawn us into a covenantal relationship with Himself, and called us out of the world together with His people in the church. And, as we will see in the pages that follow, He is the all-glorious God for whose glory we live the Christian life. Get a glimpse of this all-glorious God, and the cry of your life will invariably be the Reformers' cry: *soli Deo gloria*—"to God alone be the glory." In a nutshell, that is what the Reformed view of the Christian life is all about.

Granted, living to the glory of God is easier said than done, and left to us, it would not be done. It is not done by gimmicks that focus on us. Rather, we must look to Christ, the author and finisher of our faith. We have been united to Christ and must learn to trust that He who began a good work in us will perfect it until we are with Him in glory. The Christian life, then, is not primarily about us. It is primarily about Christ. To be even

215

more precise, it is about Christ for us and Christ in us, our hope of glory.

Glorifying God in the Christian life would be impossible apart from our union with Christ. In union with Him, we live a life of gratitude to Him for paying the penalty for our sin and crediting us with His righteousness (see chap. 16); we become progressively conformed to His image here and now, knowing that we are truly bound for glory (chap. 17); we enjoy the freedom He has granted us as we responsibly live for Him (chap. 18); we serve Him faithfully in our respective callings as His priests (chap. 19); and we learn to cultivate a distinctively biblical worldview (chap. 20). He is the Lord of glory, who has done, is continuing to do, and will one day complete His glorious work in us.

God's glorious work in us, however, depends upon His glorious work for us, particularly how He has graciously declared us righteous through faith on account of what Christ alone has done. We are sinners, to be sure. But in Christ we are more than just sinners.

Justified Sinners

In a comedy routine entitled "I Believe," made famous several years ago, a well-known comedian delivers a series of one-liners, listing various things he believes. At one point, he blurts out that he believes in "eight of the ten commandments." While the shock value of this zinger causes many in his audience to chuckle, my guess is that we would not find it too humorous to learn that he may actually have a higher view of God's law than most professing Christians today, who cannot even name eight of the ten commandments, let alone claim to believe them.

In all likelihood, this sad state of affairs is the result of culpable ignorance on the part of Christians who know all too well in their heart of hearts—where God's law is now written (Jer. 31:33–34)—that they do not measure up to that summary of God's perfect moral standards for Christian living. They know that they are far from loving God and their neighbors as they ought. They know that they have violated more than one of God's commandments and that, in the words of James, they are lawbreakers (James 2:10). And they know that there is no shelter for them in mere outward obedience, since the Lord also weighs their hearts (1 Sam. 16:7; Prov. 21:2).

After all, if our Lord's Sermon on the Mount teaches us anything, it teaches us that the demands of the law are not satisfied by avoiding certain outward actions. Those demands reach deep within us and prick our hearts as well. We may not have murdered, but we have all hated. And that, Christ says, is a violation of the sixth commandment (Matt. 5:21–26).

Sad to say, idolaters, false worshipers, blasphemers, Sabbath breakers, rebels, murderers, adulterers, thieves, liars, and the covetous are not found only outside the church halls. They are also in the pews—your pew, to be exact. Tall or short, fat or skinny, young or old, we have all broken God's holy law and continue to do so every day in thought, word, and deed.

Put differently, our tendency to break God's law, which reigned supreme in us before our conversion, survived in us when we were sovereignly and graciously drawn into covenant with God and His people. And that tendency to sin will remain in us until that blessed day when we are face-to-face with the Lord of glory.

Like most slogans on Christian bumper stickers, the one claiming that "Christians aren't perfect, just forgiven" is both true and false. It is true that "Christians aren't perfect," if by that we mean that Christians continue to sin. But this slogan is also false, for Christians are not "just forgiven." There is a sense in which they *are* perfect, having been credited with the perfect righteousness of Christ.

The truth that Christians, in this life, are both sinful and yet righteous or justified was brought to light by the Reformers when they taught that believers are *simul iustus et peccator* ("simultaneously justified and sinful"). That means that even on a good day, even in their finest Sunday suits and on their best Sunday behavior, Christians sin. Yet, it is precisely at this point that Christians can rejoice, knowing that God has already justified them, pardoned them, and declared them righteous on the basis of the finished work of Christ. Christians are not just forgiven; they are not just sinners. They are justified sinners, that is, sinners who have been justified. And that makes all the difference in the world!

The doctrine of justification is crucial to Christian faith and life. It is not only the doctrine upon which the church stands or falls, but also the doctrine upon which the Christian life—your Christian life—stands or falls. Because progress in the Christian life requires us to begin again, let us see how it all began. How were we justified as sinners, and how do we remain justified sinners on this side of glory?

MISSING THE MARK

It should come as no surprise that we are sinners both by who we are and by what we have done, both by nature and by conduct. We are sinners by nature, in that the guilt of Adam's sin was imputed or credited to us as his heirs. In the words of Paul, we "were made sinners" through Adam's disobedience (Rom. 5:19). David, you will recall, reiterated this truth when he wrote that we were "brought forth in iniquity" (Ps. 51:5) and "estranged from the womb" (Ps. 58:3).

Adam's sin was imputed (credited) to us for the simple reason that he acted as our covenant head or legal representative. When a legislator votes in favor of a particular bill, for example, he acts on behalf of his constituents at home. In a similar way, Adam's sin was a sin on behalf of his constituents, his heirs. He represented us all. Thus, what he did we were counted to have done through him (Rom. 5:12, 16–19). While we did not personally eat of the forbidden fruit ourselves, we were counted sinners as Adam's offspring and bear the sinful nature, depravity, and corruption that flow from his sin.

We are not only sinners by nature, but also sinners in that we sin. In fact, it is precisely because we are sinners that we sin each day. As a result, no one is righteous. No one does good (Rom. 3:9, 12), not even those who pride themselves on being more religious than the next guy. Even the apparent "good" that we do is but "filthy rags" (literally, "menstrual cloths") in God's sight (Isa. 64:6 NKJV). Indeed, no one is excluded from this indictment since all have sinned and continually fall short of the glory of God (Rom. 3:23). All are under the curse for failing to fulfill the righteous demands of God's law perfectly (Deut. 27:26; Gal. 3:10; James 2:10). Make no mistake: we are cursed sinners because we were made sinners through Adam's disobedience, and, because of that, we continue to sin every day.

And yet, if we would be saved, the perfectly holy and righteous God of Scripture requires that we be not only sinless, but also perfectly righteous. We are to be holy as He is holy (Lev. 11:44–45; 1 Peter 1:15–16), to be perfect as He is perfect (Matt. 5:48), and to imitate Him (Eph. 5:1). But how can we ever imitate Him? How can we ever be as perfectly holy as an all-holy God? How can we ever be sinless, since we have already sinned and continue to do so? How can we ever be perfectly righteous if we are sinners by nature? In short, how can we ever become right with God?

Is it impossible? That is what the disciples once thought, when, in a slightly different context, they despairingly cried out, "Then who can be saved?" Christ comforted them by changing their focus. Instead of focusing on man, they needed to focus on God. Rather than looking at what man must do to be saved, they needed to look at what God does for man. Salvation, according to Christ, is impossible with men, but is possible with God and only with God (Luke 18:26–27).

Man, in other words, cannot save himself. If he is to be saved at all, he must be saved by God. From beginning to end, salvation is from the Lord alone. As one pundit put it, we contribute nothing to our salvation, except the sin from which we are saved! So how is it that we become right with a sinless and perfectly righteous God? What does Scripture mean when it says that we have been justified?

THE VERDICT

In the Old Testament, to be *justified* means "to be in the right." It is primarily a legal term that declares one's standing in the eyes of the law. One is righteous or justified if one obeys the law, and wicked or condemned if one violates it. In Deuteronomy 25:1, for example, we learn that the judges before whom a controversy was brought were to "justify the righteous and condemn the wicked." Judges do not make people righteous any more than they make people wicked. They simply declare that those who have obeyed the law are just and that those who have disobeyed the law are wicked (Ex. 23:8; Ps. 51:24; Isa. 5:23; 43:9; 50:8).

When the New Testament speaks of justification, it likewise uses terms that convey the same legal sense of pronouncing or declaring someone righteous. Christ once told the Pharisees, "You are those who justify yourselves in the sight of men," even though God knew the true condition of their hearts (Luke 16:15). Although the Pharisees were fond of professing their legal righteousness to others, they were actually far from being righteous. Their talk was cheap. They honored God with their lips, but their hearts were far from Him. They declared themselves to be righteous before the law of God when they really were not righteous at all.

Justification, then, has a decidedly judicial ring to it. As we will see below, it refers to the one-time act by which God, as judge, freely and graciously imputes or credits our sin to Christ and imputes His righteousness to us. He pardons our sin and judicially declares us righteous in Him. Simply put, when God justifies the sinner, He judicially declares that all of the claims or demands of the law are satisfied with respect to the sinner on the basis of the finished work of Christ on the sinner's behalf.

Justification is thus something that God does *for* us, not something that He does *in* us. It is objective or external to us, not subjective or internal.

Justification is not the process by which we become internally righteous. Of course, we become internally righteous when God makes us spiritually alive (regeneration). We grow in this internal righteousness throughout the Christian life (sanctification), and we will be perfected in righteousness when we are completely redeemed in both body and spirit (glorification). Yet, the presence, growth, and eventual perfection of this internal righteousness is not what justification is all about.

While we are not justified by our own internal righteousness, our justification cannot be completely separated from it. In other words, there is a relationship between justification, on the one hand, and sanctification and glorification, on the other hand. Without justification, we could never be sanctified and glorified. By the same token, if we are truly justified, we will be sanctified and glorified, since God sanctifies and glorifies those whom He justifies (1 Cor. 6:11; Rom. 8:17, 29–30). He completes the work He starts in us (Phil. 1:6).

But justification and sanctification are not at all the same thing. Even though they ought never to be separated from each other, justification and sanctification are clearly distinguished in the Bible. While sanctification refers to the renewing and sanctifying grace of God by which we are made righteous, justification refers to the completed act by which God graciously declares us righteous through faith in the completed work of Christ alone on our behalf. While Roman Catholicism and other forms of non-Reformed theology play down this important distinction, the Reformed faith, taking its cue from Scripture, has always maintained it. At least three lines of argument prove that justification, in Scripture, refers to a judicial declaration about us—an external legal verdict, as opposed to an internal moral change.

First, the very language used to describe our justification is also used with reference to both the Father and the Son. Yet we know that they are already morally perfect and thus cannot be made righteous or undergo a moral transformation. Luke 7:29 (NKJV) tells us, for instance, that the people and the publicans "justified God." No Christian, however, would think for a moment that the people made God just or righteous. No, they simply acknowledged or declared Him to be righteous in His judgments. Along the same lines, Scripture speaks of Christ as justified (1 Tim. 3:16), not because He was made righteous by some kind of divine infusion (since He was already perfectly righteous), but because He was vindicated by God through the triumph of His resurrection.

Second, as we saw with Deuteronomy 25:1 and as found elsewhere, justification is often contrasted with condemnation (1 Kings 8:32; Job 9:20; 34:17; Prov. 17:15; Isa. 5:23; Matt. 12:37; Rom. 5:16; 8:33–34). And, as we have already seen, just as condemnation does not make someone wicked, so justification cannot make someone righteous. Condemnation is a declaration that someone is wicked under the law; justification is likewise a declaration that someone is righteous under the law.

Third, some passages explicitly link the idea of justification with the idea of judgment: "Who will bring a charge against God's elect? God is the one who justifies" (Rom. 8:33). The point in this passage is that God's elect cannot be condemned because they have already been declared righteous. Verse 34 makes this point clear: "Who is the one who condemns? Christ Jesus is He who died, yes, rather who was raised, who is at the right hand of God, who also intercedes for us." Those who are justified (declared righteous) cannot thereafter be condemned (Rom. 8:1). In other passages, the terms *justification* and *righteousness* are placed side by side with terms relating to judgment, which implies the judicial character of those terms. In this connection, Genesis 18:25 speaks of the just Judge who does not judge the righteous and the wicked alike (cf. Ps. 143:2).

Still other passages teach the same truth. When Abraham believed God, it was reckoned (i.e., counted or credited) to him as righteousness (Gen. 15:6; Rom. 4:3; Gal. 3:6). God would not have had to reckon His perfect righteousness to Abraham if Abraham had already had it! On the contrary, God reckoned it to him precisely because he did not already have it. And just as God reckoned His perfect righteousness to Abraham, so David could proclaim that "the man to whom the LORD does not impute iniquity" is truly blessed (Ps. 32:2). From these two Old Testament passages alone, we learn what justification is all about: God does not reckon our sin to us, but rather reckons His perfect righteousness to us (John 5:24; Rom. 4:6–9, 11; 2 Cor. 5:19–21).

The undivided testimony of Scripture is clear: justification is not a process whereby God makes the wicked internally righteous, but a one-time pronouncement in which He judicially declares the wicked righteous. The wicked have been tried and convicted of capital crimes in God's court for having violated His holy law. Yet, God not only pardons them, but does what no earthly judge can do: He declares that they are righteous. To borrow Paul's phrase, God justifies the wicked (Rom. 4:5).

THE GREAT EXCHANGE

But how can God justify the wicked or declare them righteous, if elsewhere we are told that doing so is abominable in His sight (Prov. 17:15; cf. Ex. 23:7; Isa. 5:23)? How does declaring the wicked righteous accord with

God's perfect justice and righteous wrath, which are poured out against all wickedness (Rom. 1:18)? How can God be both "just and the justifier" of the wicked (Rom. 3:26; 4:5)?

The answer, of course, is found in the very ground or basis of our justification: God credits (imputes) our sin to Christ and credits His righteousness to us. Since God will accept only sinlessness and perfect righteousness, the sinlessness and perfect righteousness by which we are put right with Him cannot come from us. Instead, it must come solely from the only One who has ever been sinless and perfectly righteous: the Lord Himself. This righteousness is what Luther referred to as the alien righteousness of Christ—not in the sense that it comes from another planet, but in the sense that it comes from outside of us; it is external to us and is imputed to us. It is given to us or credited to our account.

Think of it this way. Apart from Christ, we were totally in debt and completely bankrupt. In due time, however, Christ stepped in our place, took on our debt, and paid it off for us. Our debt was laid on Him, and His infinite wealth, in turn, was deposited in our account. This transaction is what Paul had in mind when he told the Corinthians that God had made Christ "who knew no sin to be sin on our behalf, that we might become the righteousness of God in Him" (2 Cor. 5:21). According to this passage, we are justified on the basis of this great exchange.

- Christ became sin for us, in that our sin was imputed to Him (He took on our debt); and
- His perfect righteousness was imputed to us, so that we might become the righteousness of God in Him (He deposited His infinite wealth in our account).

Why was it even necessary for Christ to take on our sin and to credit us with His righteousness? The biblical answer is that Christ had to do so in order to satisfy the double demand that the law makes on us as sinners: first, the demand that its precepts be perfectly obeyed, and second, the demand that the penalty for violating its precepts be fully paid. Left to ourselves, we could never meet this double demand. We could neither perfectly obey the law nor fully pay the penalty for violating it. But the glorious good news of the gospel is that Christ, acting in our place and on our behalf, has already satisfied the double demand of the law for us.

How so? Just as Adam, acting as our covenant head or legal representative, led us into sin and death, so Christ, the Last Adam, acting as our covenant head or legal representative, led us into righteousness and life (Rom. 5:12–21). In our place and on our behalf, Christ perfectly obeyed God's law and thereby satisfied the law's first demand. Then, He suffered the full penalty of the law against sin and thereby satisfied its second demand.

Through Him, we have actually satisfied the double demand of the law. Justification, then, is not something God pretends to do (a legal fiction), as some have wrongly seen it. God does not pretend to do anything. He actually imputes our sin to Christ as our covenant head and actually imputes His righteousness to us. When Christ died, He died for us, but, at the same time, we also died with Him (Rom. 6:5, 8; 7:4; 2 Cor. 5:14; Gal. 2:20).

FROM RAGS TO ROBES

What a tremendous truth! Because of what Christ has done for us in His life and death, we can, along with Isaiah, proclaim that our "righteousness and strength" are "only in the LORD." In Him alone, we "the offspring of Israel will be justified, and will glory" (Isa. 45:24–25). As Jeremiah proclaims, He is "the LORD our righteousness" (Jer. 23:6). Paul joins this chorus as well when he declares that Christ is "our righteousness, holiness and redemption" (1 Cor. 1:30 NIV).

Like Adam and Eve after the Fall, we too once stood naked in our shame, guilt, and wickedness. But, as with Adam and Eve, God clothed us—except this time, with something far better than man-made, fig-leaf suits. This time, He gave us His own clothes—the "garments of salvation." We are robed in His righteousness (Isa. 61:10)!

Because God has removed our "filthy garments" from us, "taken [our] iniquity away" from us, and clothed us "with festal robes" (Zech. 3:4), our justification is based on what He has done for us, not on what we have done ourselves. And this makes good sense. Our justification could not be based upon our righteousness. Even if we never sinned again, our righteousness would never satisfy the perfect and infinite requirements of divine justice for sins we have committed in the past. And even our best righteousness, as we have seen, is nothing but filthy rags in God's sight (Isa. 64:6); it is never perfect on this side of glory and thus cannot measure up to the perfect righteousness that God requires of us (Matt. 19:17; Luke 10:28; Rom. 2–3; 10:5; Gal. 3:10; 5:3; James 2:10). Contrary to popular belief, God does not grade on a curve. He requires that we be perfect, not in some watered-down sense, but in the same way that He is perfect (Matt. 5:48).

Since God requires perfection, and since we are hopelessly imperfect, our justification cannot be based on our good works. Anyone inclined to think so should remember that the one who would be justified by his works cannot merely be better than his neighbor. Nor can he simply have the scale of his life tip ever so slightly in favor of the "good" he has done. He must do far more than help old ladies cross the street and contribute to his favorite charity. He must be sinless. But no one is sinless (Rom. 3:10–24). Hence, our justification can never be based on our works or effort, even if they are well motivated (Rom. 3:20; 4:2; 10:3–4; Gal. 2:16; 3:11; 5:4; Eph. 2:8; Titus 3:5). Along with Paul, we must confess that we want to be "found in Him [Christ], not having a righteousness of [our] own . . . but that which is through faith in Christ, the righteousness which comes from God on the basis of faith" (Phil. 3:9).

We are saved by grace, not works—by the free and unmerited favor of God, not by anything that proceeds from us (Rom. 3:24–26; 4:16; 5:15–21; 11:6; Gal. 3:12). Accordingly, we cannot look inside ourselves for the ground of our justification. Rather, we must look outside ourselves to Christ. From beginning to end, our justification is rooted outside of us in the triune God: the Father justifies us ("God is the one who justifies"—Rom. 8:33), through the finished work of the Son ("and through Him [Christ] everyone who believes is freed [justified]"—Acts 13:39), by the Spirit ("but you were justified . . . by the Spirit of our God" [1 Cor. 6:11 NKJV]).

Thus, God alone justifies; He declares that satisfaction for our sins has already been made and that by grace through faith we are entitled to eternal life.

YOU GOTTA HAVE FAITH

As we have seen so far, justification should never be regarded as our work. It does not depend upon anything done in us or by us, not even the faith given to us by God. After all, we are not justified by faith through grace. Rather, we are justified by grace through faith (Eph. 2:8; Rom. 3:24ff.; 5:15–21). To be even more precise, we are justified by God, who graciously gives us the faith necessary to apprehend His grace on account of what Christ has done for us. Seen in this light, faith is simply the instrument through which we are justified, the empty hand God gives us to receive His free gift to us in Christ (Eph. 2:7–8; Acts 14:27).

Faith is not the basis or ground of our justification—Christ is. Accordingly, Scripture, when properly interpreted, never says that we are justified because of, or on account of, faith itself, but that we are justified by, through, or upon faith in what Christ has already done for us (Rom. 1:17; 3:22, 25–28, 30; 4:3, 5, 16, 24; 5:1; Gal. 2:16; 3:8–9; 5:4; Phil. 3:9). Faith is merely the instrument of our justification, which points us to Christ, who is the object of our faith and the basis of our justification. True faith involves a binding trust, whereby sinners, by God's grace alone, cast themselves in sole and total reliance upon Christ and His finished work on their behalf, knowing what Christ has done for them.

Paul had this binding trust in mind when he wrote that we are justified "by faith, that it might be in accordance with grace" (Rom. 4:16). What he is saying is that there is something special about faith, which demonstrates that justification is based on God's grace. When we cast ourselves upon Christ, when we rest and rely completely upon Him with saving faith, we thereby abandon all self-effort and demonstrate that our justification is rooted and grounded in Him alone. As John Murray has written, "It is faith alone that justifies because its specific quality is to find our all in Christ and his righteousness."[1]

ROCK OF AGES

When all is said and done, we have only to fall on our knees in praise and thanks to God for freely and graciously giving us the faith to grasp what He has done for us. The law came, in part, to terrorize and condemn us in our wickedness. But Christ came to fulfill its demands upon us. In our place and on our behalf, He fully paid our penalty for violating the law and perfectly obeyed its every precept. Indeed, our only hope is in the One whom Augustus Toplady called the "Rock of Ages."

> Rock of Ages, cleft for me,
> Let me hide myself in Thee!
> Let the water and the blood
> From Thy riven side which flowed,
> Be of sin the double cure,
> Cleanse me from its guilt and power.

Not the labor of my hands
Can fulfil Thy law's demands;
Could my zeal no respite know,
Could my tears forever flow,
All for sin could not atone;
Thou must save, and Thou alone.

Nothing in my hand I bring;
Simply to Thy cross I cling;
Naked, come to Thee for dress;
Helpless, look to Thee for grace;
Foul, I to the Fountain fly,
Wash me, Savior, or I die.

While I draw this fleeting breath,
When my eyestrings break in death,
When I soar through tracts unknown,
See Thee in Thy judgment throne,—
Rock of Ages, cleft for me,
Let me hide myself in Thee![2]

Indeed, our labors, zeal, and tears cannot do what the Rock of Ages has already done for us. We were naked, but He clothed us; helpless, but He saved us; foul, but He washed us. Through His righteousness and blood alone, we can rejoice, knowing that even though we are justified, yet sinful here and now, we will one day see Him on His judgment throne and will be glorified together with Him for all eternity. We are truly bound for glory.

STUDY QUESTIONS

1. If God will accept only sinlessness and perfect righteousness, where must the sinlessness and perfect righteousness by which we are put right with Him come from?
2. Explain from Scripture how we are justified by God's grace through faith on account of what Christ alone has done for us. Who gives this faith to us? Who is the object of this gift of faith?
3. Why is the doctrine of justification so foundational for living the Christian life? How should it affect your Christian life in particular?

Notes

1. John Murray, *Collected Writings of John Murray*, 4 vols. (Edinburgh: Banner of Truth, 1977), 2:217.
2. Augustus M. Toplady, "Rock of Ages, Cleft for Me," *A Treasury of Hymn Stories* (1776; reprint, Grand Rapids: Baker, 1992 [1945]), 63–64.

SEVENTEEN

BOUND FOR GLORY

I f justification is the beginning of the Christian life, then sanctification is its middle, and glorification is its end. Having discussed how God justifies us on the basis of what Christ has done for us, we now turn to what He does in us as He transforms us from one degree of glory to another.

BECOMING WHAT WE ARE

There is no way around it. God demands nothing less of us than the perfect righteousness revealed in His law throughout Scripture. But He not only demands perfect righteousness of us in the law, but also graciously gives us His perfect righteousness in the gospel. What, then, is the relationship between the gospel and the law in the Christian life—between what God has done for us and what He requires of us? Simply this: we do not obey His law in order to be saved; rather, we are saved in order to obey His law (Eph. 2:8–10). Once we are saved, we keep His law as our pattern for sanctification. But we must keep our obedience in proper perspective. We are not saved because of what we do, but because of who Christ is (our justification and sanctification) and because of who God has declared us to be in Him (justified and sanctified). We are free to grow in righteousness (sanctification) by God's grace only after He declares us righteous (justification).

While justification is righteousness imputed once for all, sanctification

229

is righteousness imparted progressively throughout the Christian life. The Christian life begun in the new birth and continued on in sanctification is a process whereby God helps us to become more like who He has once for all declared us to be in Christ. We are called to be in daily life who we already are in Christ—to walk, as Paul says, in a manner worthy of our calling (Eph. 4:1).

TRAVELING THE ROAD HOME

But, even then, our obedience will be imperfect on this side of glory. True, at the moment we were regenerated and justified, we experienced the definitive sanctification objectively wrought for us by Christ's death and resurrection (Rom. 6:1–11; Eph. 2:5). At the moment we were definitively sanctified, sin's dominion over us and its attendant curse were shattered once for all. We are sanctified in that we have already received Christ's "righteousness, holiness and redemption" (1 Cor. 1:30 NIV; Col. 3:1, 9–10). Simply put, in Christ we have already died (past tense) to sin. Thus, when we read verses that tell us that we have already been sanctified, it is this definitive sanctification that is in view (John 17:19; Acts 20:32; 26:18; 1 Cor. 6:11; Heb. 10:10–14, 29; 13:12; 1 Peter 1:2). This understanding of definitive sanctification as something already accomplished for us in the past explains why notoriously imperfect Christians like the Corinthians could be called saints (1 Cor. 1:2), despite the fact that they were actually quite far from being saintly. Like the Corinthians, we too are saints, not because of anything in us, but only because of what Christ has definitively done for us once for all.

Although we have already been definitively sanctified, we must still become progressively sanctified on this side of eternity. Why? Because definitive sanctification is only part of the story. When we were definitively sanctified, sin was dethroned in our lives so that it no longer reigns over us (Rom. 6:2–6, 14; 1 John 3:9; 5:18). But some sin still remains in us (Rom. 6:20; 7:14–25; 1 John 1:8–10; 2:1). While definitive sanctification occurs at one moment in time, progressive sanctification is a lifelong process of turning from sin to God, a process that will never be complete on this side of glory. Whereas definitive sanctification involves our death to reigning sin at a single point in the past, progressive sanctification is an ongoing battle to destroy surviving sin in the present. Only in future glory will we experience final sanctification—the complete absence of sin (Zech. 14:20–21; Rev. 21:2).

To understand the difference between definitive (past), progressive (present), and final (future) sanctification, consider that we were once trapped behind enemy lines. Even though Christ has already set us free from enemy dominion (definitive sanctification in the past), He has still ordered us to travel the road home (progressive sanctification in the present). Only after we have safely arrived home will we, by His grace, be completely free from the enemy (final sanctification in the future).

On this side of glory, the true Christian will travel the road home and will never use the biblical doctrine of justification as an excuse to live licentiously (Rom. 6–8). As Luther commented, we are saved by faith alone, but not by a faith that is alone. Ever so succinctly, this adage guards against denying that we are justified by God's grace through faith on account of Christ alone. It also guards against denying the inseparable union between faith and true repentance, between justification and sanctification. While no one will be saved by works, rest assured that no one will be saved without them.

But what about the apparent difficulty between what Paul teaches (that we are justified by faith alone) and what James teaches (that we are justified not by faith alone, but by faith and works)? The answer to this apparent difficulty is found by reading Paul and James in context. When we do, we discover that they are speaking about different kinds of "faith" and different kinds of "works." Paul speaks about saving faith, which is the instrument by which we are justified. James, on the other hand, speaks first about dead faith, which is really nothing more than mere intellectual assent—the kind of "faith" that demons have (James 2:19)—but which is incapable of being the instrument of our justification. James then contrasts this dead faith with saving faith: while dead faith does not produce genuine works, saving faith always does. Notice that the works associated with dead faith and the works associated with saving faith are different. When Paul says that works cannot justify us, he is speaking about legalistic works by which the sinner tries to merit God's favor through obedience to His law. When James speaks about works, he is speaking about the good works that simply evidence or demonstrate saving faith.

What, then, do we learn from both Paul and James? Simply this: the person with dead faith does not need to add works to be justified. He needs the gift of saving faith. A person with dead faith does not need to do more. He needs to be saved. As Gerhard Forde has written, "If the faith is dead it is faith that must be revived."[1] And the faith—if it is saving faith—is pregnant with, and will give birth to, good works.

Hence, if we are truly saved, that salvation will bear the fruit of good works—works commanded by God in Scripture, which conform to biblical precepts and which spring both from faith working through love and from a desire to glorify God. Faith without such works is dead (James 2:17). Good trees bring forth good fruit (Matt. 7:16–20; John 15:8, 16). Because God is at work in us to will and to work for His good pleasure, we must demonstrate our salvation—become progressively sanctified—with reverential awe (Phil. 2:12–13). Where there is no saving faith, there will be no good works, and where there are no good works, there is no saving faith. But we must never confuse the cause (saving faith) with the effect (good works). We are saved not by works, but for works (Eph. 2:8–10). And we must never forget that such works are pleasing to God only through the merit of Christ.

The Mainspring of Our Sanctification

A mainspring is the principal spring that drives a mechanical device such as a clock. It keeps the clock ticking by constantly recoiling. Like a dependable clock, the Christian life has a mainspring all its own: the believer's union with Christ. Just as justification is ours only through union with Christ, so it is with sanctification. Christ is both our justification and our sanctification (1 Cor. 1:3).[2] When we see that justification and sanctification are both effects of our union with Christ, the supposed tension between them vanishes. We need not reduce one to the other or deny that the two are biblically distinct. God, by the power of His Spirit, sanctifies those whom He justifies (1 Cor. 6:11). And He does so in Christ. Calvin was right when he wrote that "our whole salvation and all its parts are comprehended in Christ [Acts 4:12]. We should therefore take care not to derive the least portion of it from anywhere else. If we seek salvation, we are taught by the very name of Jesus that it is 'of him' [1 Cor. 1:30]."[3] Calvin then enumerated the blessings we enjoy in Him: purification in His blood, mortification in His tomb, and newness of life in His resurrection.

This theme of our union with Christ and its impact on our sanctification is fleshed out in detail by Paul in Romans 6:1–14. Recall that in Romans 5:20 he says that where sin increases, grace increases all the more. In the first verse of chapter 6, he anticipates the erroneous inference that his opponents may be tempted to draw from this truth ("Are we to continue to sin that grace might increase?"). He then directs those who may be tempted to draw this erroneous inference to the believer's union with Christ. He moves methodically through his argument step by step, so that his opponents won't miss it.

1. As believers, we enjoy union with Christ.
2. This same Christ, to whom we are united, died to sin.
3. Since Christ died to sin and we are united to Him, we have also died to sin in the past.
4. If we have died to sin in the past, we are freed from it already and cannot continue to live in it in the present.
5. Hence, we are freed from sin already and cannot continue to live in it in the present.
6. Therefore, we cannot continue in sin that grace might increase.

Notice that Romans 6 is not a passage about how we need to do something to die to sin. The whole point of Paul's argument is that in Christ we have already died to sin. Since we have already died to sin and have been freed from it in the sense that it no longer rules us, we ought to live like that is the case. We have already been definitively sanctified in the past. Now we need to become progressively sanctified in the present. We have been set free from prison. Now, by the grace of God, in union with Christ, and empowered by the Spirit, we need to travel home.

The big picture in this passage is that sin no longer reigns over us because we have been justified and definitively sanctified in Christ. Thus, this passage focuses not on our past but on Christ's. We need to stop looking at ourselves and start looking to Christ. Sound familiar? Just as our union with Christ is the mainspring of our justification, so it is the mainspring of our sanctification. We are to look out to Christ instead of in at ourselves. Many Christians turn microscopes on themselves when they need to turn telescopes on Christ. We ought not to dwell on our progress, but instead on what God has done for us in Christ. Only then can we grow in true holiness.

With this big picture in mind, we need to "count" ourselves as—to recognize that we already are—dead to sin and alive to God in Christ (v. 11). Based on Romans 6, we are not to become dead to sin. We already are dead to sin. Dying to sin is not an experience for a few truly spiritual believers. It is something that already is true for every believer.

Believers, then, should count themselves as definitively dead to sin and alive to Christ. They will also strive to live consistently with this precious truth, knowing that although they are dead to sin (definitive sanctification), sin is not yet dead in them and constantly needs to be put to death in them (progressive sanctification). Only two chapters after expounding the great truth that we have already died to sin in Christ in Romans 6 (definitive sanctification), Paul delves into our continual need to put our sinful desires to death in Romans 8:13 (progressive sanctification). Paul does the same thing in Colossians 3. Within the space of a few verses, he discusses both our once-and-done death to sin in Christ (v. 3) and our ongoing task of counting ourselves as dead to sin by putting off the old man and putting on the new man (vv. 5–11).

Paul easily moves from the past to the present, from the definitive to the progressive. Now that we have already been definitively sanctified, we need to become progressively sanctified. And this progressive sanctification requires us, by the power of the indwelling Spirit, both to put sin to death in our lives wherever it may be found (Rom. 8:13) and to practice righteousness (Gal. 5:22–23). This dual task of putting sin to death and practicing righteousness is described by Paul in Colossians 3:5–11 and Ephesians 4:22–24 as putting off the old man and putting on the new man. Elsewhere, he makes the same point by exhorting us to cleanse ourselves from all defilement of flesh and to perfect holiness in the fear of God (2 Cor. 7:1).

FORMULAS FOR FAILURE

This process of putting sin to death and practicing righteousness, putting off the old man and putting on the new man, cleansing ourselves from defilement and perfecting holiness in the fear of God, is not to be taken lightly. It requires us to be active participants in a deep-seated spiritual war being waged between God and Satan and their respective forces in the heavenly places (Eph. 6:12). This war, as we have already seen in Part Two of this book, is being fought here on earth between the seed of the woman and the seed of the Serpent (Gen. 3:15; Matt. 12:30). But it is also being waged relentlessly on and in each believer, day in and day out. The principal foes that we are called to do battle against are no less than the infamous threesome: the world, the flesh, and the Devil (1 John 2:14–17). We ought not to underestimate them, but we ought not to overestimate them, either. They are formidable, but not unbeatable. After all, we are more than conquerors through union with Christ (Rom. 8:37).

To say that we are more than conquerors is not to say, however, that becoming a conqueror in the Christian life is a simple matter of following a particular formula. Non-Reformed traditions have typically emphasized nonbiblical or extrabiblical "follow-this-formula" approaches to the Christian life. The Reformed faith, by contrast, repudiates such formulas as gimmicks that will inevitably lead to failure. Three such formulas come readily to mind.

Becoming Perfect

Since the first century, some believers have asserted that they can live the "victorious Christian life" or become perfect on this side of eternity (1 John 1:8–10). But, lest we forget, in all of human history there has been only one completely victorious Christian life—the life of Christ.

Those who claim to be living the perfect or completely victorious Christian life simply are not honest enough about the "exceeding sinfulness" of their sin. They limit sin to conscious conduct (the stuff that bubbles above the surface), even though Scripture defines it as any failure to abide by God's law, including even our "hidden faults" (the stuff that bubbles below the surface) (Ps. 19:12).

To make their supposed perfection attainable, perfectionists and victorious-life advocates also lower the divine standard of perfect holiness that God requires of us in His Word (Lev. 11:44–45; Matt. 5:48; Eph. 5:1; 1 Peter 1:15–16). But whenever we lower God's standard, we end up attacking God Himself, since the law of God reflects His perfect and unchanging character. God Himself is the standard. And because He is the same yesterday, today, and forever (Heb. 13:8), His standard is the same yesterday, today, and forever.

Redefining sin and lowering God's perfect standard are bad enough, but perfectionists and victorious-life advocates do not stop there. They also ignore major New Testament themes: namely, that we "have not already obtained it," that we have not "already become perfect," that we "stumble in many ways," and that we are to "grow up in all aspects" in Christ (Phil. 3:12–14; James 3:2; Eph. 4:14–15; cf. Phil. 1:9; Col. 1:10; 2:19; 1 Thess. 3:12; 4:1, 10; 2 Thess. 1:3; Heb. 12:5–14; 1 Peter 2:2; 2 Peter 3:18). They also ignore 1 John 1:8, where John tells us that if we say we have no sin, we deceive ourselves and the truth is not in us. The logic of this passage is all too clear: if the truth is in us and we are not deceiving ourselves, we do not say that we have no sin.

Those who pretend that they are living the victorious Christian life have apparently never read Paul's agonizing "wretched man" confession in Romans 7, or, perhaps more accurately, have read it right out of their Bibles. Were they to read Romans 7 and understand it for what it is—one of the best descriptions of the inescapable war faced by every Christian—

they would understand how often they fall short of God's perfect standard even when they know better. They would also understand how much they need to flee to the Cross. But these truths are not limited to Romans 7. Even if you think that Romans 7 describes Paul before his conversion,[4] Scripture elsewhere describes the normal Christian life as a constant struggle with sin. The same Paul who wrote Romans 7 also wrote Galatians 5:17, where the Spirit and the flesh are said to be in constant antagonism to one another throughout the Christian life. This lifelong antagonism is a fact to accept, not a condition to deny.

Contrary to the teaching echoing in some corners today, the Spirit does not prevent us from facing conflicts. It is the very presence of the Spirit that produces these conflicts. We should not be surprised at the ferociousness of the holy war we fight, since the "presence of war raging within is evidence of [our] salvation."[5] Of course, this is just another way of saying that though God's work *for* us in Christ is complete, His work *in* us is incomplete on this side of glory. And it is the incompleteness of His work in us that occasions the war within.

So the next time you hear someone claim that he is living the "victorious Christian life," do what one skeptic was rumored to have done: push the self-proclaimed "victor" aside and ask his wife! Then remember that Christ's victory is your victory in every battle you face.[6]

Letting Go and Letting God

While some tout the victorious Christian life as though it were completely attainable on this side of glory by exerting some kind of strenuous effort, others proclaim that true sanctification is only possible if we "let go and let God"—that is, if we become passive channels, allowing the Spirit to flow through us to accomplish His will in us. If we are honest enough to admit that we are struggling against sin, we are told that we are simply not "contemplating spiritual things" enough, that we are not "yielding" to God enough, that we are not being passive enough.

But Scripture does not call us to become spiritual bystanders. It calls us to resist the aggression of the Evil One actively. In Paul's words, we are to "fight the good fight" (1 Tim. 6:12) and to "suffer hardship . . . as a good soldier of Christ Jesus" (2 Tim. 2:3). How can we fight as a good soldier for Christ if we put ourselves on inactive status by letting go?

At root, this "let go and let God" notion confuses justification with progressive sanctification. It fails to see that while both justification and progressive sanctification are gifts of God, justification is passively received at one point in time, whereas progressive sanctification is actively pursued continually throughout our lives. Yes, the triune God is sovereign over our progressive sanctification: the Father sanctifies us (John 17:17; Heb. 12:10), as does the Son (Eph. 5:25–27; Titus 2:14) through the Spirit (1 Peter 1:2; 2 Thess. 2:13). But we are also responsible for our progressive sanctification, as evidenced by the fact that every command or prohibition in Scripture is directed to us to obey. The sovereign God of the universe tells us to love our neighbor, to flee immorality, to pray at all times, and He expects us to obey Him. Nowhere is the relationship between divine sovereignty and human responsibility in our progressive sanctification more clearly focused than in Philippians 2:12–13 and Colossians 1:29. In Philippians 2:12–13 Paul says—all in one breath—"Work out your salvation with fear and trembling; for it is God who is at work in you, both to will and to work for His good pleasure." And in Colossians 1:29, he writes autobiographically, "And for this purpose also I labor, striving according to His power which mightily works in me."

God works by saving us, and we work out the implications of our salvation throughout our Christian lives. God's work does not suspend ours, and our work does not suspend His. But we must not err by thinking that God simply does His part and we simply do ours, as though His work bore no relation to our work. Rather, it is precisely because God works that we work. We need to work, says Paul. And what motivates us to work is God's work in us. Divine sovereignty does not discourage human responsibility—it actually encourages it. He sovereignly empowers us to obey Him.

To help us better understand this important truth, think of a vine and its branches. The branches could not grow apart from the vine. In fact, apart from the vine, they would shrivel up and die. But because they are connected to the vine, they can grow. And we can speak of the growth we see in the branches as long as we never forget that it was the vine that made that growth possible in the first place. Christ is the vine. We are the branches. Apart from Him, we can do nothing (John 15:1–5).

In the end, this "let go" formula mistakenly equates "inner passivity as a formula for holiness with the biblical call to disciplined moral effort in the power of the Holy Spirit."[7] As J. I. Packer puts it, it is a "delusion" that will wreak havoc in the Christian life.

Going First Class

While some teach the victorious life, and others teach the passive life, still others claim that the key to living the Christian life is to become a first-class "spiritual" Christian as opposed to a second-class "carnal" Christian. This is accomplished, we are told, by yielding or surrendering the throne of our lives to Christ as Lord.

Let us get one thing straight: we do not make Christ Lord of all. He already is Lord of all. What is more, Scripture never divides Christians into first- and second-class citizens. It tells us rather bluntly that all Christians, after conversion, are both "carnal" and "spiritual"—that is, simultaneously sinful and justified. Michael Horton hits the nail on the head when he writes, "We are not either carnal Christians or spiritual Christians; rather, all Christians are simultaneously sinful and spiritual—not because of their 'surrender,' but because of Christ's. We are all in the same category, simply at different points along the way."[8]

Indeed, the ground is level at the foot of the cross. And maybe that is where those who claim to be truly spiritual need to go. Were they at the foot of the cross, gazing intently at the perfect Lamb slain for them, perhaps they would finally put their hands over their mouths, realizing that they, like Job, have spoken too soon.

TYING UP SOME LOOSE ENDS

Formulas or recipes are of no help in overcoming sin on this side of glory. Those who approach the Bible as a recipe book by recommending one part victory or one part passivity or one part surrender always end up with half-baked understandings of the Christian life. They forget that we do not have to bake anything on our own since Christ is the Bread of Life who has come down from heaven. All we need to do is feed on Him (John 6:48–51).

And this raises an important point: we can never deal realistically with the sin in our lives if we refuse to feed on Him by availing ourselves of the means He has provided for our nourishment and growth in grace. Like the apostolic church of old, we need to learn anew the importance of continually devoting ourselves to the Word, the breaking of bread, and prayer. These are the means by which the Spirit causes us to grow in the grace and knowledge of our Lord Jesus Christ.

Notice, too, the indispensable role played by the church in passages such as Acts 2:42. Strange as it may sound to Westerners, who pride themselves on their "rugged individualism," sanctification is not just an individual thing. As we have already seen in Part Three of this book, God's people grow together spiritually by worshiping Him in spirit and in truth, partaking of the sacraments, and submitting to church leaders, especially as they exercise biblical church discipline.

Finally, we would be completely remiss if we failed to note how God causes us to experience tremendous growth in grace by sovereignly planning and providentially guiding our lives in the midst of real suffering and pain. The pang of watching a loved one take her last breath, the despair of losing a job, the grief of a broken home—each, though truly sorrowful, has a unique way of deepening our trust in Him. In His wisdom, love, and power, He really does cause all things to work together for our good. Every piece of our lives really is in His gentle hand, even when He has not yet seen fit to show us how all the pieces fit together.

God has graciously provided us with the means by which we can grow in grace. We really cannot expect to grow by neglecting them, any more than we could expect to grow physically by refusing to eat.

THE MELANCHTHON PROBLEM

As we grow by availing ourselves of the means of grace that He has provided for us, we must never lose sight of the finished work of Christ; He is the author and finisher of our faith (Heb. 12:2). Once we fix our sights on Him, we can finally understand the purpose of God's law. The law condemns us and our would-be self-righteousness in order to drive us to Christ and the gospel. It then teaches us God's will for holy living. If you look at your life in light of the law and begin to doubt your salvation, you need to do what Paul did at the end of Romans 7 and throughout Romans 8: flee to the foot of the cross. We need Christ's death now that we are alive every bit as much as we did when we were dead in our trespasses and sins. While the law still guides us, it can never judicially condemn us or threaten us (Rom. 8:1, 33–34). Never again.

But we are sometimes quick to forget this precious truth, and as a result we can find ourselves sinking into the pit of despair. We can all identify with Luther's protégé, Philip Melanchthon, who once wrote to Luther, wondering whether he trusted Christ enough to be saved. Luther boldly responded to him and to us by writing, "Melanchthon! Go sin bravely! Then go to the cross and bravely confess it! The whole gospel is outside of us."[9] Luther rendered this bold advice not to counsel Melanchthon to live licentiously, as some have wrongly imagined, but rather, in "an attempt to shock Melanchthon into realizing that his only true righteousness was external to him."[10]

When the reality of Luther's shocking statement hits home, we can humbly confess that we are justified yet sinful on this side of glory. And when we do, we will discover how refreshing it is to be honest with ourselves. Although we know that no good thing dwells in us by our own creation or nature (Rom. 7:18), we know that in Christ we have truly been cleansed, justified, and sanctified, so that we can rightly say that glorification has, in one sense, already begun in us (1 Cor. 6:11).[11] While God has graciously given us a new identity with a glorious destiny, we must sadly admit that in ourselves we are utterly defiled and deserve only death and damnation. Far from getting out of Romans 7 and into Romans 8, we live in both chapters on this side of glory.

This tension in us is more than a mere skirmish. When we finally have the honesty to admit that what is going on inside us is part of the full-scale war being waged in the heavenly places, we are able to deal with our battles realistically and biblically. No longer need we pretend that the battles at hand do not exist or talk as though we were already perfect or victorious in and of ourselves. No longer need we retreat from the rigors of war by putting ourselves on inactive or passive status. No longer need we distract ourselves in the midst of hand-to-hand combat by wondering whether we have surrendered enough so that the sovereign God of the universe can be enthroned in our lives.

By honestly admitting the vicious war within, we can finally learn to fight its battles, not by relying upon our own victory, our own passivity, or our own surrender, but by relying upon Christ. We cannot win this war in our own strength or on our own merit. We need to stop looking in and start looking out. As justified sinners, we need to cast ourselves continually upon Christ, seeking refuge in His infinite mercy, imploring Him to grant us His endless strength, and asserting His perfect merit as our only merit. We must find our every solace in Christ.

FROM GLORY TO GLORY

What a privilege it is for us as justified sinners to find our every solace in Christ on this side of glory. Yet, as great as this privilege is, Packer masterfully reminds us that what is yet to come is even better.

> To know oneself, here and now, to be, in Luther's phrase, simul justus et peccator—a justified sinner, right with God and sinning still—is a wonderful privilege. But the hope set before us is yet more

wonderful, namely to be in the presence of God, seeing him and fellowshipping with him, as one who is a sinner no longer. What God plans for us in the present is to lead us toward this goal.[12]

God does sovereignly and graciously lead us toward this goal. We are, in fact, predestined for it—bound, as it were, for glory. According to Paul,

> God causes all things to work together for good to those who love God, to those who are called according to His purpose. For whom He foreknew, He also predestined to become conformed to the image of His Son, that He might be the first-born among many brethren; and whom He predestined, these He also called; and whom He called, these He also justified; and whom He justified, these He also glorified. (Rom. 8:28–30)

Paul wrote to Christians in Rome to give them comfort and assurance during times of affliction. And he did that by revealing to them that because God had eternally purposed to glorify them, they could speak of their yet future glorification in the past tense. From God's perspective, it was a done deal.

But what does our future glorification involve? For one thing, it involves far more than being in the immediate presence of God, which happens when we die (since to die is to be with Christ [Phil. 1:21; 2 Cor. 5:8]). Admittedly, to be in the presence of Christ is stupendous in its own right. Yet glorification is far more stupendous, since it refers to the moment in time when we will be completely and finally redeemed, in both body and spirit. When we are glorified, we will be conformed to the image of our risen, exalted, and glorified Redeemer. The very body of our humiliation will be conformed to the body of His glory (Phil. 3:21).[13] Indeed, our hope of glory is a tremendous comfort in times of affliction.

But our hope of glory is much, much more. It also spurs us on to growth in holiness here and now. In his first letter, John says, "When He appears, we shall be like Him, because we shall see Him just as He is" (1 John 3:2). Without dropping a beat, John then adds that "every one who has this hope fixed on Him purifies himself, just as He is pure" (v. 3). We are to live our Christian lives, says John, in anticipation of that blessed day when we will "be like Him," when His image will be perfectly restored in us for all eternity.

Having His image perfectly restored in us is what we have yearned for since the Fall. Adam was created in God's image (Gen. 1:26–27), but when he fell into sin, that image became marred or distorted. No longer was the divine image as clear as it had been. In his fallenness—and ours through him—the divine image became like the image you see when you look at yourself in a carnival mirror. You can make out some likeness, but the image is distorted, badly bent out of shape.

Yet, in His own good time, God sovereignly and graciously restored His image in us when He redeemed us. From that point on, He began the continual process of progressively renewing His image in us (Eph. 4:24; Col. 3:10). That continual renewal is what we call progressive sanctification, during which the divine image in us becomes more and more clear. On this side of glory we behold "as in a mirror the glory of the Lord" as we "are being transformed into the same image from glory to glory" (2 Cor. 3:18). We are both reflecting the glory of God and beholding His glory more and more. Reflecting and beholding God's glory involve one another. We reflect His glory because we have beheld Him who is the full "radiance of His glory" and the express image of His being (Heb. 1:3). As we gaze at His matchless glory, we are transformed into His likeness more and more, from one degree of glory to another, until that moment in time when we will be completely transfigured.[14]

On that day when we are completely transfigured, God will be fully glorified and will both exhibit and vindicate His glory. This is the "hope of the glory of God" in which Paul exults (Rom. 5:2). It is a hope that is completely grounded in Him, for only if we, by His grace, are finally sanctified, will we be able to contain the full manifestation of His glory. But it is the full manifestation of His glory "that will itself bring with it the glorification of the believer."[15] This is the "praise of His glory" (Eph. 1:12, 14), the final goal of our redemption.

As we long for that day, our only reaction should be to fall on our knees, to praise and glorify Him all the days of our lives for what He has done in us and for us in Christ. He has truly "blessed us with every spiritual blessing in the heavenly places in Christ" (Eph. 1:3)! In Christ we were justified and definitively sanctified. In Christ we are being progressively sanctified. And in Christ one day we shall be finally sanctified, when we are glorified together with Him. Christ for us and Christ in us, our hope of glory (Col. 1:27).

On this side of glory, though, we are simultaneously justified and sinful, which comes as both bad news and good news. The bad news is that we cannot do anything apart from Him. But the good news is that our only hope in the Christian life is in Him. And that is what the good news—the gospel—is all about.

STUDY QUESTIONS

1. Is Roman 6:14–20 a passage about something you need to do in your Christian life? What is it about? Even though you are united with Christ and have died to sin with Him, do you still need to put sin to death in your life (see 2 Cor. 7:1; Rom. 8:1–13; Gal. 5:22–23; Eph. 4:22–24; Col. 3:5–11)? How will you, by His grace, begin to do that today?
2. Have you been less than honest with yourself about the vicious war within? How does the Reformed view of the Christian life actually free you up to fight the battles you face every day in the strength of the Lord?
3. When will you be completely and finally redeemed in both body and spirit? How does this hope comfort you in times of affliction (see Rom. 8:28–30)? How does it spur you on to growth in holiness as taught in 1 John 3:2–3?

Notes

1. Cited by Donald Alexander, ed., *Christian Spirituality: Five Views of Sanctification* (Downers Grove, Ill.: InterVarsity Press, 1988), 78.
2. Sinclair Ferguson, "A Reformed Response [to the Lutheran View]," in Alexander, *Christian Spirituality*, 34. The remainder of this section on the believer's sanctification and union with Christ owes a great debt to Ferguson's clear and cogent presentation at pages 47–76.
3. John Calvin, *The Institutes of the Christian Religion*, ed. John T. McNeill, trans. Lewis Ford Battles (Philadelphia: Westminster Press, 1960), 2.16.19.
4. There are compelling exegetical reasons to conclude that Paul, in Rom. 7, is speaking about his life as a Christian, not about his life prior to conversion. For starters, the first section (vv. 7–13) is written in the past tense (the aorist tense), while the second section (vv. 14–25) is written in the present tense. Just as it is natural to understand the first section as autobiographical, so also is it natural to understand the second section that way. Not only would it be unnatural to read this text as referring to Paul's life before conversion, it would be without parallel in any other Pauline text. Moreover, Paul states that he loves the law of God and delights in it (vv. 15–16, 18–22). The unconverted, however, are unable to submit to the law of God (8:5, 7). They cannot understand the things of God because they do not have the spiritual discernment necessary to do so (1 Cor. 2:14), and are blind, corrupt, lawless, and at enmity with God (Eph. 2:3; 4:17ff.). Far from talking about his life prior to conversion, Paul humbly reflects on his own failures in the Christian life to point us to our only hope—the One who alone is our victory—the Lord Jesus Christ (Rom. 7:24–25). For a detailed study of this text, see J. I. Packer, "Appendix:

The 'Wretched Man' in Romans 7," in *Keep in Step with the Spirit* (Grand Rapids: Revell, 1984), 263–70. Although most Reformed theologians understand Rom. 7:14–25 to refer to Paul as a Christian, not all do. See, for example, Anthony A. Hoekema, "The Reformed Perspective," in *Five Views on Sanctification* (Grand Rapids: Zondervan, 1987), 232, 243 n. 25.

5. Jay E. Adams, *The War Within: A Biblical Strategy for Spiritual Warfare* (Eugene, Oreg.: Harvest House, 1989), 29.
6. For a detailed refutation of perfectionism as well as the teachings of the higher life and the victorious life, see B. B. Warfield, *Perfectionism*, in *The Works of Benjamin B. Warfield*, vols. 7–8 (1931; reprint, Grand Rapids: Baker, 1991).
7. J. I. Packer, *Rediscovering Holiness* (Ann Arbor: Servant, 1992), 43.
8. Michael S. Horton, "Don't Judge a Book by Its Cover," in *Christ the Lord*, ed. Michael S. Horton (Grand Rapids: Baker, 1992), 33. For a more detailed discussion of the carnal-spiritual dichotomy, see B. B. Warfield's classic refutation of Lewis Sperry Chafer's *He That Is Spiritual*, printed originally in *Princeton Theological Review* 17 (April 1919): 322–27. This review has been reprinted in Horton, *Christ the Lord*, 211–18.
9. Rod Rosenbladt, "Conclusion: Christ Died for the Sins of Christians, Too," in Horton, *Christ the Lord*, 199.
10. Ibid., 200.
11. Ferguson, "A Reformed Response," 67.
12. Packer, *Rediscovering Holiness*, 60.
13. John Murray, *Redemption: Accomplished and Applied* (Grand Rapids: Eerdmans, 1955), 175.
14. Ibid.
15. Ibid.

EIGHTEEN

FREE AT LAST

So far we have ascended a rather majestic mountain to get a panoramic view of the Christian life from the vantage point of the Reformed faith. Bordered at one end by our justification and at the other by our eventual glorification, the view is quite breathtaking. In between these borders, however, are some noteworthy sights we ought not to miss from afar. Of course, we will not pause to note every one of them exhaustively in the pages that follow, since we have already caught a glimpse of some of them in previous chapters.

Now that we have seen the big picture, adjusted our compasses, and highlighted our maps, it is time to descend to the valley below and explore three separate but noteworthy sights: the freedom we responsibly enjoy in Christ (chap. 18), the priesthood we exercise in our respective callings (chap. 19), and the worldview we cultivate as we learn to glorify Him in all that we think and do (chap. 20). In this chapter, we turn to our freedom in Christ.

IN THE CARDS

When I think of the freedom we enjoy in Christ, I am suddenly reminded of my childhood, when my Sunday school class—a motley crew of five-year-olds—was about to earn its stripes. During the worship service, we were going to recite the Twenty-third Psalm by heart (although at age five I could not quite figure out what my heart had to do with it!).

Although we were far from perfect, our church rather charitably kept its end of the deal by presenting us with our very own Bibles. I treasured that Bible since it was my first, but I distinctly remember putting it away shortly after I got it because it made me feel a bit uncomfortable. My discomfort never really registered fully until several years later, when, as a college student who had become acquainted with the basics of the Reformed faith, I found that Bible packed away in a box. After I dusted it off and opened it, I became somewhat dismayed by something the publisher had written on the inside back cover: a list of sins to avoid, including, if you can believe it, playing cards. Immediately I recalled the source of my discomfort: this "Bible" had told me that I could not play crazy eights with my sister!

Unfortunately, the list of vices in my first Bible is not alone. There are plenty of others just like it, which, if not printed in the backs of Bibles, are etched in the membership requirements of well-intentioned churches or Bible colleges and on the minds of otherwise sincere believers. And just as some "Bibles," churches, and believers tout long lists of extrabiblical rules for "holy" living, so others brandish fancy time charts "demonstrating" that believers are completely unbridled by any rules at all, since rules, they say, were only for Old Testament times.

If those who are busy creating extrabiblical rules and deleting truly biblical rules were just to stop and read the Bible itself, perhaps, just perhaps, they would see a precious truth that formed a cornerstone of Reformation thought: Christ came to set us free, but such freedom or liberty is ours only if we truly abide in the Word of God. Only then will we know the truth. Only then will we really be free—free from the penalty and curse of sin, and free to obey God. That is what the Reformed doctrine of Christian liberty is all about.

Laying a Firm Foundation

Christ alone is the Lord of all. Nothing is outside of His lordship, dominion, or control. The universal lordship of Christ knows no distinction between the sacred and the secular realms. As we shall see in the next two chapters, we are His royal priests, and as such are to consecrate every area of our lives to Him and present ourselves as living sacrifices to Him (Rom. 12:1–2). Whether we eat or drink or whatever we do, we are to do all in His name and to His glory (1 Cor. 10:31; Col.

3:17). We are, in Paul's words, to "live for the Lord" (Rom. 14:7–8).

Living for the Lord in a God-glorifying way, though, does not require us to enroll in a monastery and spend the rest of our lives chanting in candlelit rooms, as though Christ were not Lord of all vocations and we could not be His royal priests in the real world (1 Peter 2:9). Nor does living for the Lord require us to renounce marriage or certain foods, as though Christ were not Lord of all things and the One through whom God made all things good (Gen. 1:4, 10, 12, 18, 21, 25, 31; 1 Tim. 4:4; John 1:3). And it certainly does not require us to beat and flog our "flesh" and engage in other demeaning acts, as though Christ were not Lord of our bodies and we were not the temples in which His Spirit dwells (1 Cor. 3:16; 6:19–20).

What does living a truly God-glorifying life require? It requires us to submit to Christ alone as Lord (James 4:12), and to order our lives according to His Word, which is the final authority for all that we believe and do (Acts 17:11). If Christ alone, speaking through Scripture, is our final authority, then He alone can bind our consciences. When it comes to living a God-glorifying life, then, we must speak when Scripture speaks and remain silent when Scripture is silent.

FROM ONE EXTREME TO ANOTHER

Strange as it may seem, however, many Christians have it all backwards: they either remain silent when Scripture speaks, or speak when Scripture is silent.

Remaining Silent When Scripture Speaks

Those who remain silent when Scripture speaks ignore true godliness by rejecting what God requires of them in His Word. And we have seen that He requires a lot (perfection, to be exact!). Those who ignore God by ignoring His Word and the claims that it makes on their lives are known as antinomians (*anti*—"against," *nomos*—"law"). Antinomians wrongly believe that the Christian life is a one-way street, in which they enjoy all the privileges of membership without any corresponding obligations or responsibilities. Antinomianism, if unchecked, usually leads to licentiousness. If the Christian life is one without any obligations or responsibilities, then anything goes.

In the end, antinomianism is based on the assumption that liberty (freedom *from* sin) means license (freedom *to* sin). Hence, while antinomianism operates under the pretense of Christian liberty, it ends up destroying Christian liberty altogether. The antinomian is like a fish that decides, in the name of freedom, to beach itself because its environment of water is too stifling. Of course, a beached fish is not really free at all, since a beached fish is a dead fish! In like manner, the antinomian rejects the liberating environment of God's Word and launches out on his own course, only to destroy liberty altogether. Or think of railroad trains, which are really free only when they run on the tracks made to guide them safely along. A train without tracks is a derailed train, and a derailed train is a disaster. Whether you think of the Word of God as water for a fish or tracks for a train, it provides the true bounds of Christian freedom. We are only free when we live in accordance with the law of God. This is why James twice calls it the law of liberty (James 1:25; 2:12).

Because the antinomian destroys true liberty while trying in vain to pursue it, he is not really free at all. He is still a slave to sin and subject to its dominion. Only by abiding in the Word, the perfect law of liberty, can we be truly free (John 8:31; James 1:25; 2:12). Oh, that more Christians would learn to be hearers and doers of the Word—those who listen to the Word and whose lives speak when Scripture speaks!

Speaking When Scripture Is Silent

While antinomians remain silent when Scripture speaks, others speak when Scripture is silent by inventing extrabiblical rules or codes of conduct for being put right with God or as a means of becoming truly holy. In other words, they prohibit what Scripture does not prohibit, or command what Scripture does not command. These people are known as legalists.

Not every legalist, however, intentionally adds to Scripture. Some legalists, in fact, honestly believe that their rules and codes are scriptural. Still other legalists just assume that their rules accord with Scripture because that is what they were always taught or how they have always lived. Yet, no matter which way legalism is sliced, the result is the same: legalism speaks when Scripture is silent and mandates that others do the same.

In its extreme form, legalism has led many believers to abuse their bodies in an attempt to become "truly" spiritual. They have beaten and mutilated their bodies, refused to bathe, denied themselves sleep, sat endlessly atop poles, and remained celibate without the gift of celibacy. This is known as abusive asceticism. Although some legalists reel in horror at such behavior, they cannot deny that legalism and abusive asceticism are twins born of the same dualistic heresy that the body is bad and the spirit is good.

In other words, legalists and abusive ascetics are closer than might appear at first glance. While legalists generally denounce pleasures or entertainments (drinking, dancing, moviegoing, etc.), abusive ascetics generally go one step further by also denouncing necessities (hygiene, rest, etc.). What unites legalism and abusive asceticism, however, is that both speak when Scripture is silent and both usually impose their rules on others in an ill-advised attempt to unlock the supposedly hidden secrets of holiness.

Seen in this light, abusive asceticism is simply legalism with a vengeance. And both are unbiblical with a vengeance, since both destroy true liberty altogether. Contrary to those who tout legalism and abusive asceticism as paths to the holy life, the Holy Spirit—apart from whom no holiness is possible—minces no words. Speaking through Paul, the Holy Spirit gives us a taste for how pernicious the twin evils of legalism and abusive asceticism are. He informs us that they emanate from deceitful spirits and doctrines of demons as well as from the hypocrisy of liars whose consciences are seared as with a branding iron (1 Tim. 4:1–2).

Believe it or not, that is the good news. The bad news is that the commandments and teachings of men do not prevent us from sinning at all. Not one bit. Self-made religion, self-abasement, and severe treatment of the body may appear to be wise or religious, but Scripture forthrightly says that they are actually of no value whatsoever in warring against fleshly indulgence (Col. 2:20–23). That is a sobering thought, indeed.

Life in the Balance

As those who have been truly liberated by Christ's sovereign work on our behalf and graciously called by the Holy Spirit into covenant with God and His people, we cannot afford to remain silent when Scripture speaks. Nor can we afford to speak when Scripture is silent. We must always remember that we have been called to steer clear of both antinomianism and legalism as well as their offspring, licentiousness and abusive asceticism. Christ came so that we might have life and have it more abundantly (John 10:10). And whatever else can be said about the abundant life, it is a life that is free from man-made rules and that submits to the lordship of Christ as revealed in His Word.

As such, the abundant life is a life characterized by both freedom and responsibility. From the Christian perspective, these two poles are not opposed to each another. Rather, they involve one another, since we are called to be both free and responsible. In Christ, we are to be responsibly free and freely responsible. True Christian liberty, therefore, involves freedom from sin and its curse (liberty) and freedom to live for God by obeying His Word (responsibility). Paul put it so well when he told the Galatians that though they had been "called to freedom," they were not to turn their freedom "into an opportunity for the flesh, but through love" were to "serve one another" (Gal. 5:13).

FROM A DIFFERENT POINT OF VIEW

But how do we tell the difference between that which we are free to do and that which is an opportunity for the flesh? Obviously, we must do what God has commanded (e.g., loving one another). We must also refrain from doing what He has prohibited (e.g., committing adultery). At the same time, we are completely free to enjoy what God permits (e.g., eating meat).

But what about the seemingly difficult cases like drinking, dancing, moviegoing, playing cards, and a host of other activities that some Christians have opposed? Although God commands us to glorify Him in all that we do and to do everything in the name of Christ as we live for Him (1 Cor. 10:31; Col. 3:17; Rom. 14:7–8), no one would seriously contend that God commands us to drink, dance, attend movies, or play cards. So, when it comes to such activities, the payoff question is: Does the general command to glorify God in all that we do prohibit us from such activities, or does it permit us to partake of them, provided that we can do so to His glory?

To answer this question, it would be helpful to think for a moment about two controversies that raged in the early church: whether one should eat meat at all, and whether one should eat meat that has been offered to idols. Since eating meat was not, in and of itself, commanded or forbidden, believers struggled over whether they could permissibly eat it when it was served to them. Consider, if you will, the following passages, some of which arose or were invoked in the very context of these controversies:

> The earth is the LORD's, and all it contains, the world, and those who dwell in it. (Ps. 24:1)

There is only one Lawgiver and Judge, the One who is able to save and to destroy; but who are you who judge your neighbor? (James 4:12)

Listen to Me, all of you, and understand: there is nothing outside the man which going into him can defile him; but the things which proceed out of the man are what defile the man. . . . For from within, out of the heart of men, proceed the evil thoughts and fornications, thefts, murders, adulteries, deeds of coveting and wickedness, as well as deceit, sensuality, envy, slander, pride and foolishness. All these evil things proceed from within and defile the man. (Mark 7:14–15, 21–23)

I know and am convinced in the Lord Jesus that nothing is unclean in itself. . . . All things indeed are clean. (Rom. 14:14, 20)

All things are lawful for me, but not all things are profitable. All things are lawful for me, but I will not be mastered by anything. . . . All things are lawful, but not all things are profitable. All things are lawful, but not all things edify. (1 Cor. 6:12; 10:23, 26)

But the Spirit explicitly says that in later times some will fall away from the faith, paying attention to deceitful spirits and doctrines of demons, by means of the hypocrisy of liars seared in their own conscience as with a branding iron, men who forbid marriage and advocate abstaining from foods, which God has created to be gratefully shared in by those who believe and know the truth. For everything created by God is good, and nothing is to be rejected, if it is received with gratitude; for it is sanctified by means of the word of God and prayer. (1 Tim. 4:1–5)

If you have died with Christ to the elementary principles of the world, why, as if you were living in the world, do you submit yourself to decrees, such as, "Do not handle, do not taste, do not touch!" (which all refer to things destined to perish with the using)—in accordance with the commandments and teachings of men? These are matters which have, to be sure, the appearance of wisdom in self-made religion and self-abasement and severe treatment of the body, but are of no value against fleshly indulgence. (Col. 2:20–23)

Although these passages speak for themselves, perhaps it would be helpful to hold the microphone up to them just long enough to hear that they argue loudly and clearly in favor of the Reformed view of Christian liberty by teaching us at least five important truths.

First, Christ alone is Lord over the earth and all it contains (Ps. 24:1; 1 Cor. 10:26). If Christ is Lord over all areas of life, then He alone can bind the consciences of those made in His image; in the words of James, there is only one Lawgiver and Judge (James 4:12a). Because Christ alone lays down the rules for being Christlike, we ought not to judge one another by laws and rules that Christ has not explicitly or implicitly promulgated in His Word (James 4:12b). And we ought not to allow other believers or institutions to impose man-made rules upon us either.

Second, even as Christ is Lord of all and the sole Lawgiver and Judge, so He is the One through whom God created all things (John 1:3). And how does Scripture describe God's creation? It plainly tells us that God Himself declared that His creation was good (Gen. 1:4, 10, 12, 18, 21, 25, 31). Notice that Scripture does not say that God created all things "well"— an adverb describing how God created the universe. Rather, it says that God created all things "good"—an adjective describing the creation itself. God, to be sure, created all things well, but Scripture, at this point, emphasizes the goodness of the creation itself. And the goodness of the creation was not limited to the way things were before the Fall. While the Fall profoundly affected the creation (Rom. 8:18–22), even after the Fall Paul unhesitatingly affirmed its goodness: "Everything created by God is good" (1 Tim. 4:4a).

Third, because the creation is good in and of itself, there is nothing intrinsically evil about it. Thus, nothing outside of us can defile us (Mark 7:14–15). Paul says the same thing elsewhere, with a slightly different twist. After noting that everything created by God is good, he establishes a general principle that nothing is to be rejected (1 Tim. 4:4b). He also tells us that "nothing is unclean in itself," and then puts it positively: "All things indeed are clean" (Rom. 14:14, 20). Similarly, "all things are lawful" (1 Cor. 6:12, 10:23).[1] Scripture dresses the same general principle in slightly different garb: Nothing out there is evil in and of itself. Nothing is to be rejected. Nothing is unclean. All things are clean. All things are lawful. Why? Because God made them all. As C. S. Lewis once quipped, "God likes matter; He invented it."[2]

Fourth, although God has repeatedly told us that we are free in Christ, we must not turn our freedom into an opportunity for the flesh (Gal. 5:13; 1 Peter 2:16). In Christ, we are free from sin and at the same time are free to obey God as His bondservants. We are not to use our freedom as a cloak for evil. Instead, we are to exercise our freedom within the boundaries established by Christ, our only Lawgiver and Judge (James 4:12). The outer boundary of our freedom is set by biblical commandments and prohibitions, which set forth the things we must do and must refrain from doing. But when it comes to the things that we are free to do, we must realize that Scripture itself places certain limits on the way we do them.

Toward this end, Paul says that nothing is to be rejected if it is received with gratitude and sanctified by the Word of God and prayer (1 Tim. 4:4). Of course, this principle implies that if we are to reject anything, we are to reject it because it is not received with gratitude or is not sanctified by the Word of God and prayer. As we exercise our freedom in Christ, we must do so with the right motive (in this case, gratitude) and within the context of Scripture and prayer, which is to say that we must be convinced that whatever we are doing is genuinely within the boundaries of our freedom as defined in Scripture. After all, whatever is not from faith is sin (Rom. 14:23). Why? Because it is wrong to do even the right thing with an improper motive—to do something that you think is wrong, even if it may really be all right in and of itself.

But we must also make sure that we properly examine the consequences of our behavior, keeping in mind that our ultimate goal as believers is to glorify God and to advance His kingdom on earth. We should not do anything that would thwart that goal or that might harm us or those around us. While Scripture tells us that all things are lawful, it also tells us that we must not allow ourselves to be mastered by anything other than our one true Master (1 Cor. 6:12; Matt. 6:24). Moreover, we should only do those things that are profitable—those things that edify us and those who have been put under our care (1 Cor. 6:12). Finally, we must not cause a weaker brother to stumble (Rom. 14:1–15:3; 1 Cor. 8:7–13; 10:13–23) by influencing him to do something that he believes to be sinful. A primary consideration in biblical ethics is how others will be affected by what we do. While there is nothing wrong with looking out for our own legitimate interests, we must also take into account the interests of others (Phil. 2:4).

Fifth, those who add to the claims that Scripture makes on our lives slap God in the face by attempting to usurp His lordship. They also reject the goodness of God's creation and deny our freedom in Christ. In essence, they assume that the infallible Word of God, which equips us "for every good work" (2 Tim. 3:16–17), somehow needs to be supplemented by the fallible word of man. What usually happens is that the word of man ends up supplanting the Word of God! It is no wonder that Scripture lays it on the line by describing those who promulgate man-made rules as having fallen away from the faith. According to Paul, legalists pay attention to deceitful spirits and doctrines of demons and are seared in their own consciences by the hypocrisy of liars. Paul uses some of the strongest words in all of Scripture to denounce those who are in the business of manufacturing rules for "holy living," since to do so is to deny the faith by denying the sufficiency of God and His Word. To top it off, such rules, as we have already noted, are totally useless in fighting sin. As Christians we dare not add to, or take away from, the Word of God, which alone is our standard for all that we believe and do (Deut. 4:2; Rev. 22:18–19).

A TIME TO PLAY?

At this point, it might be helpful to illustrate the Reformed view of Christian liberty by looking at life as a playground that God has created for His children to enjoy, as long as they do so to His glory. But God has also built a fence around the playground and forbidden us to wander beyond it. What is within the playground is generally permissible, but what lies beyond it is forbidden.

But a playground would not be a playground if it did not have its rules (e.g., "no pushing," "take turns," etc.). God's playground is no exception. We must always seek to understand those rules, including the primary rule to glorify Him by playing on the playground and not wandering beyond the fence.

That is, we must understand and apply the relevant biblical principles to the various situations that we face in life. Biblical principles include those things which Scripture commands, commends, prohibits, and permits. But we cannot understand and apply biblical principles in a vacuum. We must understand and apply them in light of who we are as God's people (e.g., our motivations, capabilities, strengths and weaknesses, likes and dislikes) and in light of the situations or problems we encounter (e.g., the facts before us, as well as the short- and long-term consequences of our actions).

Some of us, for instance, may like to play on the swings, while others may avoid them because they would get dizzy on them. And those who like to ride on the swings should do so safely, without harming themselves or others, and should not be selfish or force others to swing. This, of course, is just another way of saying that though something may be permissible in and of itself (e.g., eating meat), it may not be good or desirable for every-one (e.g., those who have scruples) or under every circumstance (e.g., if it causes a brother to stumble).

SOME CONCLUDING THOUGHTS

Seen in this light, only the Reformed view of our freedom in Christ safe-guards both liberty and responsibility by simultaneously steering us clear of both antinomianism (which is based on a distorted view of liberty) and legalism (which is based on a distorted view of responsibility). This is not to suggest that everyone who adheres to the Reformed view agrees on what should be done in every case. Nor is it to say that the Reformers them-selves or their heirs always adhered to, or lived consistently with, this po-sition. While Reformed believers may be inconsistent or may reach different conclusions on some issues, more often than not they agree that many of the activities or entertainments that non-Reformed believers use as bo-geymen are permissible if done within the limits prescribed in Scripture.

Unfortunately, however, non-Reformed lists of dos and don'ts often go beyond what we do to entertain ourselves after putting in a hard day's work. Often, such lists also include work itself, since many in the non-Reformed camp assume that you cannot really serve and glorify God in "secular" employment. Having already explored our freedom in Christ, we turn next to explore what the Reformers called our priesthood as believ-ers. We will learn that we are to serve and glorify God wherever He has called us in life.

STUDY QUESTIONS

1. How do some Christians live their lives so as to remain silent when Scripture speaks? How do some Christians live so as to speak when Scrip-ture is silent? Have you ever fallen into these traps for the unwary? What can you do today to prevent such error in the future?
2. Through whom did God make all things, according to John 1:3? Is the creation good (see Gen. 1:4, 10, 12, 18, 21, 25, 31)? Even though the creation was dramatically affected by the Fall (Rom. 8:18–22), does Paul, in 1 Timothy 4:4, still affirm the basic goodness of God's creation even after the Fall? How does this truth change the way you look at God's creation?

3. Does our freedom in Christ mean that we can do whatever we want, whenever we want, to whomever we want (see Gal. 5:13; 1 Peter 2:16)? What does it mean? Explain how we can be free in Christ, yet be His bondservants (1 Peter 2:16). What are some of the limits that Christ places on the way we exercise the freedom that we enjoy in Him (see Rom. 14:1–15:3; 1 Cor. 6:12; 8:7–13; 10:13–23)? Do you exercise your freedom within such limits?

Notes

1. Some New Testament scholars see this statement, "All things are lawful," as a motto for Corinthian libertinism, which Paul proceeds to refute by placing true Christian liberty in its proper perspective. (I.e., you say that all things are lawful, but I say that not all things are profitable; you say that all things are lawful, but I say that I will not be mastered by anything.) Other scholars see this phrase as a general principle of Christian liberty, subject to the limits of profitability and mastery stated thereafter. Happily, this is not the only place where Scripture teaches us the goodness and acceptability of all things in and of themselves. Besides, both views get to the same place; they just get there by following different routes. In the words of Paul, though we are free in Christ, we ought not to use our freedom as an opportunity for the flesh (Gal. 5:13).
2. Cited in Alan Maben, "When World Denial Becomes Worldliness," *Modern Reformation*, March/April 1992, p. 6.

NINETEEN

ANSWERING THE CALL

So much for the tweed coat, button-down oxford, and loafers. They are not for this professor. In his attempt to claim solidarity with the common man, he wears boots, disparagingly known as "longhorns" in farming country. He struts around his class, spurning any accommodation to the "evil" capitalism that would actually pay him more than the janitor who cleans his lecture hall at night. Once, in a well-known article, this Harvard Law School professor went so far as to suggest that the professors at the law school trade places with the janitors. But he never bothered to ask the janitors if they wanted to trade places with the professors.

One day, however, a student in this professor's class did just that. And he published his results in the *Wall Street Journal*, where he reported that the janitors, on the whole, were not too pleased with this lofty professorial suggestion, since lurking behind it was the arrogant assumption that being a professor was more dignified than being a janitor. So while the professor may have tried to safeguard the dignity of janitors as people, he did so at the expense of denigrating their vocation. In the end, the professor promoted what he had apparently set out to deny—the notion that professors are better or more dignified than janitors.

Over against such well-intentioned but misguided attempts to preserve the dignity of those who pursue various vocations stands a clarion truth of Scripture, a truth proclaimed by the Reformers, called the priesthood of all believers—as well as the related doctrine of callings. When properly understood, these doctrines restore true dignity to believers who pursue different vocations, by teaching that all believers are God's royal priests and, as such, are to serve and glorify Him no matter what legitimate vocation He sovereignly calls and providentially guides them to pursue.

GETTING TO THE ROOT OF THE PROBLEM

In contrast to the Reformers, many Christians today believe that some vocations are more dignified than others in the sight of God. Of course, this belief stems from a failure to see that the Christian life is an integrated whole. And that stems from a failure to see that Christ is Lord over all areas of life. For if Christ is Lord over all areas of life, we can ill afford to carve up our lives in this world into "sacred" and "secular" slices. The Roman Catholic Church of the Reformation era carved up life in this way and, to no one's surprise, viewed the priesthood as the highest calling that one could pursue. Priests were simply cut from a different cloth than the laity. There was the priesthood (the "spiritual estate") and then there was everyone else (the "temporal estate").

Unfortunately, the descendants of medieval Catholicism are still around today, even in some professedly Protestant circles, where they dress their spiritual-temporal distinction in slightly different garb. This brand of Protestantism, you see, is not brash enough to come right out and call some people priests and others the laity. But if you look long and hard enough, you will find the same kind of pecking order.

The new Protestant priesthood consists of those in "full-time Christian service." If you really want to serve God in this life, we are told, you will become a missionary to a foreign land. And, if you do not mind being just one rung lower on the Protestant pecking order, you can become an inner-city pastor. Still lower are suburban pastors and so on until you come to the rest of us clustered together in the pews. They have the ministry; we just have jobs.

Sadly, this pecking order is more prevalent than we care to admit. Once I visited a respected evangelical seminary, since I was considering attending seminary after graduating from law school. When I informed the admissions director of my plans, he somberly but sternly told me that he had quit his career as a successful businessman to go into the "ministry" (read: "full-time ministry"). He then informed me that if I were really serious about the ministry, I could not live with "one foot in the world and one in the church."

This admissions director should have known better. So should the evangelical community at large. The Christian life is an integrated whole. It should not be artificially broken up into spiritual (sacred) and temporal (secular) compartments. As Christians, we are called to glorify God in all that we do—even in mundane activities like eating and drinking (1 Cor. 10:31). Whatever we do, we are to do it in Christ's name, giving thanks through Him to the glory of God the Father (Col. 3:17). Simply put, we are to live for the Lord (Rom. 14:7–8).

If our entire life is to be lived as an integrated whole to the glory of God, we cannot treat some areas of life as though they were less important or less dignified than others in the eyes of God. But that is precisely what some Christians do. As Paul Helm once wrote, some Christians act "as if Christian responsibility ceases at the church porch, as if the Christian gospel has nothing to do with the pavement outside and the roads . . . beyond."[1] He then goes on to note, quite correctly, that

> nowadays the idea of a calling or vocation, where it is used at all, is limited to special occupations such as nursing or social work. But the biblical view is that any lawful occupation may be a calling and more than this, that the whole of a person's life is a calling from God. . . . It is the product of His providential ruling. . . . Such an idea was prominent at the Reformation, but is now largely forgotten.[2]

Because our Protestant memories are sometimes lacking, we would all do well to sit up and heed what the Reformers and their heirs had to say about our lives and vocations as callings from God—about our priesthood as believers.

Are we really God's priests? How do we become priests and how should this truth change our lives? Allow Scripture, as illuminated by the Reformers and their heirs, to answer these all-important questions.

OUR GREAT HIGH PRIEST

Since our sovereign God stands at the center of the biblical message, we must never forget that our priesthood, from beginning to end, is rooted and grounded in our great high priest, Jesus Christ, whose priesthood was ordained not by man, but rather by God. In fact, God swore with a binding oath—in the Covenant in the Godhead—that Christ was, is, and will forever be our eternal high priest according to the order of Melchizedek

(Heb. 5:6; 6:26; 7:26–27). As our eternal high priest—as the God-man—Christ is the sole mediator between God and man (1 Tim. 2:5), having offered Himself as our sacrifice once for all. He did so, as we have already seen, to expiate or cleanse us from the guilt of our sin, propitiate or turn away God's wrath against our sin, reconcile or restore us to God (who was alienated from us by our sin), and redeem or ransom us from the bondage and curse of sin and death.

But Scripture does not simply teach us that our great high priest died to make atonement on our behalf; it also teaches us that because of His death, we have been made priests in and for Him. The same priest "who loves us, and released us from our sins by His blood," also "made us to be a kingdom, priests to His God and Father" (Rev. 1:5–6). What a glorious truth! Christ, by His death as our great high priest, not only atoned for our sins, but also, as Calvin so aptly put it, received us "as his companions" in this great priestly office.[3]

THE PRIESTLY CALLER

Just how did Christ receive us as His companions in this great priestly office? Scripture tells us that God bestowed His favor upon us, chose us for Himself, and called us to be His covenant people and His royal priests. Simply put, we would not be His priests had He not first called us to be His chosen people. This is why almost every passage that speaks of us as priests also speaks of us as those who have been called by God as His chosen people.

In his first epistle, for example, Peter applies the attributes reserved for God's Old Covenant people to us as New Covenant believers, and explicitly proclaims that we, too, are the covenant people of God. In the Old Testament, we learn that God mercifully called the children of Israel to be His people and promised them that if they walked in obedience to His covenant, they would be His "own possession," "a kingdom of priests," and a "holy nation" (Ex. 19:5, cf. Deut. 14:2, 21). Conjuring up this imagery and applying these attributes to New Testament believers as the new Israel, Peter writes,

> But you are a chosen race, a royal priesthood, a holy nation, a people for God's own possession, that you may proclaim the excellencies of Him who has called you out of darkness into His marvelous light; for you once were not a people, but now you are the

people of God; you had not received mercy, but now you have received mercy. (1 Peter 2:9–10)

In the same vein, the four living creatures and the twenty-four elders in the book of Revelation sing that the Lamb was slain and with His blood purchased for God "men from every tribe and tongue and people and nation. And Thou hast made them to be a kingdom and priests to our God; and they will reign upon the earth" (Rev. 5:9–10).

In these passages, we learn about the mercy and grace of God, who called us to be His royal priests. In particular, we learn three important truths. First, God, by the atoning blood of Christ, has mercifully called us out of every tribe and tongue and nation to conversion—or, as Peter puts it, out of darkness into His marvelous light. Second, we have also been called into covenant with Him to be His chosen people and His royal priests. Third, as His royal priests we are to serve Him daily by proclaiming His excellencies (our priestly function) and reigning upon the earth to His glory (our kingly function). By God's grace, we are both kingly priests and priestly kings. As such, we are to serve Him daily as we reign for Him.

CALVIN AND JOBS

Since we are to serve and glorify God daily as His royal priests, the idea of a priesthood of all believers should not be relegated to the status of a time-worn theological slogan. It is a cornerstone of Reformed theology, which should change how we live our lives each and every day, including how we pursue our vocations.[4] Properly understood, the priesthood of all believers does not do away with God-given authority in the family, the church, the workplace, and the state. But the priesthood of all believers does teach us that our lives and vocations are callings from God, thereby obliterating the distinction between the spiritual (sacred) and the temporal (secular). All believers are priests, no matter what their calling in life might be.

Luther put it well when he wrote,

> Just as those who are now called "spiritual," that is, priests, bishops, or popes, are neither different from other Christians nor superior to them, except that they are charged with the administration of the word of God and the sacraments, which is their work and office, so it is with the temporal authorities. They bear the sword and rod in their hand to punish the wicked and protect the good.

A cobbler, a smith, a peasant—each has his own work and office of his trade, and yet they are all alike consecrated priests and bishops. Further, everyone must benefit and serve every other by means of his own work or office so that in this way many kinds of work may be done for the bodily and spiritual welfare of the community, just as all the members of the body serve one another [1 Cor. 12:14–26].[5]

According to Luther, the distinction between priests and laymen is functional. While priests have their calling and perform various functions, so do laymen. Laymen, in fact, are also consecrated by God to serve Him as His priests in their divinely ordained "offices." Whatever our office happens to be, Luther reminds us that we are to serve one another humbly and contribute selflessly to the life of the body.

Calvin wrote that because our human nature would otherwise lead us "hither and thither," God has appointed assignments or stations for everyone in this life, which act to limit us—to serve as boundaries for us. He called these assignments or stations "callings" and believed that our lives are best ordered when we do not transgress them.

Accordingly, your life will then be best ordered when it is directed to this goal [God's calling]. For no one, impelled by his own rashness, will attempt more than his calling will permit, because he will know that it is not lawful to exceed its bounds. A man of obscure station will lead a private life ungrudgingly so as not to leave the rank in which he has been placed by God. Again, it will be no slight relief from cares, labours, troubles, and other burdens for a man to know that God is his guide in all these things. The magistrate will discharge his functions more willingly; the head of the household will confine himself to his duty; each man will bear and swallow the discomforts, vexations, weariness and anxieties in his way of life, when he has been persuaded that the burden was laid on him by God. From this will arise also a singular consolation; that no task will be so sordid and base, provided you obey your calling in it, that it will not shine and be reckoned very precious in God's sight.[6]

According to Luther and Calvin, all believers have equally received the treasures that God has given, from the cobbler to the smith to the peasant. No vocation stands over and above any other. No vocation is more sacred than any other. God has given believers different offices or callings—from the dock worker to the doctor, from the messenger to the manager, from the electrician to the executive. All legitimate vocations are vehicles through which God will do His work.

EXCUSES, EXCUSES

The fundamental problem, though, is that many believers never realize that their vocations are an important part of their Christian calling.[7] As a result, they fail to see their vocations as vehicles through which God will do His work through them as His priests. Believers are endowed with the incredible privilege of ministering for God daily wherever He has called them. But because some believers lose sight of their priestly calling, they slosh through their tasks day after day, week after week, losing valuable opportunities to serve God and glorify Him as priests in their vocations.[8]

Working for the Weekend

Sometimes Christians dress up their slosh-through-the-week mentality in rather pious garb. Some, for example, are fond of thinking that they have to get through the workweek so they can pursue their real calling to minister to others at church on Sunday. Somehow they have forgotten that their calling—their ministry—includes what they do Monday through Friday. We are not to work primarily to minister; we are primarily to minister as we work.

Sadly, those who slosh through the week often fail to live up to the standard of excellence that is to adorn their Christian profession. While they set out to advance the gospel, they end up undermining it, because they neglect to perform the tasks set before them to the glory of God (1 Cor. 10:31; Col. 3:17).

In fact, this problem is not limited to Christian employees. Some Christian employers similarly think that putting a fish or a cross on their letterhead is a substitute for competence. And the Christians who hire them sometimes put up with their incompetence. Of course, the solution to this problem is not necessarily for us to hire unbelieving employers or for an employer to hire an unbelieving employee; it is for the believing employer or employee in that situation to become competent. And there is no better starting point than for the believer to remind himself that his ministry to God and others does not start and stop on Sundays.

Working to Witness

Still other Christians fail to fulfill their divine calling during the week because they view their jobs simply as mission fields—going so far as to spend company time to witness to unbelieving colleagues or patrons, all the while thwarting their witness and possibly harming their business in the process.

The story is told of a well-respected missionary who, before going to the mission field, worked as a cobbler by day and studied for the mission field at night. Apparently motivated by his evening studies, he demonstrated an admirable desire to share the gospel with nearly everyone who entered the shop. When told one day that he was causing some of the shop's patrons to go elsewhere, he replied that such was of no concern to him since his primary task was to build the kingdom of God. He then added that he only fixed shoes "to pay the expenses." The cobbler-would-be-missionary's reply misses the point: one way he should have advanced the kingdom of God was by doing his best during the day to repair shoes to the glory of God. While he had an admirable zeal for souls, as a cobbler he needed to cultivate an equal zeal for soles!

The bottom line is that God has given us enough time to do everything He has called us to do. If you feel compelled to witness on company time, you should make up that time, which rightfully belongs to your employer. The Lord, after all, never calls His priests to steal time from their employers (Ex. 20:15; Rom. 3:8).

Similarly, there are those who claim that they cannot think about work-related things because they are too busy thinking about spiritual things. They actually think that they are worshiping God and being more heavenly-minded than the Christian down the production line who concentrates on his work and puts forth his best effort from nine to five. Richard Steele warns those so inclined not to neglect their "necessary affairs upon pretense of religious worship."[9] Thomas Shepard renders the same advice to Christians who claim that religious thoughts distract them at work: "As it is sin to nourish worldly thoughts when God sets you at work in spiritual, heavenly employments, so it is, in some respects, as great a sin to suffer yourself to be distracted by spiritual thoughts when God sets you on work in civil . . . employments."[10]

We ought not to think that we are slighting God when we put our minds to our work. In fact, we slight God when we do not put our minds to our work, since we are to serve and glorify Him through our work. The problem, as Os Guinness has correctly observed, is not that most Christians are not where they ought to be. It is that most Christians are not what they ought to be where they are. They are not serving and glorifying God as His priests in the workplace. In the words of Paul, they are not working "heartily, as for the Lord rather than for men." Somewhere along the way, they have forgotten that it is "the Lord Christ whom you serve" (Col. 3:23–24).

Those who have forgotten whom they serve in the workplace need to draw deeply from the well of the Reformers and their heirs on this point. Luther, for example, wrote that what seem to us to be secular works actually praise God and represent an obedience with which God is well pleased. "There are no limits at all," he continues, "to this idea of calling. Wherever you are, whatever you are doing, you are able to please God in a concrete way and glorify His name and witness to Him by working."[11] Thus, we should not primarily work to witness in the narrow sense, but rather should primarily witness in the broad sense through our work. Only then can we offer a powerful witness that will honor God, please Him, and truly glorify His holy name.

Working to Move On

Other Christians become slack in their attitudes at work because they believe that they will never have an opportunity to move on—or, sometimes, because God may already be preparing them to move on. Students with part-time jobs or full-time workers in promotion training programs, for example, often struggle with this problem, since they know that they will be moving on in the near future. The "underemployed" and those with unfulfilled performing arts or athletic backgrounds also struggle in this way, since they are not doing what they feel they were specifically trained to do.

Paul tells us that we are not necessarily locked into one calling for our entire lives. In 1 Corinthians 7:21–22, he speaks about remaining where we currently find ourselves until the opportunity to move on to another calling presents itself. In particular, he instructs those who are called by God as slaves not to worry if they cannot become free, but to become free if they are ever able to do so. Based on Paul's exhortation, it is not wrong to change your calling, as long as God presents the opportunity to you and as long as you are not making changes for the wrong reasons (greed, envy, impatience, etc.). But regardless of whether such an opportunity presents itself, God wants you to function as His priest to His glory now in your present calling.

Think of your present calling as a seating assignment on an airplane. When you board a plane, you are given a specific place to sit. While you may have to sit in that seat for the entire flight, you may be given an opportunity to move to an empty seat before the end of the flight. But until the opportunity to change seats presents itself, your only seat is where you are currently sitting. And you should serve and glorify God as you sit there now. While you may not be bound to stay forever where God has currently assigned you, you should not fail to pursue God's call in your current assignment. Just think of Noah. He glorified God as an ark builder before the Flood, a shipman and zoo keeper during the Flood, and as a farmer and gardener after the Flood. But then again, it helps to live to the ripe old age of 950!

Working as a Curse

Some think that they are called to minister for God only on Sundays, while others view the workplace only as a mission field or have become frustrated with their present assignments. There are still others who fail to serve and glorify God during the workweek as priests because they have mistakenly concluded that work is the result of the Fall. Accordingly, they have taken an unbiblically low view of work.

But work is not a post-Fall institution. God put Adam in the Garden of Eden to be its caretaker (Gen. 2:15) before the Fall. He also commanded Adam to "subdue" the earth and to "rule" over creation (Gen. 1:27–28) before the Fall. Lest anyone forget, Genesis 1 and 2 come before Genesis 3! To be sure, God's curse upon Adam encompassed his work; he would have to toil all the days of his life (Gen. 3:17–19). But even then, the curse, properly understood, affected only the circumstances of his work, not the institution of work itself (Gen. 5:29). Adam worked before the Fall, and he had to work after it. The difference was that in the post-Fall world he had to work harder and sweat more.

While those who take an unbiblically low view of work forget that God ordained man to labor before the Fall, they also forget the high view of work found in Scripture even after the Fall. The fourth commandment, as found in Exodus 20:8–11 and Deuteronomy 5:12–15, for example, commands us to work ("six days shalt thou labor and do all thy work") every bit as much as it commands us to rest ("in it [the Sabbath] thou shalt not do any work"). It is no accident that believers who scorn the Lord's Day frequently end up scorning work, and vice versa. Somewhat ironically, those who scorn the Lord's Day often end up resting six days a week and working on the seventh!

Scripture's high view of work can also be found in the many proverbs that extol industriousness or diligence and condemn slothfulness or laziness (e.g., Prov. 10:4–5, 26; 12:11, 24, 27; 13:4; 14:23; 19:15, 24; 20:4; 21:5, 25; 22:13; 24:30–34; 26:13–16; Eccl. 9:10). Solomon observes that we are to enjoy ourselves in our labor as well as the fruit of such labor, since this enjoyment is a gift from God and His reward to us (Eccl. 5:18–20).

And then there are Paul's injunctions to do our work to please the Lord (Eph. 6:5–8; Col. 3:22–24), to refrain from being busybodies and to work quietly for our own bread (1 Thess. 4:11–12; 2 Thess. 3:7–12), to labor for ourselves and those in need (Eph. 4:28), and to provide for those under our care lest we deny the faith and prove ourselves to be worse than unbelievers (1 Tim. 5:8, 13–16).

From cover to cover, then, Scripture frowns on the notion that work is simply post-Fall drudgery. It is a pre-Fall institution which, even after the Fall, is both commanded and commended in Scripture. If even slaves are to do their work heartily as for the Lord (Eph. 6:5–8; Col. 3:22–24), we have no excuse. Their chains were real. Ours are only imaginary.

No more sloshing. No more pious excuses. We should begin today to seize the opportunities that God has given us. We should commit ourselves to pursuing our respective vocations with vigor and zeal, viewing them as opportunities to serve and glorify our great high priest. "The main end of our lives," wrote William Perkins, "is to serve God in the serving of men in the works of our callings."[12] In other words, when we fulfill our callings and serve others in them, we thereby serve and glorify God, which is our primary purpose in life.

We are not just Christians who happen to be carpenters, dentists, or professors. We are called to be Christian carpenters, dentists, and professors. We are not just Christians on Sunday. We are called to be Christians every day, including Monday through Friday. We are not just Christians at church and in the prayer closet. We are called to be Christians everywhere, including the workplace.

Seen in this light, our callings are not mere occupations—ways of occupying us or passing time. They are vocations, that is, callings from God, by and through which we serve and glorify Him. Humbly recognizing the tremendous privilege that God has bestowed on us through our great high priest, we should begin today to view our legitimate vocations—no matter what they may be—as one sphere of life through which we are to exercise our divinely ordained priesthood.

Promoting the Cause

But many Christians turn south precisely at this point by thinking that if their vocations do not overtly promote the Christian cause, they are somehow letting God down or failing to fulfill His will for their lives. They fail to see that if they function as His priests by fulfilling His calling in their lives, they are promoting the Christian cause already. They do not need to be doing "religious" things full-time to glorify God.

You do not have to try freedom of religion cases to be a Christian lawyer. You do not have to paint the Last Supper to be a Christian artist. You do not have to sing hymns to be a Christian singer. You do not have to sell Bibles to be a Christian salesperson. Christians who think that you do have sold out to the ministry-job pecking order. And where the ministry-job pecking order is found, mediocrity is soon to follow. We have become addicted to mediocrity, not only in the arts, but in all of life, in part because we have lost sight of our priestly calling.

"Where are today's Bachs, Handels, Miltons, Rembrandts, Durers, Cranachs, Herberts, and Donnes?" asks Michael Horton, ever so tellingly. Some of them, he replies, may be working two or three jobs to put food on the table, while others were persuaded to go into full-time ministry, thinking that only by doing that would they ever glorify God fully. To those who are tempted to think that full-time ministry is somehow the highest or best calling in life, Horton responds by observing,

> When Christians begin to see that it is as godly to be a businessperson, lawyer, homemaker, artist, rubbish collector, doctor, or construction worker, as it is to be a missionary, evangelist, pastor, youth leader, or an employee of a Christian organization, they will once again become salt and light. Once a Christian woman realizes that it is just as spiritual to sing at the Met as it is to sing in the church choir, we will begin to see a new generation of liberated Christians calling attention to their Maker and Redeemer. . . . When all believers become priests once again, we will see the end of full-time Christian ministry as a separate and superior calling.[13]

Do you think that full-time ministry is a separate and superior calling? Do you really think that singing at the Met is as spiritual or as God-glorifying as singing in the church choir?

Have you sold out to the ministry-job pecking order? Do you need eyes to see what the Reformers and their heirs saw? According to Luther, the work of the ministry, in the sight of God, is "in no way superior to the works of the farmer laboring in the field, or of a woman looking after her home."[14] Along the same lines, Perkins once wrote that the work of a shepherd in tending sheep "is as good a work before God, as is the action of a judge in giving sentence, or a Magistrate in ruling, or a Minister in preaching."[15] And William Tyndale made the same point when he observed that in God's eyes there is no difference between washing dishes and preaching the gospel.[16] How is that for bringing the truth home?

What About You?

Have you been called to wash dishes? To work in the field? To sing at the Met? What is God's calling in your life, and how are you to discern that calling?

A good starting point is to ask yourself what biblical desires God has given you. What, after all, do you enjoy doing, and are such enjoyments biblical? If you do not enjoy working with numbers and have no desire to do so, rest assured that God probably has not called you to be an accountant or a mathematician. By the same token, even if you enjoy working with numbers, working as a bookie would be unbiblical. God does not call anyone to do anything contrary to His Word.

Another helpful thing to do is to assess the responsibilities that God has given you and the commitments that you have made. You may desire to stand on the street corner playing your saxophone from dawn till dusk, but you may have a family to feed and rent to pay. Remember that God never calls you to do something that would cause you to shirk the responsibilities that He has placed on you and the commitments that you have undertaken. If you are shirking your responsibilities and commitments, think again: the one who does not provide for his family, as we have already seen, is worse than an unbeliever (1 Tim. 5:8), and the one who biblically binds himself must swear to his own hurt (Ps. 15:4). While it is true that some callings involve financial sacrifice, we must never confuse sacrificing personal gain with shirking personal responsibility. Sacrificing is admirable; shirking is abominable.

You should also look around you to see where God has led you so far in life. Does your education and experience prepare you for a particular vocation in keeping with your desires and responsibilities? Becoming a brain surgeon, for instance, would be a pretty difficult task if you have never been to medical school.

At the same time, we should remember that God has given us all different gifts and abilities. These, John Murray says, are an index to His will and hence to His calling in our lives.[17] Steele once wrote that God does not call us now "by audible words, but by bestowing real and suitable gifts" on us.[18] If you are wondering whether you are being called to a particular vocation, stop and ask yourself whether you have the basic gifts required by that calling or whether you and others see those basic gifts developing in you. God never calls anyone to a particular vocation without giving him or her the gifts required by that vocation.

Two serious implications follow from this truth. First, if God gives us gifts for our callings, we need to discern those gifts and use them for His service and glory. To whom much is given, much is required. Second, because God has not given the same gifts to everyone, we should not think that God has called everyone to do the same thing in life. Parents, for example, need to learn that God has not necessarily bestowed the same gifts on their children in equal measure, and hence has not necessarily called each of them to follow the same academic or professional path.

While God calls some to labor with their minds, He calls others to labor with their hands, and still others to labor with both. When God called Adam to be a caretaker of the Garden, Adam did not think that such a task was somehow beneath his dignity as a vice-regent created in God's image. He did not complain about his job description and threaten to quit unless he could spend more of his work day on the more intellectual aspects of his calling (e.g., categorizing the animals). Neither should we. From the very beginning, the call to care for the Garden and the call to categorize the animals existed side by side. One was not superior to the other. Adam's job description included both manual and intellectual labor. Murray was right when he wrote that if many had been taught to appreciate what they derisively called "menial labor," they "would have been saved from the catastrophe of economic, moral, and religious ruin because they would have been preserved from the vain ambition of pursuing vocations for which they were not equipped and which on sober and enlightened reflection, they would not have sought."[19]

What about you? Can you learn anything from Christ the carpenter? From Peter, James, and John the fishermen? From Paul the tentmaker? What are your gifts and what are they telling you about God's calling in your life?

Sometimes we cannot reflect soberly on our gifts or calling without the wise counsel of others. In the abundance of counselors, Solomon tells us, there is victory (Prov. 11:14; 15:22; 24:6). Maybe one reason for the vocational failure of many is their tendency to ignore counsel from their parents or their peers or their pastors. Sometimes fathers do know best—as do mothers, brothers, and sisters—both at home and in the body of Christ. This is especially true of those who are presently pursuing the calling we may be considering. Along these lines, Richard Baxter reminds us that we should "choose no calling . . . without the advice of some judicious, faithful persons of that calling. For they are best able to judge in their own profession."[20]

As we begin to pursue and fulfill our callings by assessing our desires, responsibilities, experiences, and gifts, and by seeking the wisdom and counsel of others, we should also remember to pray to, and take comfort in, the God who sovereignly calls and providentially guides our lives every step of the way. We are to trust in Him with all our hearts and to acknowledge Him in all that we do, and He will direct our paths (Prov. 3:4–5; 16:3). We may have our plans, but it is the Lord who directs our steps (Prov. 16:9). His job is to call, guide, and direct us. Our job is to trust in Him, assess the life and vocation to which He has called us, and live our lives responsibly and humbly before Him, knowing that every calling shines and will, as Calvin observed, "be reckoned very precious in [His] sight."[21]

BEING ALL THAT YOU CAN BE

The priesthood of all believers, rightly understood, leaves no room for arrogance, complacency, discontent, or envy among God's people. No believer has more privilege or status in the sight of God because of the vocation he pursues. In Paul's words, there is neither slave nor free man, since they are both one in Christ (Gal. 3:28). From God's perspective, those who, true to their calling, vigorously pursue any legitimate vocation, stand before Him with equal dignity and integrity. "All lawful callings," Helm reminds us, "are equally valid and worthwhile because each one has God as its source and the service of God as its object."[22]

And, as Luther observed, "We are all of the spiritual estate, all are truly priests. . . . But they do not all have the same work to do."[23] Indeed, different vocations may impose different work or duties on those who pursue them, and one vocation may even pay more than another. But the person who receives higher pay does not necessarily have more dignity than the one who receives less pay. That is not what really counts.

What really counts, what ultimately distinguishes one person from another, what really makes someone somebody, is Christ. As John Barkley once noted, "The only real farmer is a Christian farmer; the only real doctor is a Christian doctor; the only real man is a Christian man; and the only real woman is a Christian woman; and so on covering every detail and aspect and station in life. Apart from Christ we are not what we ought to be."[24] Apart from Christ, we are nobody and can do nothing (John 15:5). But by His grace, we are somebody and can do everything He calls us to do (Phil. 4:13).

Thus, "being all that you can be" does not characterize one particular vocation rather than another. It comes as a direct result of being a Christian, of knowing the great high priest, Jesus Christ, and doing what He has called you to do. The priesthood of all believers should not only focus us inward to serve and glorify God as we vigorously pursue our respective vocations. It should also focus us outward to let our light so shine before men everywhere, even in the workplace, so that they, too, can become somebody—children of God—and glorify their Father in heaven (Matt. 5:16).

Becoming somebody does not come from trading places with others. It comes from knowing—or, rather, from being known by—our great high priest, who traded places with us by dying in our stead, bestowing His grace and mercy upon us, and calling us to serve and glorify Him as His royal priests.

And that is a message that even our professor in longhorns needs to hear.

STUDY QUESTIONS

1. What are some of the reasons you have given for failing to do your utmost to glorify God during the workweek? Are these reasons biblical? When was the last time you reminded yourself at the start of the workday that you are at work to glorify God as you minister for Him? Why not start doing so today?
2. Do you have to be doing overtly "religious" things to be a Christian on the job? Explain. Is it as spiritual to sing at the Met as in the church choir? What does the Bible say?
3. What are some ways in which you can discern the gifts and calling of God in your life?

Notes

1. Paul Helm, *The Callings: The Gospel in the World* (Edinburgh: Banner of Truth, 1987), x.

2. Ibid., xiii.

3. John Calvin, *The Institutes of the Christian Religion*, ed. John T. McNeill, trans. Lewis Ford Battles (Philadelphia: Westminster Press, 1960), 2.15.6.

4. While the rest of this chapter will focus on applying the doctrine of the priesthood of all believers to our vocations, this is by no means the only application of the doctrine. Much of the Christian life, in fact, can be seen through the lens of this doctrine. While Old Testament priests offered sacrifices in anticipation of Christ's all-sufficient sacrifice on Calvary (Hebrews; 1 Peter 3:18), we as New Testament priests are to look back to Calvary and offer our very lives as living sacrifices to God, thus consecrating every area of life to serve and glorify Him (Rom. 12:1–2). Thus, our whole Christian life consists of priestly service to God. Whereas Old Testament priests interceded on behalf of the people, we as New Testament priests are to intercede through praying for one another as well as by admonishing, instructing, and encouraging one another.

5. Martin Luther, *An Open Letter to the Christian Nobility of the German Nation Concerning the Reform of the Christian Estate*, in *Three Treatises*, based on the American edition of Luther's Works (1520; reprint, Philadelphia: Fortress, 1966), 130.

6. Calvin, *Institutes*, 3.10.6.

7. Helm, *The Callings*, 96.

8. While most Christians fail to see work as part of their calling and thus fail to work heartily as for the Lord, still others go to the opposite extreme and see work as their only calling—and thus fail to fulfill their responsibilities in their personal life, the home, the church, and society at large. Just as the Puritans have much to say to those who do not take work seriously enough, so they have much to say to those who go to the opposite extreme and allow their work to crowd out the other aspects of their lives. In his masterpiece, *The Christian Man's Calling*, George Swinnock cautions that we ought to order our "affairs relating to heaven and earth, to God and [our] family that they may not interfere or cross each other" ([1868; reprint, Edinburgh: Banner of Truth, 1992], 307–8). He goes on to observe that the "faithful and wise steward will give every one their portion, their meat in due season; as he will give his body and his family their portion every day, so he will give God and his soul their portion every day" (pp. 309–10). He is then quick to add that "there is a time for all things" such that we do "not so much as want time as waste time" (p. 310). What is so refreshing about Swinnock's view is its balance in avoiding the family-over-work or work-over-family extremes advocated by some today. The biblical view is that each aspect of our calling is to receive its due. Al-

though this chapter will focus primarily on our calling at work, we should not lose sight of the biblical balance required of us in our personal lives, families, churches, workplaces, cultures, and countries. All of life is "holiness to the Lord," as will be discussed in more detail in the following chapter.

9. Leland Ryken, *Worldly Saints: The Puritans as They Really Were* (Grand Rapids: Zondervan, 1986), 34, citing R. H. Tawney, *Religion and the Rise of Capitalism* (New York: Harcourt, Brace, 1926), 245.

10. Ryken, *Worldly Saints*, 34, citing Perry Miller, *The New England Mind: The Seventeenth Century* (1939; reprint, Cambridge, Mass.: Harvard University Press, 1954), 44.

11. Luther's *Commentary on Genesis*, at 3:13, as quoted by Alister McGrath, "The Protestant Work Ethic," taped lecture (Anaheim, Calif.: Christians United for Reformation, 1993).

12. William Perkins, *A Treatise of the Vocations, or, Callings of Men, with the Sorts and Kinds of Them, and the Right Use Thereof* (Cambridge: John Legat, 1603), 911. (Modern English is supplied in this quotation and hereafter.)

13. Michael Horton, *Putting Amazing Back into Grace: An Introduction to Reformed Theology* (Nashville: Thomas Nelson, 1991), 197.

14. Ryken, *Worldly Saints*, 228 n. 3, citing W. R. Forester, *Christian Vocation* (New York: Scribner, 1953), 148.

15. Perkins, *A Treatise of the Vocations*, 913.

16. William Tyndale in *The Parable of the Wicked Mammon*, quoted in Ryken, *Worldly Saints*, 25.

17. John Murray, *Principles of Conduct* (1957; reprint, Grand Rapids: Eerdmans, 1984), 86.

18. *The Religious Tradesman or Plain and Serious Hints of Advice for the Tradesman's Prudent and Pious Conduct; From His Entrance into Business, to His Leaving It Off* (1603; Harrisonburg, Va.: Sprinkle Publications, 1989), 27.

19. Murray, *Principles of Conduct*, 35.

20. Richard Baxter, *Baxter's Practical Works*, vol. 1: *A Christian Directory*. (1673; reprint, Ligonier, Pa.: Soli Deo Gloria Publications, 1990), 378.

21. Calvin, *Institutes*, 3.10.6.

22. Helm, *The Callings*, 61.

23. Luther, *To the Christian Nobility of the German Nation*, in *Three Treatises*, 14.

24. Quoted in Cyril Eastwood, *The Priesthood of All Believers: An Examination of the Doctrine from the Reformation to the Present Day* (London: Epworth, 1960), 73.

TWENTY

TO GOD BE THE GLORY

U p to this point, we have examined several major themes that distinguish the Reformed view of the Christian life from its non-Reformed counterparts. We began by looking at what God has already done for us in our justification and definitive sanctification, what He continues to do in our progressive sanctification, and what He has yet to do in our final sanctification or glorification. For the past two chapters, we have focused on two particular Reformed themes, namely, our freedom in Christ and our priesthood as believers.

As we noted from the outset and have seen along the way, what unites the various themes on the Reformed view of the Christian life is the way each reminds us that our primary purpose in life is to do all to the glory and enjoyment of God. But whenever we hear that all-too-familiar "do all to the glory of God" language, we dutifully nod in agreement, even though we may never have taken time to understand what that language really means.

When we say that our primary reason for living is to glorify God, we do not mean that we add more glory to the all-glorious God of the universe or somehow make Him more glorious in His essence. After all, you cannot add a drop of water to a full bucket. Although "the God of glory" (Acts 7:2) is infinitely and perfectly glorious, He has nonetheless chosen to glorify Himself in the sense of demonstrating His own essential glory. This He does both in creation and in redemption.

Aware of how God glorifies Himself in creation, the psalmist pro-

275

claims that "the heavens are telling of the glory of God; and their ex-
panse is declaring the work of His hands" (Ps. 19:1). And we learn of the
glory of God revealed in redemption through the pen of the apostle
Paul, who tells us that God patiently endured "vessels of wrath prepared
for destruction" in order to "make known the riches of His glory upon
vessels of mercy, which He prepared beforehand for glory" (Rom. 9:22–
23). Thus, God reveals His glory not only in the heavens, but also by
pouring out His mercy on His appointed vessels of mercy—those whom
He has sovereignly and graciously converted, drawn into a covenantal
relationship of union and communion with Himself, called out of the
world to His church, and declared righteous on the basis of the finished
work of Christ alone on their behalf. In other words, God glorifies Himself by what He does for us as His appointed vessels of mercy. He also
glorifies Himself by what He has done, is now doing, and has yet to do in
us in our Christian life.

When He summons us to glorify Him in our Christian life, He ushers
us into His presence to become so intoxicated with His glory that we respond by honoring Him for who He is and what He has done for us and in
us as His people. When we are called upon to glorify Him in this sense, we
are called upon to reflect or declare His glory in our very lives, to live so as
to "ascribe to the LORD the glory due His name" (1 Chron. 16:29; Ps. 29:2).
We glorify God in this sense when we praise Him (Pss. 50:23; 86:12), fear
and worship Him (Rev. 14:7; 1 Chron. 16:29; Ps. 29:2), refrain from sinning against Him in our bodies (1 Cor. 6:20), grow strong in our faith in
Him (Rom. 4:20), bear much fruit for Him (John 15:7–8), and obey Him
in doing good works (Matt. 5:16). There are no limits to glorifying God in
our lives. We are to do everything with the purpose of glorifying Him (1
Cor. 10:31). We are to live by reflecting and declaring His glory in everything we believe and do.[1]

And glorifying Him in this way involves enjoying Him as never
before. If we strive to live for His glory, we will set our sights on Him
and enjoy Him anew each day. We will proclaim, along with David, that
even amidst failing health, God is the strength of our heart and our
portion forever (Ps. 73:25–26). Although we are empty and insufficient
in and of ourselves, our fullness and sufficiency are found in Him and in
Him alone. While we experience true but imperfect joy now in union
and communion with the Lord of glory, we eagerly look forward to the
day when we shall be in His all-glorious presence and enjoy Him forever.
In that day, the partial will be done away. We shall be face-to-face with
the Lord of glory, and in His presence we shall experience "fullness of

joy" (Ps. 16:11). As Thomas Watson reminds us, we "shall never enjoy ourselves fully till we enjoy God eternally."[2]

BRINGING THE TRUTH HOME

Looking forward to that day when our joy will be made full, we seek to live here and now so as to reflect or declare God's glory and enjoy Him, albeit imperfectly, in everything we do. By reminding us that we exist to glorify and enjoy God both now and forever, the Reformed faith stresses the inescapable connection between what we know about the all-glorious God of Scripture and how we are to live for His glory. It is not enough to know about His glory. We are to live for it. The glory of God is not a lifeless truth we shelve, like groceries we bring home from the market and tuck away in the back of the pantry, never again to be seen. As with all truths of the Reformed faith, the glory of God ought to be brought home. But once home, it ought also to be preserved, prepared, and savored, thereby nourishing, strengthening, and sustaining every part of our being.

In other words, the truths of the Reformed faith should carry their life-giving nutrients to every area of our lives. They should so transform our lives that the Reformers' motto, *soli Deo gloria* ("to God alone be the glory"), seasons everything we believe and do. Understanding the connection between believing and doing, faith and practice, doctrine and life, knowing the truth and living it, has long led those of Reformed persuasion to see that the Reformed faith is a system of truth that impacts every area of life. Our understanding of the all-glorious God of Scripture, if it is a true understanding, cannot but dominate our entire lives, not just in theory, but also in practice.

So it was with Abraham Kuyper, who rightly described the Reformed faith as a "high and holy calling to consecrate every department of life and every energy at its disposal to the glory of God."[3] Kuyper ought to know. Among his many noteworthy accomplishments, he was the founder of a leading political party and a university, as well as a prolific theologian, articulate pastor, influential journalist, distinguished professor, and able prime minister. Through it all, he learned that he was to submit every area of his life to the lordship of Christ. He was fond of saying that there was not one inch of creation over which Christ didn't say "mine," and, as a result, he consistently lived his life as if to say "yours."

Kuyper is not alone. The Reformers before him changed the world and influenced culture in ways almost unimaginable in our day when the church is often seen either running with open arms to embrace and ape the world in the name of relevance (what I shall call "apism"), or running away from the world to escape from it in the name of holiness (what I shall call "escapism"). Even worse, many Christians escape from the world by creating their own subcultures, and, once ensconced within them, they end up simply aping the world, as is too often the case today with what passes for "Christian" music, television, entertainment, and the like.

In contrast to the apist-escapist tendencies often displayed by the modern church, the Reformers and their heirs, by the grace of God, sought to glorify God in everything they believed and did, whether in the lecture hall, art studio, orchestra chamber, courtroom, laboratory, body politic, pulpit, or pew. They did not try to escape from the world. But neither did they uncritically ape it. Although they were in the world with all of its risks and opportunities, they were not of it. They knew that the Father would not take them out of the world, but they took comfort in the fact that He would keep them from the Evil One (John 17:15). To borrow Luther's phrase, they lived in the world *coram Deo* ("in the presence of God") and realized that there was no area of their lives where, in the words of Calvin, they did not have *negotium cum Deo* ("business with God").

What can we learn from the Reformers on this score? Exactly how should we, like the Reformers, conduct our business with God as we live continually in His presence? By glorifying Him in everything we do, said the Reformers. Hence, believers of Reformed persuasion have long made "it an all-embracing purpose to glorify God in all walks of life."[4] But glorifying God in all walks of life does not just happen automatically. Although it cannot take place apart from divine sovereignty, it nonetheless takes concerted effort on our part, requiring us, by His grace, to apply biblical truth faithfully and consistently to all areas of life.

A faith that is truly Reformed according to the Bible, yet always re-forming according to the Bible—a truly Reformed faith—demands that those who embrace it learn how to cultivate a consistently biblical view of the world and every aspect of their lives in it. It shuns escapism by affirming the goodness of God's creation (1 Tim. 4:4). It also stands opposed to apism by remembering that God's good creation is still fallen (Rom. 8:18–22). To God's fallen creation, a truly Reformed faith proclaims the need for redemption, thus taking seriously its evangelical task to make disciples of all nations. But it does not stop there. It goes further, by fulfilling its cultural task in God's good creation, which is to teach Christ's disciples to observe all that He has commanded by filling the earth, subduing it, and ruling it to His glory wherever they are as His vice-regents and royal priests (Matt. 28:18–20; Gen. 1:27–28; 1 Peter 2:9). While Christ is Lord of our hearts in redemption, His lordship by no means ends there. He is Lord of all, including the creation—the world in which we live and the culture all about us. And as Lord of all, He rules everywhere, everyone, and everything for His glory in accordance with His Word.

Because the Reformed faith has always underscored the lordship of Christ and His consequent claim to every area of life, it is not surprising that it has given birth to a distinctively Christian way of looking at the world and our lives in it, a world-and-life view, or simply a worldview. In the pages that follow, we will conclude our survey of the Reformed view of the Christian life by examining how the lordship of Christ should transform every area of our lives and cause us to cultivate a distinctively Christian worldview, so that we fully glorify and enjoy God.

LORD OF ALL

In the beginning was God, the One who created the heavens and the earth out of nothing (Gen. 1:1), as well as everything in them (Ex. 20:11; Neh. 9:6). All things are "from Him and through Him and to Him," which is why all glory is to be ascribed to Him for ever and ever (Rom. 11:36). "The earth," declares David, "is full of Thy possessions" (Ps. 104:24). He owns the cattle on a thousand hills (Ps. 90:10), a symbol of the whole earth, which, the psalmist says elsewhere, belongs to the Lord (Ps. 24:1). In fact, absolutely everything belongs to Him (1 Chron. 29:11; Gen. 14:19; Ex. 9:29; Deut. 4:39; 10:14; Job 41:11).

As the eternal Creator and possessor, He alone has jurisdiction or control over everything. There are no boundaries to His authority. He is not like a law enforcement officer whose authority is limited to certain territorial boundaries. God's authority knows no boundaries. His jurisdiction is absolute. All that is in heaven and on earth is His because He is exalted as Lord above all and has dominion over all (1 Chron. 29:10–11). He has absolute authority and dominion everywhere, over everyone and everything. His reign, we are told, extends to the ends of the earth (Pss. 59:13; 103:19; Neh. 9:6). The Lord has "established His throne in the heavens; and His sovereignty rules over all" (Ps. 103:19). He possesses all authority in heaven and on earth (Matt. 28:18), and accomplishes His will in heaven and on earth (Matt. 6:10). Not only does He rule everywhere, but His rule will never end. His throne is everlasting (Pss.

93:1–2; 97:1–2; 99:1–2). He is, and forever will be, preeminent in all things (Col. 1:18).

THE NEW BATTLE FOR THE BIBLE

The preeminent Creator, possessor, and ruler—the Lord of the universe and everything in it—has told us that He is to have preeminence in our lives by being glorified in all. But glorifying and enjoying Him would not be possible at all, were it not for the fact that He has revealed to us how we are to glorify and enjoy Him, how we are to order our lives before Him so as to bring Him glory and enjoy Him in all that we believe and do. In times past, God revealed Himself in many ways, but He has revealed Himself to us finally and fully in His Son (Heb. 1:2) and in the written testimony that bears witness to His Son, the Scriptures of the Old and New Testaments. In the Scriptures we learn how to glorify and enjoy God, because they teach us what we are to believe about God and what conduct He requires of us. We are also privileged to have resident within us the very Spirit of God, who illuminates His Word and who also enables and empowers us to obey it in every area of our lives and in every situation we face. Contrary to popular belief, the Spirit does not guide us apart from Scripture. He guides us through Scripture, which He inspired for that very purpose (John 14:26; 16:13; 17:17; 2 Tim. 3:16–17).

Today, however, it seems that many Christians are looking for guidance in all the wrong places. When recently asked to identify what they would be most likely to base an important moral or ethical decision on, a surprisingly large number of those who claim to be Christians did not even bother to mention the Bible.[5] And many of those who mentioned the Bible showed by their answers to other questions that it was not really their standard for everything they believe and do.[6] Furthermore, the same survey revealed that one in four who claim to be born again admitted that they never read the Bible at all. Among evangelicals, the numbers are better, but still bleak.[7]

Clearly, something is wrong. While reading the Bible is no guarantee that we will understand and obey it, one disturbing question remains: How can the Bible be the standard for what we believe and do if we do not even read it to know what it says? As evangelicals, we may have won the battle for the Bible over its inerrancy, but we are perilously close to losing the battle over its sufficiency. Apparently, some believers are willing to admit that the Bible is perfect, but then turn right around and ignore it.

Somewhere along the way, evangelicals, as the heirs of the Reform-ers, have forgotten the formal principle of the Reformation: *sola Scriptura.* Scripture is the supreme standard for everything we are to believe and do. Nothing is to be put on a par with it, since, as we have already seen, when we try to supplement Scripture, we eventually end up supplanting it. At the time of Christ, the Pharisees placed tradition alongside Scripture, only to have their traditions end up trumping Scripture. Today, cheap substi-tutes abound. Many Christians would never have the audacity to say that these cheap substitutes actually trump Scripture. But when faced with the hand that Scripture deals them, they often turn around and play the fol-lowing trump cards: "The Bible is not a textbook about . . ." "The Bible is about faith, not about . . ." "The Bible was written to save sinners, not to tell us what to do about . . ." "The Bible is silent about . . ."

One after another, the trump cards keep coming, thereby showing how little those who play them understand the lordship of Christ over all of life and the consequent authority and sufficiency of His Word for all of life. We must turn to Scripture not only for important ethical and moral decisions, but also for every decision we make. Scripture was inspired so that we would be completely equipped for "every good work," so that we would lack nothing (2 Tim. 3:16-17).

Do you really believe that Scripture is sufficient to equip you to do everything that God requires of you? Do you believe that absolutely every area of your life is to be holy to the Lord (1 Peter 1:15, 22–25)? Do you believe that godliness is profitable for all things (1 Tim. 4:8)? Not even our thoughts escape the domain of Christ's lordship. In the words of Paul, we are to destroy everything that opposes the knowledge of God by "tak-ing every thought captive to the obedience of Christ" (2 Cor. 10:5). This means that our thoughts about art, science, history, mathematics, eco-nomics, psychology, philosophy, and so on, are to be taken captive to Christ, since He is the One in whom "all the treasures of wisdom and knowledge" are hidden (Col. 2:3), the One who is before all things and in whom all things consist or cohere (Col. 1:16–17).

We are to let the Word of Christ richly dwell in us, so that whatever we do in word or deed, we do it "in the name of the Lord Jesus, giving thanks through Him to God the Father" (Col. 3:17). Even when it comes to otherwise commonplace activities like eating and drinking, we are to glorify God; indeed, whatever we do, we are to do to His glory (1 Cor. 10:31). We are to live or die for the Lord (Rom. 14:7–8). We are to love the Lord our God with all of our hearts, souls, minds, and strength, and our neighbors as ourselves (Matt. 22:37; cf. Deut. 6:5).

How Should We Then Live?

Because we are to love and glorify God in all of life in accordance with Scripture, it follows that Scripture, in the most important sense, is never silent.[8] Admittedly, "Scripture doesn't tell us in detail how to speak French or to repair autos or to paint a portrait or to run a business."[9] But, as John Frame has noted, it does tell us that "in all of these activities we must be seeking to glorify our great God."[10]

Far from being a compendium of minute details or exhaustive applications, Scripture speaks to us primarily through principles, which, when properly interpreted, apply to the minute details of life. Our task in building a distinctively Christian worldview, then, is to apply Scripture faithfully to every area of life, to apply biblical principles to the situations we face every day. Admittedly, our task is not always easy. Sometimes, in fact, it requires painstaking study and may even be quite difficult (2 Tim. 2:15; 2 Peter 3:16–17). But it is our task nonetheless.

The Puritans understood that their task was to build a Christian worldview, even though that term had not yet been coined. But they said the same thing when they insisted that all of our lives and relationships must become "holiness to the Lord." In the words of J. I. Packer, the Puritans well understood that "every part of the Christian's life—his relationship to God and God's creation; all his relationships with others, in the family, the church, and the world; and also his relationship to himself, in self-discipline and self-management across the board—must become 'holiness to the Lord.' "[11]

Writing in the nineteenth century, J. C. Ryle described this Puritan notion of holiness to the Lord as "faithfulness in all the duties and relations in life." This is a sign of truly holy persons, who aim to do everything well and who strive to be "good husbands and good wives, good parents and good children, good masters and good servants, good neighbors, good friends, good subjects, good in private and good in public, good in places of business and good by their firesides."[12]

Notice that the Puritan notion of holiness to the Lord was not an exercise in mental gymnastics, but rather was the stuff of which individual lives and social institutions were made. They sought the truth in order to live it in the prayer closet, the living room, the pew, the shop, and the marketplace. They saw all of life in relation to Christ as Lord, which is why they sought to live all of life as holiness to Him.

Today, by contrast, we often limit Christ's lordship to certain areas of our personal life and neglect His lordship over life and culture in general. At best, we declare that only part of our lives needs to be holy. To our detriment, we have neglected our rich Reformation heritage, which, according to Kuyper, "demands that all life be consecrated to His service in strict obedience," and which refuses to confine faith to "the closet, the cell, or the church."[13] We would do well to learn from H. Henry Meeter, who wrote that the truly Reformed believer "declares that not only with his soul for eternity, but as well in matters that concern his body in time, he belongs to his faithful Savior Jesus Christ. . . . [H]e must obey in all walks of life."[14] Concurring with Kuyper and Meeter, Clarence Bouma rightly claims that the Reformed under-standing of the lordship of Christ

> calls for a Christian witness in every realm of life. A witness in the home, in the church, in the school, in the state, and in every other social sphere. Preaching the gospel and reforming society are not exclusive. To live for the glory of God in every relationship of life, to be a soldier for the King in every legitimate realm of human endeavor—this belongs to the very essence of being a true, full-orbed Christian, and it is the Calvinist—the true Calvinist, not his caricature—who stands committed to this task.[15]

Bouma can speak of the all-encompassing nature of true salvation because of the all-encompassing extent of the sin from which we have been saved. Prior to salvation, we were totally depraved, not in the sense that we were as bad as we could have been, but in the sense that every aspect of our lives was adversely affected by the corruption and pollution of sin. If sin affected every aspect of life, then salvation from sin—if it is true salvation—must also affect every aspect of life. Salvation from sin, therefore, begins in the heart but does not end there. Every facet of man's being before God and others is saved. Thus, those who are truly saved will, by God's grace, love Him with all their hearts, souls, strength, and minds, and love their neighbors as themselves. Concerning the totality of our salvation, Meeter has observed,

> When God saves man, he saves the whole man. The whole man must, therefore, be devoted to God's cause—not only when he is at church, but when he is transacting business or engag-ing in political or social activities of any sort. No sphere of his life may be excluded. Life as a whole must be God-directed; poli-tics, social and industrial relations, domestic relations, education,

science and art must all be God-centered. . . . God must control the whole of life.[16]

In light of Christ's claim to be Lord of all, we must honestly ask ourselves the insightful question that Herbert Schlossberg and Marvin Olasky have put to the Christian community: "Will we live out our faith in every area of life by showing that Christ is not only Lord of our lives personally but just as much Lord over all of life and culture?"[17] That question is simply an expanded version of Francis Schaeffer's now-famous question, "How should we then live?" Of course, the word "then" in Schaeffer's question is pregnant with meaning and gives birth to the following full-grown question: Since Christ is Lord of all, and as such demands obedience to His Word in every area of life, how should we then live in every area of our lives? How should we then live in our personal lives, families, churches, workplaces, cultures, and countries? How about you? How should you then live? Can you honestly say that as far as it depends on you, you live your life in your family, workplace, culture, and country as holiness to the Lord? Since Christ is Lord of all of life and lays claim to all of your life, how should you then live? How will you then live?

Choose This Day

Because Christ is Lord of all and therefore demands our utmost allegiance and loyalty in all areas of life, Frame correctly notes that "there is no compartment of life where we may assert our autonomy, where we may serve ourselves. We must do all to the glory of God. All of life, therefore, not just formal worship, is religion—service to God. In all our decisions, we decide either for Christ or against Him."[18]

There is no room for indifference or impartiality here. We are either for Christ or against Him, either paying homage to the Son or committing treason against Him. As the Reformed theologian A. A. Hodge soberly reminds us,

> Since the kingdom of God on earth is not confined to the mere ecclesiastical sphere, but aims at absolute universality, and extends its supreme reign over every department of human life, it follows that it is the duty of every loyal subject to endeavor to bring all human society, social and political, as well as ecclesiastical, into obedience to its law of righteousness.

He goes on to say,

> It is our duty, as far as lies in our power, immediately to organize human society and all its institutions and organs upon a distinctively Christian basis. Indifference or impartiality here between the law of the kingdom and the law of the world, or of its prince, the devil, is utter treason to the King of Righteousness. The Bible, the great statute-book of the kingdom, explicitly lays down principles which, when candidly applied, will regulate the action of every human being in all relations. There can be no compromise. The King said, with regard to all descriptions of moral agents in all spheres of activity, "He that is not with me is against me."[19]

If in any area of your life you are not for Christ, you are against Him. If you do not gather with Him, you scatter. About this antithesis, Jay Adams has written,

> From the Garden of Eden with its two trees (one allowed, one forbidden) to the eternal destiny of the human being in heaven or hell, the Bible sets forth two, and only two ways: God's way and all others. Accordingly, people are said to be saved and lost. They belong to God's people or the world. There was Gerizim, the mount of blessing, and Ebal, the mount of cursing. There is the narrow way and the wide way, leading either to eternal life or destruction. There are those who are against and those who are with us, those within and those without. There is life and death, good and bad, light and darkness, the kingdom of God and the kingdom of Satan, love and hatred, spiritual wisdom and the wisdom of this world.[20]

In the Garden, God declared total war against Satan, a war that is waged in the heavenly places by angels and demons, and waged on earth by the seed of the woman and the seed of the Serpent. Do not fool yourself. There are only two alternatives. There is no demilitarized zone, no middle ground, no neutrality. "No one can serve two masters; for either he will hate the one and love the other, or he will hold to one and despise the other" (Matt. 6:24). Like the children of Israel about to enter the Promised Land, we too must choose this day whom we will serve.

Prepared for Glory

No matter what we choose, make no mistake: God will be glorified. As the God of glory, He glorifies Himself in all that He does, even when it comes to those who choose against Him, those whom Paul has no qualms about calling vessels of wrath prepared for destruction. In fact, Paul tells us that God patiently puts up with these vessels of wrath to "make known the riches of His glory upon vessels of mercy, which He prepared beforehand for glory, even us, whom He also called" (Rom. 9:23–24).

This passage presents us with a unique biblical antithesis, since it joins an antithesis in the mind of God before time began with an antithesis in time at the consummation of the ages. From the beginning, God prepared vessels of wrath and vessels of mercy. Yet, He prepared them for far different destinies: destruction and glory. But the point we ought not to miss is that God demonstrates His glory in both types of vessels. When the curtain goes down, God will be glorified by both vessels of wrath and vessels of mercy—though, admittedly, they have different roles to play in the divine drama. God, says Paul, has so scripted this drama that He uses even the rebellion of the vessels of wrath prepared for destruction to make the riches of His glory known to His vessels of mercy, whom He has prepared for glory.

And who are these privileged vessels of mercy that are prepared for glory? They are those whom He has called to conversion, the covenant, the church, and the Christian life (vv. 24–29). You, dear Christian, are a vessel of mercy. You were prepared beforehand for glory. To you He has made known the riches of His glory. This is why He calls on you to glorify Him here and now by declaring and reflecting His eternal and infinite glory and truly enjoying Him in everything you do, a task you could not fulfill if you were left to yourself.

Once again, we are forced to take our eyes off of ourselves and look to Him, the One who is the full radiance of the Father's glory—the Lord of glory. By living each day in union with Him as our risen and exalted Lord of glory, we eagerly anticipate that day when we shall be with Him in glory. On that day, we shall see Him as He is in all His glory, and we will be glorified together with Him both in body and in spirit for all eternity. Then and only then will we fully declare and reflect His glory. Indeed, He is our hope—our only hope—of glory. To Him be the glory for ever and ever. Amen.

STUDY QUESTIONS

1. When Scripture commands us to glorify God, does it somehow command us to add more glory to God? Why not? How does God glorify Himself? How are we to glorify God? Do you glorify God in this way?
2. Name some ways in which the modern church has aped or escaped from the world we live in and the culture all about us. In what ways have you aped or escaped from the world and your culture? Should Christians ever be apists or escapists? What can you do today to avoid being an apist or an escapist?
3. Since Christ is Lord of all, how should your life reflect that fact? How should you then live in your personal life, family, church, workplace, culture, and country? How will you then live?

Notes

1. For more on our primary purpose to glorify and enjoy God, see Thomas Ridgely, *Commentary on the Larger Catechism* (1853; Edmonton: Still Waters Revival Books, 1993), 3–9; Thomas Boston, *Commentary on the Shorter Catechism* (1853; Edmonton: Still Waters Revival Books, 1993), 9–14; Thomas Vincent, *The Shorter Catechism Explained* (1674; Edinburgh: Banner of Truth, 1980), 13–15; Thomas Watson, *A Body of Divinity* (1692; Edinburgh: Banner of Truth, 1986), 6–25; G. I. Williamson, *The Shorter Catechism for Study Classes*, vol. 1 (Phillipsburg, N.J.: Presbyterian and Reformed, 1970), 1–4.
2. Watson, *A Body of Divinity*, 26.
3. Abraham Kuyper, *Lectures on Calvinism* (1931; Grand Rapids: Eerdmans, 1987), 24.
4. H. Henry Meeter, *The Basic Ideas of Calvinism*, ed. Paul A. Marshall, 6th ed. (Grand Rapids: Baker, 1990), 21.
5. George Barna, *Absolute Confusion: How Our Moral and Spiritual Foundations Are Eroding in This Age of Change*, The Barna Report, vol. 3 (Ventura, Calif.: Regal, 1993), 245–46.
6. Ibid.
7. Ibid.
8. Frame, "The Lordship of Christ and the Regulative Principle of Worship," unpublished paper, 4.
9. Ibid.
10. Ibid.
11. J. I. Packer, *Rediscovering Holiness* (Ann Arbor: Servant, 1992), 106.
12. J. C. Ryle, *Holiness*, Christian Life Classics, vol. 3 (Lafayette, Ind.: Sovereign Grace Trust Fund, 1990), 37.
13. Kuyper, *Lectures on Calvinism*, 24.

14. Meeter, *Basic Ideas of Calvinism*, 76.
15. Clarence Bouma, "The Relevance of Calvinism for Today," in *God-Centered Living or Calvinism in Action* (Grand Rapids: Baker, 1951), 20.
16. Meeter, *Basic Ideas of Calvinism*, 48.
17. Herbert Schlossberg and Marvin Olasky, *Turning Point: A Christian Worldview Declaration* (Westchester, Ill: Crossway, 1987), 8.
18. John Frame, *The Amsterdam Philosophy: A Preliminary Critique* (Phillipsburg, N.J.: Presbyterian and Reformed, 1972), 4.
19. A. A. Hodge, *Evangelical Theology: A Course of Popular Lectures* (1890; reprint, Edinburgh: Banner of Truth, 1976), 283–84.
20. Jay E. Adams, *A Call to Discernment: Distinguishing Truth from Error in Today's Church* (Eugene, Oreg.: Harvest House, 1987), 31.

CONCLUSION: A NEW SONG

B ack to basics" is a familiar cry today. Whether echoing from school halls, capital buildings, or assembly lines, the cry to get back to basics calls on those who hear it to recognize a problem and to remedy it. But not just any remedy will do. The remedy must involve returning to what really counts, recovering the essentials, reclaiming lost ground—hence, getting back to basics.

If ever the modern church needed to get back to basics, it is today. Even a casual observer of the contemporary evangelical scene could not miss the obvious: the church—or at least what goes for the modern evangelical church—is in trouble. It is no wonder that some of the most noted evangelical scholars of this century have written jeremiads, chronicling the modern church's drift from biblical truth toward heresy and neopaganism.

A LESSON FROM THE PAST

Nearly five centuries ago, the medieval church, like the modern church, had long since drifted from the truth. At that time, however, God graciously raised up a group of heralds who called the church back to basics. The Reformers, as those heralds came to be called, wanted to reform the church by calling her back to the basics of true biblical faith. Throughout the sixteenth century, the term *Reformed* applied to their message and, in

289

fact, to all Protestant churches, as did the term *evangelical*. To be Reformed or evangelical in those days meant that one shared the Reformers' ardent desire to reform the church according to Scripture. Over time, however, the Swiss Reformers came to be called Reformed in a special way, because they were committed to the task of reforming not only the church, but all of life, according to Scripture. When they claimed to be "reformed, yet always reforming," they were claiming to be reformed according to Scripture, yet always reforming according to Scripture in every area of life.

The reformation they spoke and wrote about was not a matter of doctrine divorced from life. It was a matter of doctrinal truths intended to transform lives: reformation for the sake of transformation. Not content with just knowing the truth, they wanted to zealously live consistently with it to the glory of God. With their biblical knowledge, they taught an ignorant and superstitious church, and with their zealous lives, they awoke a slumbering and lethargic church.

ZEAL AND KNOWLEDGE

Unlike the heralds of the Reformed faith in days gone by, the church to-day, on the whole, has failed to balance zeal and knowledge. On one side of the spectrum are those who zealously busy themselves doing all sorts of things, even though what they do often stems from a deep-seated igno-rance of what Scripture really teaches. They have no idea what it means to be reformed according to Scripture, yet always reforming according to Scrip-ture. In Paul's words, "they have a zeal for God, but not in accordance with knowledge" (Rom. 10:2).

At the same time, though, we must sadly admit that there are also many Christians—including many in the modern-day Reformed camp— at the opposite end of the spectrum, who have plenty of knowledge but no real zeal. They, too, have no idea what it really means to be reformed according to Scripture, yet always reforming according to Scripture. To borrow from Paul again, they have the kind of "knowledge" that puffs up (1 Cor. 8:1).

What is dangerous about these extremes is their tendency to spawn an unteachable spirit among those caught within their webs. Misguided zealots refuse to be taught, because to them, doctrine does not matter at all. And lifeless intellectuals refuse to be taught, because all that matters to them is doctrine.

Happily, we are not forced to choose between these two extremes.

Our only choice, if we are to heed Paul's admonition, is to demonstrate a zeal in accordance with knowledge. Put differently, our knowledge of the truth should cause us to live for it zealously, and our zeal for living the truth should cause us to grow in our knowledge of it. We are to have a knowledgeable zeal and a zealous knowledge.

Theology never exists in a vacuum. One way or another, all theology affects the way we live. The question is not whether it will do so, but how. J. I. Packer has made the same point by observing that "all theology is spirituality," by which he means that all theology "has an influence, good or bad, positive or negative, on its recipients' relationship or lack of relationship to God."[1] He notes, "If our theology does not quicken the conscience and soften the heart, it actually hardens both; if it does not encourage the commitment of faith, it reinforces the detachment of unbelief; if it fails to promote humility, it inevitably feeds on pride."[2] Elsewhere, he expresses the same idea by reminding us of the ultimate purpose of theology: "Theology is for doxology and devotion—that is, the praise of God and the practice of godliness. It should therefore be presented in a way that brings awareness of the divine presence. Theology is at its healthiest when it is consciously under the eye of God of whom it speaks, and when it is singing to his glory."[3]

Those who make it their business to theologize are warned by Packer's challenging words to think long and hard about what effect their theology will have on those who hear and read it. But those who hear and read it ought also to mind the same warning. For even a theology that sings to the glory of God can be turned into a monotonous humdrum by those who hear it. In other words, the problem may not necessarily be with the theology per se—or even with the theologian, for that matter. Sometimes the problem is with the self-proclaimed virtuoso who fails to sing along with an otherwise splendid melody.

THE REFORMED MELODY

In the preceding pages, we have introduced you to, or perhaps reacquainted you with, the melody sung by those who call themselves Reformed. And what a God-glorifying melody it is! Starting with the sovereign and gracious God who has revealed Himself in Scripture, we have seen that He sovereignly planned all things according to His purposes, including how He graciously drew us to Himself in conversion. God the Father appointed us to eternal life, God the Son bought us with the price of His own precious blood, and God the Spirit opened our hearts, enabling us to turn to Him in faith and repentance. From beginning to end, our conversion is the result of His sovereign and gracious work in and for us as His people.

But God's sovereignty and graciousness do not stand alone. They are exercised toward us as His people in a covenantal way; that is, He has established a redemptive relationship of union and communion with His people and their offspring. This divine bond between God and His people precedes the beginning of time, when the triune God covenanted to be in union and communion with a people. At Creation, God promised Adam, as the representative of the entire human race, eternal life on the condition of faithful obedience, but Adam rebelled against that sovereign and gracious covenant. Even then, God continued to display His marvelous grace. Although the seed of the woman would be at war with the seed of the Serpent, God promised to redeem the seed of the woman through one of her descendants, who would forever crush the Serpent and his seed. From that point on, God unfolded and expanded this marvelous promise through Noah, Abraham, Moses, David, and the Prophets. Then, in the fullness of time, the anticipation emanating from the Garden pointed to the manger, the Cross, and eventually the empty tomb. Christ, the seed of the woman, crushed the Serpent and continues to do so by ransoming us as His people from our slavery to sin, uniting us in marriage as His bride, avenging us against the seed of the Serpent, and regaining our lost inheritance. He continues to work on our behalf and has also promised us that the gates of hell will not prevail against us. Not only will He be our God and the God of our seed after us, but we shall be His people, both now and forever.

The sovereign graciousness of God and His covenantal dealings with His people and their seed lie at the heart of the Reformed view of the church. When God sovereignly and graciously converts us and draws us into covenant with Himself, He also draws us into covenant with His people, the church. He calls us out of the world and brings us both to Christ and to His church to worship Him in spirit and in truth together with His people. For our growth in grace, He graciously gives us the proclamation of His Word to call us to repentance and greater obedience. He also gives us the water and the wine to point us to Christ, seal the redemptive benefits we possess in Him, mark us out as those who are His, and challenge us to even greater faithfulness to Him and to one another. At the same time, He, as the chief shepherd, also vests His undershepherds with authority to rule His church representatively on His behalf by declaring the demands His Word makes on us, thus challenging us to grow in holiness together through mutual discipline in the body.

As those who are converted, drawn into covenant with God, and called to His church, we are to live our Christian life by glorifying and enjoying Him both now and forever. We are to live in such a way as to honor Him for who He is and what He has done for us. But we are incapable of living the Christian life apart from the One who makes it possible—Christ. We need to take our eyes off of ourselves and look to Him, the author and finisher of our faith. We have been united to Him and must learn to trust that He who began a good work in us will perfect it until we are with Him in glory. He is the One who was made sin for us, that we might become the righteousness of God in Him—the One who, by His Spirit, enables us to become progressively conformed to His image from one degree of glory to another, the One who set us free from the dominion and bondage of sin and has made us free indeed, the One who invites us to be His companions as royal priests in our respective callings, and the One whom we are to glorify in everything we do by submitting to Him in all areas of our lives. Apart from Him we could do nothing. Left to ourselves, we would be undone. But in Him we are blessed with every spiritual blessing in the heavenly places. The Christian life, then, is Christ for us and Christ in us, our hope of glory.

SING A NEW SONG

Having heard the melody sung aloud, we bid you to come and sing along with it. You need not worry about going at it solo. You can follow the lead of the many voices who can help you stay on pitch: Calvin, Witsius, Perkins, Ames, Baxter, Owen, Gillespie, Bunyan, Cotton, Boston, Turretin, Ursinus, Charnock, Shepard, Sibbes, Watson, Burroughs, Bates, Binning, Whitefield, Spurgeon, Newton, Edwards, Howe, Zanchius, the Hodges, the Alexanders, Girardeau, Breckenridge, Thornwell, Dabney, Toplady, Shedd, Ryle, Kuyper, Warfield, Bavinck, Berkouwer, Machen, Schaeffer, Van Til, Young, Wilson, Murray, Berkhof, Hoekema, Hoeksema, Vos, Ridderbos, Lloyd-Jones, and others too numerous to mention. Some of them, to be sure, have varied the theme presented in these pages just a bit, but all have sung or continue to sing the same basic song.

Amidst the cacophony ringing today, is it not time for the church to follow the psalmist by singing a new song to the Lord? This new song, however, is really nothing more than the old song about how God beautifies the afflicted with salvation (Ps. 149:4), takes pleasure in them by mak-ing them His covenant people (v. 4), is praised by them in the congrega-tion of the godly ones (v. 1), and enables them to exult in His glory as they conquer His enemies with the power of His Word (vv. 5–9). It is a song about conversion, the covenant, the church, and the Christian life—a song about true reformation, which should transform our lives from this time forth and forever.

Indeed, all theology is for doxology and devotion. He is the Lord, and we exist to glorify and enjoy Him all the days of our lives. And that is about as basic as it gets. Oh, how we need to get back to basics!

Soli Deo gloria!

Notes

1. J. I. Packer, *A Quest for Godliness: The Puritan Vision of the Christian Life* (Wheaton, Ill.: Crossway, 1991), 15.
2. Ibid.
3. J. I. Packer, *Concise Theology: A Guide to Historic Christian Beliefs* (Wheaton, Ill.: Tyndale House, 1993), xii.

CONTRIBUTORS

David G. Hagopian graduated from the University of California, Irvine, in June of 1985, with a Bachelor of Arts in history and a minor in classical Greek (magna cum laude, Phi Beta Kappa). Thereafter, he earned his Juris Doctor degree from the University of Southern California, graduating Order of the Coif.

Mr. Hagopian is currently a business litigator in the California office of Dorsey and Whitney law firm and is a member of the California State Bar, the Orange County Bar Association, the Christian Legal Society, and the Federalist Society for Law and Public Policy.

In addition to pursuing his legal career, Mr. Hagopian also served as a senior editor of, and contributing author to, *Antithesis: A Review of Contemporary Christian Thought and Culture* and has written for other publications. He is also a founding member of Redeeming Grace Presbyterian Church in Orange County, California.

Mr. Hagopian lives in southern California with his wife, Jamie, and his three children, Brandon, Kirstin, and Anallyce.

Douglas M. Jones III received his Bachelor of Arts in philosophy from the University of California, Irvine, in 1986 and his Master of Arts in philosophy from the University of Southern California in 1990.

In addition to being a Fellow of Philosophy at the New St. Andrews College, Mr. Jones has taught at the University of Southern California, the University of Idaho, and Lewis-Clark State College. He served as the editor of *Antithesis* and is currently the managing editor of *Credenda/Agenda*. He has written *Huguenot Garden* (Canon Press) and has contributed to *And It Came to Pass* (Canon Press). He is also ordained as a ruling elder in the Orthodox Presbyterian Church.

Mr. Jones lives in Idaho with his wife, Paula, and his three children, Amanda, Chelsea, and Mac.

Roger Wagner received his Bachelor of Arts from Westmont College in 1970 and his Master of Divinity from Westminster Theological Seminary (Philadelphia) in 1973. He is currently a Doctor of Ministry candidate at Westminster Theological Seminary in California.

Mr. Wagner has written various articles for publications such as the *Journal of Pastoral Practice* and *Antithesis,* is an ordained minister in the Orthodox Presbyterian Church, and serves as the pastor of Bayview Orthodox Presbyterian Church in Chula Vista, California.

Mr. Wagner lives in southern California with his wife, Sherry, and his three children, David, Benjamin, and Sarah.

Douglas J. Wilson received his Bachelor of Arts in philosophy in 1977, his Master of Arts in philosophy in 1979, and his Bachelor of Arts in classical studies in 1988, all from the University of Idaho.

Mr. Wilson has written several books, including *Recovering the Lost Tools of Learning* (Crossway Books), *Reforming Marriage* (Canon Press), *Standing on the Promises* (Canon Press), *Introductory Logic* (Canon Press), *Latin Grammar* (Canon Press), *Persuasions* (Canon Press), *Finding the Faith* (Canon Press), *Pursuit of the Cross* (Canon Press), and *Easy Chairs/Hard Words* (Canon Press). He has also contributed to *And It Came to Pass* and has published numerous articles, columns, and book reviews in publications such as *World, Antithesis, Credenda/Agenda, Reformation and Revival Journal,* and *Practical Homeschooling.* He is the editor of *Credenda/Agenda.*

Mr. Wilson is a Fellow of Philosophy at the New St. Andrews College and has also taught at the University of Idaho and Lewis-Clark State College. He is a founding school board member and instructor in ethics at Logos School. He is also a teaching elder with Community Evangelical Fellowship in Moscow, Idaho, and is a frequent conference speaker.

Mr. Wilson lives in Idaho with his wife, Nancy, and his three children, Bekah, Nathan, and Rachel.

FOR FURTHER READING

The extended bibliography given below has been provided as a guide to some of the works relied upon by each author and to other helpful works. This bibliography, of course, is by no means exhaustive. Also, the authors do not necessarily endorse everything written in each book.

PART ONE: BACK TO CONVERSION

Adams, Jay. *The Grand Demonstration*. Santa Barbara, Calif.: EastGate Publishers, 1991.

Bavinck, Herman. *The Doctrine of God*. Translated by William Hendriksen. 1951. Reprint, Edinburgh: Banner of Truth, 1991.

Berkhof, Louis. *Vicarious Atonement Through Christ*. Grand Rapids: Eerdmans, 1936.

Berkouwer, G. C. *Faith and Perseverance*. Translated by Robert D. Knudsen. Grand Rapids: Eerdmans, 1958.

Boettner, Loraine. *The Reformed Doctrine of Predestination*. Phillipsburg, N.J.: Presbyterian and Reformed, 1963.

Bridges, Jerry. *Trusting God*. Colorado Springs: NavPress, 1988.

Calvin, John. *Institutes of the Christian Religion*. 1536. Edited by John T. McNeill. Translated by Ford Lewis Battles. 2 vols. Philadelphia: Westminster, 1960.

Chantry, Walter. *Man's Will—Free Yet Bound*. Canton, Ga.: Free Grace Publications, 1988.

Charnock, Stephen. *The Doctrine of Regeneration*. 1840. Reprint, Hertfordshire: Evangelical Press, 1980.

———. *The Existence and Attributes of God*. 2 vols. 1684. Reprint, Grand Rapids: Baker, 1990.

Cheeseman, John, Philip Gardner, Michael Sandgrove, and Tom Wright. *The Grace of God in the Gospel*. Edinburgh: Banner of Truth, 1976.

Clark, Gordon H. *Predestination*. Jefferson, Md.: Trinity Foundation, 1987.

Custance, Arthur. *The Sovereignty of Grace*. Phillipsburg, N.J.: Presbyterian and Reformed, 1979.

Edwards, Jonathan. *On the Freedom of the Will*. In *The Works of Jonathon Edwards*, vol. 1. Edinburgh: Banner of Truth, 1974.

Gill, John. *The Cause of God and Truth*. 1735–38. Reprint, Grand Rapids: Baker, 1980.

Girardeau, John L. *Calvinism and Evangelical Arminianism Compared as to Election, Reprobation, Justification, and Related Doctrines*. 1890. Reprint, Harrisonburg, Va.: Sprinkle Publications, 1984.

Hodge, A. A. *The Atonement*. 1867. Reprint, Memphis, Tenn.: Footstool Publications, 1987.

Kuiper, R. B. *God-Centered Evangelism*. Edinburgh: Banner of Truth, 1961.

Luther, Martin. *The Bondage of the Will*. 1525. Old Tappan, N.J.: Revell, 1957.

Machen, J. Gresham. *The Christian View of Man*. 1937. Reprint, Edinburgh: Banner of Truth, 1965.

———. *God Transcendent*. 1949. Reprint, Edinburgh: Banner of Truth, 1982.

Morris, Leon. *The Atonement*. Downers Grove, Ill.: InterVarsity Press, 1983.

Murray, John. *The Atonement*. Phillipsburg, N.J.: Presbyterian and Reformed, n.d.

———. *Calvin on Scripture and Divine Sovereignty*. Grand Rapids: Baker, 1960.

———. *The Imputation of Adam's Sin*. Grand Rapids: Eerdmans, 1959.

———. *The Sovereignty of God*. Philadelphia: Committee on Christian Education, 1943.

Murray, John J. *Behind a Frowning Providence*. Edinburgh: Banner of Truth, 1990.

Packer, J. I. *Evangelism and the Sovereignty of God*. Downers Grove, Ill.: InterVarsity Press, 1961.

———. "Introductory Essay" for *The Death of Death in the Death of Christ*, by John Owen. 1647, 1852. Reprint, Edinburgh: Banner of Truth, 1959.

———. "John Owen's *The Death of Death in the Death of Christ.*" In *The Quest for Godliness: The Puritan Vision of the Christian Life*. Wheaton, Ill.: Crossway, 1990.

———. *Knowing God*. Downers Grove, Ill.: InterVarsity Press, 1973.

Palmer, Edwin. *The Five Points of Calvinism*. Grand Rapids: Baker, 1972.

Pink, A. W. *The Sovereignty of God*. 1930. Reprint, Grand Rapids: Baker, 1990.

Rice, N. L. *God Sovereign and Man Free*. Harrisonburg, Va.: Sprinkle Publications, 1985.

Seaton, W. J. *The Five Points of Calvinism*. 1970. Reprint, Edinburgh: Banner of Truth, 1993.

Smeaton, George. *Christ's Doctrine of the Atonement*. 1870. Reprint, Edinburgh: Banner of Truth, 1991.

———. *The Doctrine of the Atonement According to the Apostles*. 1870. Reprint, Peabody, Mass.: Hendrickson, 1988.

Sproul, R. C. *Chosen by God*. Wheaton, Ill.: Tyndale House, 1986.

Steele, David N., and Curtis C. Thomas, *The Five Points of Calvinism*. Phillipsburg, N.J.: Presbyterian and Reformed, 1963.

Storms, C. Samuel. *Chosen for Life*. Grand Rapids: Baker, 1987.

Warfield, B. B. *The Plan of Salvation*. 1915. Reprint, Boonton, N.J.: Simpson Publishing Co., 1989.

———. "Predestination in the Reformed Confessions." In *The Works of Benjamin B. Warfield*, vol. 9: *Studies in Theology*. 1932. Reprint, Grand Rapids, Mich.: Baker, 1981.

Zanchius, Jerome. *The Doctrine of Absolute Predestination*. 1779. Reprint, Grand Rapids: Baker, 1977.

PART TWO: BACK TO THE COVENANT

Allis, Oswald. *Prophecy and the Church*. Philadelphia: Presbyterian and Reformed, 1945.

Campbell, Roderick. *Israel and the New Covenant*. 1954. Reprint, Phillipsburg, N.J.: Presbyterian and Reformed, 1981.

Clowney, Edmund P. *The Unfolding Mystery: Discovering Christ in the Old Testament*. Phillipsburg, N.J.: Presbyterian and Reformed, 1988.

Crenshaw, Curtis, and Grover Gunn. *Dispensationalism Today, Yesterday, and Tomorrow*. Memphis: Footstool Publications, 1985.

Davis, John Jefferson. *The Victory of Christ's Kingdom: An Introduction to Postmillennialism*. Moscow: Canon Press, 1995.

Frame, John. *The Doctrine of the Knowledge of God*. Phillipsburg, N.J.: Presbyterian and Reformed, 1987.

Fuller, Daniel. *Gospel and Law: Contrast or Continuum? The Hermeneutics of Dispensationalism and Covenant Theology*. Grand Rapids: Eerdmans, 1980.

————. *The Unity of the Bible*. Grand Rapids: Zondervan, 1992.

Gentry, Kenneth. *He Shall Have Dominion: A Postmillennial Eschatology*. Tyler, Tex.: Institute for Christian Economics, 1992.

Gerstner, John. *Wrongly Dividing the Word of Truth: A Critique of Dispensationalism*. Brentwood, Tenn.: Wolgemuth & Hyatt, 1991.

Hendriksen, William. *The Covenant of Grace*. Grand Rapids: Baker, 1932.

Kik, Marcellus J. *An Eschatology of Victory*. Phillipsburg, N.J.: Presbyterian and Reformed, 1975.

Morin, Terry, ed. *And It Came to Pass: Symposium on Preterism*. Moscow, Idaho: Canon Press, 1992.

Murray, Iain. *The Puritan Hope: Revival and Interpretation of Prophecy*. Edinburgh: Banner of Truth, 1971.

Murray, John. *The Covenant of Grace*. London: Tyndale Press, 1954.

Poythress, Vern. *Understanding Dispensationalists*. Grand Rapids: Zondervan, 1987.

Ridderbos, Herman N. *The Coming of the Kingdom*. Phillipsburg, N.J.: Presbyterian and Reformed, 1962.

Robertson, O. Palmer. *The Christ of the Covenants*. Phillipsburg, N.J.: Presbyterian and Reformed, 1980.

Sartelle, John P. *Infant Baptism: What Christian Parents Should Know*. Phillipsburg, N.J.: Presbyterian and Reformed, 1985.

Vos, Geerhardus. *Biblical Theology: Old and New Testaments*. 1948. Reprint, Grand Rapids: Eerdmans, 1985.

Witsius, Herman. *The Economy of the Covenants Between God and Man: Comprehending a Complete Body of Divinity*. 1822. Reprint, Escondido, Calif.: Den Dulk Christian Foundation, 1990.

PART THREE: BACK TO THE CHURCH

Adams, Jay. *The Handbook of Church Discipline*. Grand Rapids: Zondervan, 1986.

————. *The Meaning and Mode of Baptism*. Phillipsburg, N.J.: Presbyterian and Reformed, 1975.

Bannerman, James. *The Church of Christ: A Treatise on the Nature, Power,*

Ordinances, Discipline and Government of the Christian Church. 1869. Reprint, Edmonton: Still Waters Revival Books, 1991.

Burroughs, Jeremiah. *Gospel Worship*. 1648. Reprint, Ligonier, Pa.: Soli Deo Gloria Publications, 1990.

Chantry, Walter. *Call the Sabbath a Delight*. Edinburgh: Banner of Truth, 1991.

Cunningham, William. *Discussions on Church Principles: Popish, Erastian, and Presbyterian*. 1863. Reprint, Edmonton: Still Waters Revival Books, 1991.

Eyres, Lawrence R. *The Elders of the Church*. Phillipsburg, N.J.: Presbyterian and Reformed, 1975.

Gillespie, George. *A Dispute Against English Popish Ceremonies Obtruded on the Church of Scotland*. 1637, 1660, 1844. Reprint, Dallas, Tex.: Naphtali Press, 1993.

Girardeau, John L. *Instrumental Music in the Public Worship of the Church*. 1888. Reprint, Havertown, Pa.: New Covenant Publication Society, 1983.

Kuiper, R. B. *The Glorious Body of Christ*. 1966. Reprint, Edinburgh: Banner of Truth, 1987.

Murray, Iain. *The Reformation of the Church: A Collection of Reformed and Puritan Documents on Church Issues*. Edinburgh: Banner of Truth, 1964.

Murray, John. *Christian Baptism*. Phillipsburg, N.J.: Presbyterian and Reformed, 1980.

Wray, Daniel E. *Biblical Church Discipline*. 1978. Reprint, Edinburgh: Banner of Truth, 1988.

PART FOUR: BACK TO THE CHRISTIAN LIFE

Adams, Jay. *The War Within*. Eugene, Oreg.: Harvest House, 1989.

Alexander, Donald L., ed. *Christian Spirituality: Five Views of Sanctification*. Downers Grove, Ill.: InterVarsity Press, 1988.

Baxter, Richard. *The Practical Works of Richard Baxter*, vol. 1: *A Christian Directory*. 1673. Reprint, Ligonier, Pa.: Soli Deo Gloria Publications, 1990.

Bolton, Samuel. *The True Bounds of Christian Freedom*. 1645. Reprint, Edinburgh: Banner of Truth, 1978.

Bridges, Jerry. *Transforming Grace: Living Confidently in God's Unfailing Love*. Colorado Springs: NavPress, 1991.

Buchanan, James. *The Doctrine of Justification.* 1867. Reprint, Edinburgh: Banner of Truth, 1991.

Clowney, Edmund P. *Called to the Ministry.* Phillipsburg, N.J.: Presbyterian and Reformed, 1964.

Downame, George. *The Christian's Freedom.* 1935. Reprint, Ligonier, Pa.: Soli Deo Gloria Publications, 1994.

Eastwood, Cyril. *The Priesthood of All Believers: An Examination of the Doctrine from the Reformation to the Present Day.* London: Epworth, 1960.

Ferguson, Sinclair. *The Christian Life: A Doctrinal Introduction.* 1981. Reprint, Edinburgh: Banner of Truth, 1989.

———. *Discovering God's Will.* Edinburgh: Banner of Truth, 1982.

Frame, John. "Doctrine of the Christian Life." Unpublished course syllabus, n.d.

———. *Medical Ethics.* Phillipsburg, N.J.: Presbyterian and Reformed, 1988.

Gentry, Kenneth L., Jr. *Lord of the Saved.* Phillipsburg, N.J.: Presbyterian and Reformed, 1992.

Helm, Paul. *The Beginnings: Word and Spirit in Conversion.* Edinburgh: Banner of Truth, 1986.

———. *The Callings: The Gospel in Today's World.* Edinburgh: Banner of Truth, 1987.

Hodge, Charles. *The Way of Life: A Guide to Christian Belief and Experience.* 1841. Reprint, Edinburgh: Banner of Truth, 1978.

Horton, Michael S., ed. *Christ the Lord: The Reformation and Lordship Salvation.* Grand Rapids: Baker, 1992.

———. *Putting Amazing Back into Grace: An Introduction to Reformed Theology.* Nashville: Nelson, 1991.

Kevan, Ernest. *Salvation.* Hertfordshire: Evangelical Press, 1973.

Kuyper, Abraham. *Lectures on Calvinism.* 1931. Grand Rapids: Eerdmans, 1987.

Luther, Martin. *The Freedom of a Christian.* 1520. In *Three Treatises.* Philadelphia: Fortress, 1966.

———. *An Open Letter to the Christian Nobility of the German Nation Concerning the Reform of the Christian Estate.* 1520. In *Three Treatises.* Philadelphia: Fortress, 1966.

Machen, J. Gresham. *What Is Faith?* 1925. Reprint, Edinburgh: Banner of Truth, 1991.

McGrath, Alister E. *Justification by Faith.* Grand Rapids: Zondervan, 1988.

———. *Justitia Dei.* Cambridge: Cambridge University Press, 1986.

Martin, A. N. *A Life of Principled Obedience*. Edinburgh: Banner of Truth, 1992.

———. *Living the Christian Life*. Edinburgh: Banner of Truth, 1986.

———. *The Practical Implications of Calvinism*. 1979. Reprint, Edinburgh: Banner of Truth, 1983.

Meeter, H. Henry. *The Basic Ideas of Calvinism*. 1939. Reprint, Grand Rapids: Baker, 1990.

Murray, John. *Principles of Conduct: Aspects of Biblical Ethics*. 1957. Reprint, Grand Rapids: Eerdmans, 1984.

———. *Redemption: Accomplished and Applied*. Grand Rapids: Eerdmans, 1955.

Packer, J. I. *Keep in Step with the Spirit*. 1984. Grand Rapids: Revell, 1993.

———. *A Quest for Godliness*. Wheaton, Ill.: Crossway, 1990.

———. *Rediscovering Holiness*. Ann Arbor, Mich.: Vine Books/Servant Publications, 1992.

Perkins, William. *A Treatise of the Vocations, or, Callings of Men, with the Sorts and Kinds of Them, and the Right Use Thereof*. Cambridge: John Legat, 1603.

Reisinger, Ernest C. *What Should We Think of the Carnal Christian?* Edinburgh: Banner of Truth, 1992.

Ryken, Leland. *Worldly Saints: The Puritans as They Really Were*. Grand Rapids: Zondervan, 1976.

Ryle, J. C. *Holiness*. Reprinted in *Christian Life Classics*, edited by Jay P. Green. Lafayette, Ind.: Sovereign Grace Trust Fund, 1990.

Schlossberg, Herbert, and Marvin Olasky. *Turning Point: A Christian World View Declaration*. Wheaton, Ill.: Crossway, 1987.

Sproul, R. C. *Pleasing God*. Wheaton, Ill.: Tyndale House, 1988.

Steele, Richard. *The Religious Tradesman or Plain and Serious Hints of Advice for the Tradesman's Prudent and Pius Conduct; From His Entrance into Business to His Leaving It Off*. 1603. Reprint, Harrisonburg, Va.: Sprinkle Publications, 1989.

Swinnock, George. *The Works of George Swinnock*, vols. 1–3: *The Christian Man's Calling*. 1868. Reprint, Edinburgh: Banner of Truth, 1992.

Van Til, Henry. *The Calvinist Concept of Culture*. 1959. Reprint, Phillipsburg, N.J.: Presbyterian and Reformed, 1972.

Warfield, B. B. "Benjamin B. Warfield on Lewis Sperry Chafer: A Review of *He That Is Spiritual*." In *Christ the Lord*, by Michael S. Horton. Pp. 211–18. (Originally printed in *Princeton Theological Review* 17 [April 1919]: 322–27.)

SYSTEMATIC THEOLOGIES AND MULTIVOLUME WORKS

Berkhof, Louis. *Systematic Theology*. 1939. Reprint, Grand Rapids: Eerdmans, 1991.

Boice, James M. *Foundations of the Christian Faith*. Downers Grove, Ill.: InterVarsity Press, 1986.

Boston, Thomas. *The Complete Works of the Late Rev. Thomas Boston*. 12 vols. Reprint, Wheaton, Ill.: Richard Owen Roberts, 1980.

Bradford, John. *The Writings of John Bradford*. 1848, 1853. Reprint, Edinburgh: Banner of Truth, 1979.

Bunyan, John. *The Works of John Bunyan*. 3 vols. 1854. Reprint, Edinburgh: Banner of Truth, 1991.

Calvin, John. *Institutes of the Christian Religion*. 1536. Edited by John T. McNeill. Translated by Ford Lewis Battles. 2 vols. Philadelphia: Westminster Press, 1960.

Clarkson, David. *The Works of David Clarkson*. 3 vols. 1864. Reprint, Edinburgh: Banner of Truth, 1988.

Dabney, Robert L. *Lectures in Systematic Theology*. 1878. Reprint, Edinburgh: Banner of Truth, 1988.

Edwards, Jonathan. *The Works of Jonathan Edwards*. 2 vols. 1834. Reprint, Edinburgh: Banner of Truth, 1990.

Gill, John. *A Complete Body of Doctrinal and Practical Divinity*. 1769–70. Reprint, Paris, Alaska: Baptist Standard Bearer, 1989.

Gillespie, George. *The Works of George Gillespie*. 2 vols. 1640. Reprint, Edmonton: Still Waters Revival Books, 1991.

Hodge, A. A. *Evangelical Theology*. 1890. Reprint, Edinburgh: Banner of Truth, 1990.

————. *Outlines of Theology*. 1860. Reprint, Edinburgh: Banner of Truth, 1983.

Hodge, Charles. *Systematic Theology*. 3 vols. 1871–73. Reprint, Grand Rapids: Eerdmans, 1982.

Hoeksema, Herman. *Reformed Dogmatics*. 1966. Reprint, Grand Rapids: Reformed Free Publishing Association, 1985.

Howe, John. *The Works of John Howe*. 3 vols. 1724. Reprint, Ligonier, Pa.: Soli Deo Gloria Publications, 1990.

Murray, John. *Collected Writings*. 4 vols. 1976. Reprint, Edinburgh: Banner of Truth, 1989.

Newton, John. *The Works of John Newton*. 6 vols. 1820. Reprint, Edinburgh: Banner of Truth, 1988.

Owen, John. *The Works of John Owen*. 16 vols. 1850–53. Reprint, Edinburgh:

Banner of Truth, 1987.

Packer, J. I. *Concise Theology*. Wheaton, Ill.: Tyndale House, 1993.

Shedd, W. G. T. *Dogmatic Theology*. 3 vols. 1888–94. Reprint, Grand Rapids: Zondervan, 1950.

Shepard, Thomas. *The Works of Thomas Shepard*. 1853. Reprint, Ligonier, Pa.: Soli Deo Gloria Publications, 1991.

Sproul, R. C. *Essential Truths of the Christian Faith*. Wheaton, Ill.: Tyndale House, 1992.

Strong, Augustus Hopkins. *Systematic Theology*. Chicago: Judson, 1947.

Thornwell, James Henley. *The Collected Writings of James Henley Thornwell*. 4 vols. 1875. Reprint, Edinburgh: Banner of Truth, 1986.

Toplady, Augustus. *The Works of Augustus Toplady*. 1794. Reprint, Harrisonburg, Va.: Sprinkle Publications, 1987.

Turretin, Francis. *Institutes of Elenctic Theology*. Translated by George Musgrave Giger. Edited by James T. Dennison, Jr. 3 vols. 1679–85. Phillipsburg, N.J.: Presbyterian and Reformed, 1992—.

Warfield, B. B. *The Works of Benjamin B. Warfield*. 10 vols. 1932. Reprint, Grand Rapids: Baker, 1991.

CREEDS, CONFESSIONS, AND CATECHISMS

Boston, Thomas. *Commentary on the Shorter Catechism*. 2 vols. 1853. Reprint, Edmonton: Still Waters Revival Books, 1993.

Clark, Gordon H. *What Do Presbyterians Believe?* 1956. Reprint, Phillipsburg, N.J.: Presbyterian and Reformed, 1989.

The [Westminster] Confession of Faith, The Larger Catechism, The Shorter Catechism, etc. 1646. Glasgow: Free Presbyterian Publications, 1990.

Hodge, A. A. *The Confession of Faith*. 1869. Reprint, Edinburgh: Banner of Truth, 1983.

Hoeksema, Herman. *The Triple Knowledge*. 3 vols. Grand Rapids: Reformed Free Publishing Association, 1971.

Hoeksema, Homer. *The Voice of Our Fathers: An Exposition of the Canons of Dordrecht*. Grand Rapids: Reformed Free Publishing Association, 1980.

Noll, Mark A. *Confessions and Catechisms of the Reformation*. Grand Rapids: Baker, 1991.

Ridgely, Thomas. *Commentary on the Larger Catechism*. 2 vols. 1853. Edmonton: Still Waters Revival Books, 1993.

Schaff, Philip. *The Creeds of Christendom with a History and Critical Notes*.

3 vols. 1931. Reprint, Grand Rapids: Baker, 1985.

Shedd, W. G. T. *Calvinism: Pure and Mixed*. 1893. Reprint, Edinburgh: Banner of Truth, 1986.

Watson, Thomas. *A Body of Divinity*. 1692. Reprint, Edinburgh: Banner of Truth, 1986.

Williamson, G. I. *The Heidleberg Catechism: A Study Guide*. Phillipsburg, N.J.: Presbyterian and Reformed, 1993.

————. *The Shorter Catechism for Study Classes*. 2 vols. Phillipsburg, N.J.: Presbyterian and Reformed, 1970.

————. *The Westminster Confession of Faith for Study Classes*. Phillipsburg, N.J.: Presbyterian and Reformed, 1964.

Witsius, Herman. *Sacred Dissertations on the Apostles' Creed*. 2 vols. 1681, 1823. Reprint, Escondido, Calif.: Den Dulk Christian Foundation, 1993.

Vincent, Thomas. *The Shorter Catechism Explained from Scripture*. 1674. Reprint, Edinburgh: Banner of Truth, 1984.

INDEX OF SCRIPTURE

307